D1333054

A Diamond Fell Into
My Pocket

A Diamond Fell Into My Pocket

by

Morris Spurling

as told to

Paul Drewitt

The Extraordinary Adventures of
'Morry the Head', the Most Audacious Jewel
Thief the World Has Ever Known

LITTLE, BROWN AND COMPANY

A *Little, Brown* Book

First published in Great Britain in 1997
by Little, Brown and Company

Copyright © Paul Drewitt, 1997

The moral right of the author has been asserted.

All rights reserved.
No part of this publication may be reproduced,
stored in a retrieval system, or transmitted, in any
form or by any means, without the prior
permission in writing of the publisher, nor be
otherwise circulated in any form of binding or
cover other than that in which it is published and
without a similar condition including this
condition being imposed on the subsequent purchaser.

A CIP catalogue record for this book
is available from the British Library.

ISBN 0 316 88112 0

Typeset in Berkeley Book by
Palimpsest Book Production Limited,
Polmont, Stirlingshire
Printed and bound in Great Britain by
Clays Ltd, St Ives plc.

Little, Brown and Company (UK)
Brettenham House
Lancaster Place
London WC2E 7EN

Contents

1

Carpet Slippers and a Pipe

Friday, February 16, 1996

An air of tension gripped the courtroom. The few spectators in the public gallery gasped as the woman prosecutor read out the long list of previous convictions exposing nearly half a century of crime. An elderly woman strained her eyes to see the inoffensive slim old man standing in the dock. Although she was used to being entertained every day by the shocking stories of crime described by the lawyers in the busy courtroom she still found it hard to believe what was being said about this bald-headed pensioner. Was Morris Spurling really this racy dilettante man-about-town? A criminal who had spent his life mixing with the rich and famous in the world's smartest casinos while funding his pleasures with audacious thefts of diamonds and other jewels from places as far apart as London, Sydney, Johannesburg, Zurich and New York?

The man in the dock stood quietly with his head bowed, fiddling with his walking stick, his bags packed ready for another spell in prison. He looked every inch the penitent sinner.

Despite the inauspicious circumstances, it was as though he was making his first appearance in court. His face adopted the look of a naughty dog as his barrister, Leslie Spittle, told the court it was only in fiction that a Raffles-type jewel thief ended up in the South of France with a blonde on one arm and a yacht in the bay.

The barrister strode into the centre of the courtroom and holding his arms aloft in supplication he asked the judge to look at the pathetic creature in the dock. 'In front of you is the reality. You see before you a pitiful creature. At the age of sixty-seven he has no money, no family really. As he would put it: "It's not worth the candle."'

The lawyer paused for effect before continuing to paint the portrait of a life ruined by crime and gambling. 'It is a pathetic, sad picture. He is amusing, intelligent, irritating and frustrating. But he is not without hope.'

Teesside Crown Court had not heard such a strange case for some time. Here was a living member of the London Under-world who had spent his entire life, less the years in the womb, the cradle and the pushchair, living off the proceeds of crime.

The old woman's ears pricked up as she heard the revelations of his daredevil exploits. The court was told how he had stolen diamonds in South Africa valued at £400,000 pounds. That was twenty years earlier and he had been sentenced to nine years in jail. He had committed jewel robberies on nearly every continent. In Nice, in the South of France, he had been jailed for six years. At least two countries had sent him packing, banished never to return.

There had been no inkling that such a story would be heard when the public had assembled that morning for their daily dose of true crime. In front of them was an elderly man arraigned in court for stealing five gold chains from a jeweller's shop in Thirsk in North Yorkshire. A chance encounter five months earlier had led to his arrest. On arriving in Thirsk, Spurling had been stopped by a policeman on traffic duty for not wearing a seat belt. A few hours later the same policeman had been called to investigate the theft of the five gold chains from the jeweller's. On seeing the security video he immediately recognised the thief as Spurling, whose car registration number he had noted earlier in the day.

Morris Spurling was described in court as a 'Raffles-type character' who was now in much reduced circumstances and living in one room in a hostel in Milton Keynes. The court heard it was a world away from the glamorous high life he had led in the resorts of the French Riviera, the nightclubs and casinos of Atlantic City, New Jersey, or Las Vegas in the Nevada desert, Sydney in Australia or Sun City in Africa.

A weak smile played across the criminal's lips as he heard himself described by the nickname the Underworld had long ago granted him: 'Morry the Head'. A name given to him for the most obvious of reasons, his head being almost totally devoid of hair. The international crime-busting organisation Interpol had listed 'Morry the Head' among its most wanted criminals many times in the past half a century. He had been sentenced to more than four decades in prison in half-a-dozen countries.

His barrister, Mr Spittle, was now pleading for The Head's freedom. He described a life committed to gambling. His client had never really profited from his crimes, just handed the money back to the bookmakers and the casino owners. 'He has realised that if he does not stop offending, then all he has got left is his final years as a guest of Her Majesty. He ought to take up smoking a pipe, buy a pair of carpet slippers and leave other people's jewellery alone.'

After hearing The Head's promise to retire from his half-century of international crime, the judge addressed him directly. 'I am going to take an exceptional course and place you on probation for two years,' said the Assistant Recorder, Gordon Nuttal. 'At your time of life I am going to give you that chance.'

The figure in the dock visibly shuddered with relief as he heard the news of his freedom. He mumbled his thanks to the judge before turning in the dock and hobbling out of court.

Outside, in the brisk fresh February air, he wiped away a tear as he leaned on his stick and spoke to the small group of reporters. 'I'm a silly old thing,' he told them. 'It is time to give it up.' And turning away with his usual request for 'no photographs' he made his way around the courthouse to the car park where his ten-year-old Vauxhall was waiting for him, surrounded by the BMWs of the lawyers in court that day. With a heavy heart he drove out trying to gather his thoughts.

The traffic on the four-hour journey back to Milton Keynes was unusually light that afternoon and he made good time. As the old banger dragged him slowly back to his solitary room, 'The Head' felt a deep depression coming over him. The whole week had been spent in preparation for another prison sentence. He had packed his bags confident in the knowledge he would be spending the next few months inside. Now, he was remaining free but with the knowledge that another conviction would mean he would almost certainly be going back to jail, with the keys well and truly thrown away. He would have to change. His promise to the judge, which had gained him his freedom, would have to be honoured, despite the lure of gambling.

'The Head' arrived back in Milton Keynes during the early evening. He went upstairs with a suitcase in one hand and his walking stick in the other. In his wallet was £10, all he had left in the world. But the following morning all the jewellers in the world would be safe because 'Morry the Head' was going straight. It would be a small bet indeed at his regular betting shop. The girl behind the counter might once again be pleased to see him. Recently she had avoided looking into his eyes. He knew she felt guilty for having taken the vast amount of money he had spent in bets over the previous four years. At least £100,000 had gone over that counter.

Once inside the room, Morris Spurling placed his suitcase beside the bed. He did not have enough space in the small wardrobe to hang all his clothes. Most of the floor was taken up by the bed and hard wooden chair.

Morry sat on the bed, kicked off his shoes and poured himself a glass of red wine. The man who had told reporters outside the court that he had 'more stories in me than Hemingway' was starting to reflect on some of them.

Although time played tricks with his memory the key moments in his life as an international jewel thief returned to amuse and haunt 'The Head' in his lonely room in a Buckinghamshire hostel.

2

The Early Years

63 years earlier

It was Christmas 1933 and Britain was in the heart of the terrible Depression. The backstreets of London were filled with shabby-looking characters wearing worn-out old clothes, shambling along looking apologetic for being alive. Children roamed the streets barefoot, begging for food. But Oxford Street was a world away from the rest of London as the wealthy hurriedly shopped for last-minute presents in the few days before Christmas.

I was in a blue romper suit walking along towards Selfridges with my parents holding my hands as they laughed and joked with me. I can't remember whether it snowed that year but I seem to recall a few flakes falling on my hair with my parents quickly brushing them off before they could melt. I was excited, on my way to see Father Christmas who I knew would have a decent present and a good old chuckle to keep me happy.

We entered the store and since it was a special occasion I had to have my hair cut. My parents were very formal about such matters. So first we went to the Barber's Shop where haircuts were a special treat for youngsters. They had a marvellous old wooden rocking horse and children would be allowed to sit on it while the barber cut their hair. I had lovely thick long locks of brown hair, all frizzy curls. The barber called me Freddie Bartholomew after the child star of that time and he cut my hair in a similar style. I think he also gave me a sweet because I behaved myself so well.

That day we all waited outside the store for my uncle to turn up in his old Packard, a big American car he had bought to show off in. He used to buy me anything I wanted. I think if I'd asked for the Empire State Building he'd have bought it and had it transported over to Britain for his little nephew.

I was born Morris Spurling on April 6, 1928, the only child of upper middle-class Jewish parents, Benjamin and Marie. They had been trying for a baby for many years before I came along and that meant they spoiled me. My first home was in a fairly ordinary middle-class town house in Tottenham, 46 Ravensdale Road. My parents had been born in the East End. My grandparents were both Russian, from Vilna in Estonia. They escaped before the Russian Revolution in 1917, seeing Britain as a safe place to work and practise their living as general tailors and garment makers. My granny called round every Tuesday night with a penny bar of Nestlé's chocolate.

Life was full of fun those days. We never seemed to want for anything. We weren't exactly in the most affluent part of London but we had more than enough money to cushion the effects of The Depression. There were plenty of people well able to afford the clothes sold by my parents. So money was not a problem.

My father was a tailor and my mother was a manufacturer of ladies' dresses, a gown-maker. She was in partnership with her brother, Alexander Gordon, who was a very well-off man who had worked his way up to the top of the gown business. He was an orthodox Jew and on the Jewish Board of Deputies. His company was named after him and run out of a huge building in Great Portland Street off Oxford Circus in London, next to where Rymans was on the Oxford Street end of the road. During the Second World War an aerial torpedo bomb hit the next building and brought down his as well.

My mother was the driving force of the partnership and quite wealthy as a result of it, although nowhere near as affluent as my uncle. They had a hundred girls working for them, machinists, cutters, all going flat out making dresses for Britain and for export. The warehouse was part of the same building. In the back they were making the clothes which were then sold in the shop at the front which opened onto the street.

I used to drive around the streets of Tottenham in the working miniature of a sports car, a Sunbeam Talbot. It must have cost a fortune.

No child could have asked for more love nor for a richer environment in which to grow up. I longed for nothing either from my parents or from my uncle. As an only child who had come along late I was showered with love and attention. Some days I would sit in the front of the shop with my mother bouncing me up and down on her knees as I commented on the customers. But there is one memory which gives me a clue as to why I developed as I did.

I can't have been more than about six and had gone to bed early as six year olds do. A few hours later I woke up to hear laughter coming from the dining room. It sounded like quite a party and being an adventurous and curious little boy I got out of bed and went to the half-open door. I slipped through and slid onto the hallway, creeping along to the point where I could see inside the dining room. The door was ajar, presumably to hear if I called out for Mummy or Daddy during the evening. The dining-room light had been pulled down and was giving off enough light to illuminate a green baize cloth on which a deck of cards was spread. My mother, father, uncle and another couple of friends were engrossed in a game of poker. One was a boxing promoter and another was also in the garment trade. They seemed so adult and to be having so much fun I wanted to go down and join in. I sat on that hallway with my little legs tucked through the banisters for what seemed like hours that night. Maybe the enjoyment of it seeped into my subconscious. I don't know. Anyway, card playing was to become a major part of my life and I sometimes wonder whether the experience of that night had a lot to do with it.

Later I was to learn that it was my mother who hosted the card parties. She gave them regularly, several times a week. She was a gambler and so was my father. The result of their ways was that we had to move out of our house into a rented flat in Haringey. Money seemed to flow in and out of our house at a rate of knots. When I was seventeen and times were difficult, I even had an Austin Healey Sprite sports car. Maybe it was my uncle and his vast wealth which was paying for such treats.

As I grew up I started to understand the problems with their gambling. My father was always behind with the payments and the bills. I found out he was spending a lot of time at the dog track. My mother began to have murderous rows with him. Then one Passover I had my first experience of what gambling can do to a person.

It's an old Jewish custom on Seder Night, the first night of the eight-day festival, for the youngest of the household to open the door at a certain stage of the service to allow the Angel to enter. That year it was my turn to open the door. But instead of the Angel entering there stood two bailiffs with a warrant to take away the furniture for debts owed by my father.

Much of my childhood was spent in Tottenham until 1940 when I was evacuated to Wales during the Blitz. At the age of nearly twelve I was packed off with my suitcase and a load of other children and sent to the countryside near Cardiff. My foster people were the directors of Fry's Chocolates at Somerville in Bristol. I lived at a place called Radyr. It was a lovely little town. I even sang in the church choir. Fancy that, a Jewish boy singing in a Catholic church. That wasn't the only time that happened to me. Much later I was singing in a Catholic church inside a French prison.

As a boy I had a fine voice and one year on holiday in Littlehampton even won a singing competition. I thoroughly enjoyed my years in Wales. From time to time my mother used to come down and see me. The foster people were lovely individuals and as a family they could not have done more to make me welcome. After the RAF had seen off the Luftwaffe it was deemed safe for me to return to London.

I was a good all-round scholar. I excelled at history, geography and maths and came top of the class in everything except science. I was also sports mad and represented the Home Counties as a swimmer. I could have had a career there had I been bothered to apply myself just a little bit harder. I didn't like football but I adored cricket, in fact I was something of a fanatic about the sport. Every Saturday morning my father took me to the synagogue in Egerton Road. I would be wearing the traditional Sabbath clothes of a dark suit, white shirt and dark tie. But underneath would be my cricket whites. The minute the service was over I would rush like mad to the playing fields for a game of cricket. I was an exceptionally good spin bowler and played for North London boys against the rest of the country. After Craven Park Road School I went on to the senior school, Downhills Central. I was captain of cricket at both schools. My notoriety as London's best spin bowler preceded me. As soon as I got to the senior school, the captain said: 'You're now in charge.'

However, I was a lousy batsman. We reached the finals of one competition for North London teams and were matched against the best team in North London, called Belmont. All our batsmen went in and everyone was bowled out for none. I was number nine or ten and their terrific fast bowler sent the ball hurtling down towards me. I shut my eyes, swung the bat and hit a four. Our final score was just that, four. And I got clapped off the field as the star batsman. Then I took six wickets but we didn't win the match.

By now I had started to play truant from school, bunking off at every opportunity. One day that led me down the road to my first venture into gambling. There was an amusement arcade at Wood Green where I had met a young girl. I used to go up there every day just to see her. When I was waiting for her to turn up I used to while away my time by playing the one-armed bandits. Soon my few shillings would start disappearing into the machines. I never won, you can't beat those machines. Nevertheless, I found the attraction so strong I could not give up. I became hooked. I must have been about fourteen. Soon my money ran out and although my parents were extremely generous in giving me pocket money it never seemed to be enough to feed those machines. So I started thieving from my mother's handbag. I think she knew but she didn't admonish me. Then one day the postman came with a registered envelope which I opened. There was money in it for my mother from one of her accounts and I took that out. That's really when I starting thieving for real.

My cricketing days came to an end because of the thirst for gambling. I was the captain and consequently I was in charge of the funds to buy equipment. One day a master discovered there was not a single penny for bats, balls, pads or gloves. I couldn't stump up a good enough excuse and he rightly chucked me out of the team for embezzling the cricket fund. Looking back on those days I would not describe myself as a thief despite the fact I was thieving. It was more a case of pocketing loose cash when I came across it. Those were strange days during the war and if you were clever enough you could live two lives without anyone bothering. It wasn't that people didn't care, just that they had other more worrying things on their minds.

I left school when I was fourteen, which annoyed my parents. They wanted me to have a tip-top education and they had been pleased with my first-class school results.

I didn't escape totally unaffected by the Second World War. The worst time came when I lost my best friend in a land-mine explosion. Siddy Nead was his name. The land mine blew up right beside the school we went to, so the whole neighbourhood was in shock. I tried not to think too much about Siddy's death but he's never far from my mind. It's an awful thing to have your life snatched away from you when you're a plucky little nipper chock-full of life. After that happens to a close friend of yours you can't help but wonder what life is all about. Maybe Siddy's death has had something to do with the 'devil may care' attitude I have taken throughout my three careers of gambling, stealing and womanising.

My father was an air raid warden, Home Guard. It's a good job he never had to save anybody's life because he was always too busy playing cards. Many a night we spent under the table in the dining room when the bombs came down. It was either there or down Turnpike Lane underground station which was the official bomb shelter for our neighbourhood.

Just before I left school I learnt my most valuable lesson in life. I had my first fight when I was at school, and I lost it. I knew I was not a fighter. I was a lover, not a fighter. I was in the hundred yards' sprint and I won it and a fellow got annoyed. So I squared up to him although I was only as big as a threepenny bit. He hit me and I fell down and like a fool I got up. And he hit me again. And this time when I fell down I stayed down.

My uncle tried to persuade me to go into business but I spent the best part of the years between 1942 and 1944 roaming the streets and dance halls. When I was about fifteen there were three main dance halls which I regularly visited: the Royal at Tottenham, the Lyceum by the Aldwych and the Paramount, where everybody used to go.

So two years passed and they were so unmemorable I have forgotten them except to say I was probably mixing with the wrong crowd, even then.

3

Going to the Dogs

It all came to a head when I turned sixteen and my parents finally got fed up with me bunking off and roaming the streets. They called a family conference and a second uncle of mine who was also a wealthy businessman told me I would now be managing a menswear shop he owned in the Whitechapel Road in the East End. I was fashion mad and after a bit of complaining realised I might quite take to running a men's hosiery and fashion shop. The name of it was Gilbert's and it was just across the road from the London Hospital. He needed someone to look after it for him because he lived in Dunstable and only came up to town once or twice a week. So at the tender age of sixteen I became the manager of a menswear shop. A real job with a real future. If I'd had a head for business maybe I might now be a tycoon, who knows? It wasn't to turn out like that but from the first day I gave it all I got, little knowing it was to become my introduction to crime.

For a while everything went smoothly. I ran the shop like a proper business and my uncle was clearly pleased at how well everything was going. Then came the fateful day when I had my first real encounter with gambling and stealing. Two things happened in that shop within a few hours of each other and my reaction to both put me well on the road to a life of crime.

The first event came as I was idling away my time in the shop hoping for customers when in walked two black men. They were dressed like wealthy businessmen and spoke like gentlemen and looked as though they had money to burn.

Now the fashion in those days was for Van Heusen shirts and it didn't take long for me to realise I might make a good sale here.

One of the men came right up to me and said: 'Hiya, Boy.'

'Hallo.'

'We would like a couple of shirts.'

'OK.'

'Hey,' said the second one, 'you got a couple of Van Heusens?'

Several boxes of these shirts were piled up on the higher racks. So I got out my little ladder and climbed up to where I had stacked the Van Heusens. They couldn't make up their minds and kept on asking to see more and more. I was climbing higher and higher up my little ladder and bringing down more and more of these shirts. Suddenly I hear a voice behind me: 'What are they?' I turn around and see he's pointing even higher. Well, being a young lad and keen to do my job well I promptly went even further up this ladder and dragged down several boxes from the very top of the shelves. I can tell you I was getting quite excited by now. I couldn't imagine how many shirts they were going to buy.

This went on for quite some time. Every time I came down the ladder with an armful of shirts they would ask: 'And what are they up there?'

'Oh, they're . . .'

'Well, show us them.' And it was off up me little ladder once more.

The upshot of all this activity was that they could not decide which of all the shirts they wanted to buy. They ummed and ahhed for a little while and then told me they would come back the next day and decide.

They left the premises and I started to put back all the boxes. The strange thing that occurred to me was that after bringing down seventeen boxes there were only fifteen to put back. I thought it quite odd and so I searched the whole shop for the other two boxes. Then the penny dropped and I realised what had happened. That was my first experience of what is known in the trade as 'hoisting'. I couldn't believe what had happened. Right in front of my eyes they had taken two boxes of shirts, most likely selling them for a tidy profit. Little did I know then that I would turn out to be one of the world's best hoisters.

Later on that day my friend Sid came into the shop and we got talking and he could see there was a problem.

'What's wrong, Morry?'

'I'm in trouble.' I told him the story. A smile spread across his face. He thought for a moment and then said: 'That's no problem. Come with me and we'll catch the trolley bus from Aldgate to Clapton.'

'For what?' I asked.

'Clapton Dogs.'

'Clapton Dogs! What are they?'

'A dog track.'

'What happens there?'

'Come with me and I'll show you. We'll get back the money lost on those shirts.'

Reluctantly I said: 'All right.'

'But we'll need a bit of money to place a bet.'

So I opened the till, took out what was there, shut the shop, and caught the 653 trolley bus which took us right from

Whitechapel Road to Clapton Dog Track, whereupon I had the first bet of my life. I remember it as if I had laid out the money two hours ago. I even remember the name of the dog, Blackwater Cutlet.

That first bet was two shillings to win and ten shillings a place on the Tote. Blackwater Cutlet won! I was overjoyed. That was my misfortune. I can't remember what I won, it would be about two quid, but I know that dog started me on the road to ruin by winning. That was the end of a normal boy's life. I was completely and utterly hooked.

Years later I was at the Clapton Dog Track in the middle of winter when it was colder than Moscow at Christmas. That January I was so short of money but so determined to win I took off my overcoat and sold it for a fiver in order to have a bet. Needless to say I didn't win and had to hitch a lift home in the freezing cold with no coat.

As a consequence of that first win, Gilbert's menswear shop was no longer top of my list of priorities. I used to close the shop on the days when my uncle was up at Dunstable and go off to the dogs. No one knew since I was the only person working in the shop. Up to that moment I had been doing well. I had sold loads of shirts, ties, socks and shoes. I had been running a respectable business.

Clapton Dogs never lived up to its promises. I never got to win after Blackwater Cutlet. That didn't stop me from trying. I used to go there so often I needed to start dipping my hand in the till on a regular basis. I was taking the money out of the till to go to the dog track but unable to win enough to convince my uncle I was not stealing. Of course it took a lot of time for him to find out since he only came down on a Monday and a Friday to collect the money.

He still didn't catch on when I started an unofficial sale in midsummer. Shirts were going very cheap after my misfortune at the dogs because I was selling them all for myself at half price. No money was going in the till. The amount of money I was taking from the shop could not be hidden for ever and one day my uncle came down unexpectedly and realised what had been going on. He was so angry he went red in the face, blue in his language, picked me up by my shirt collar and the belt of my trousers and chucked me out the front door into the crowds walking down the Whitechapel Road. And then he drove straight across London to tell my mother. I had lasted just six months, which for me must be an all-time record for holding down a job. It also coincided with the end of my first real romance which also fell apart because of my gambling.

While in the East End I had fallen in love with a girl who was the daughter of a chemist. Ray Waldman and her father had a shop in Brick Lane and I started going out with her. We either went to the local cinemas or we used to go dancing. One night she turned up carrying a bag of money which she'd been told to put in a safe.

'I'll put it in the safe for you,' I told her.

'OK.'

Of course I didn't put it in the safe. I proceeded to take it to Romford Dog Track and promptly lost it all. It was a hundred pounds which in 1945 was a lot of cash considering you could buy several houses in London for that amount of money.

Needless to say the romance got broken off and I was lucky not to get put away. Around that time I started mixing with some real characters. I suppose you would call them gangsters but to my teenage mind they were just a group of people having a lot more fun than anyone else.

4

Entering the London Underworld

My mentor was a man called Albert Dimes. His real name was Dimeo.

Albert was one of the leaders of the London gangs, he liked me and so I started to work for him. I was good at maths and obviously you need to be acquainted with maths to be a bookmaker, to understand figures. I made a book for him at all the Point-to-Points and all the illegal gambling events.

Legal gambling only started in 1961, I think that was when betting shops came in. When the Gaming Act was passed in 1960 one of the first to take advantage was Albert Dimes. I was to work for Albert in one of the first legal betting shops, in Frith Street in Soho. But in the mid-Forties, Frith Street was where all the illegal action was.

I was up to my eyes in every bit of skulduggery and mixing with people who were into everything.

This is where I met 'The Swan' who was later to play such an important part in my life. We got into every lark there was, loads of scams.

I used to ring up a wine merchant and say: 'I'm having a birthday party. My name is so and so.' I used to know who had an account with them. If you had an account with Berry Brothers and Rudd or whatever you could order two thousand pounds' worth of wine.

'Shall we deliver it, sir?'

'No. I'll send a taxi round for it.'

The taxi went round. En route I used to stand outside a block of flats, wave down the cab, give him a tenner and take the wine and sell it.

There were so many scams. You would stand outside a jeweller's in Hatton Garden and the postman comes with a registered packet. You say: 'Oh. That's for me isn't it?'

'Yes. Mr Lewis? Would you sign for it?'

'Of course.' And that was it. People were more trusting and it was an era of naivety, if you like to call it that. There were no drugs, people weren't on the alert.

If we had no money we used to go into the West End and put hundreds and hundreds of pounds' worth of clothes in bin bags and just walk out of the shops. There wasn't the technology there is today and so no security tags to set off alarms when we left with our haul. We'd sell them in ten minutes, to bookmakers, gangsters, if you like to call them that, anybody who had money. Anybody would buy anything at a third of the price, as they would today.

All sorts of things appertained to the Yanks. I was about sixteen or seventeen and on the corner of Shaftesbury Avenue there was what they called The Rainbow Room, which was the American Forces hostel. There were all sorts of rackets going on with cigarettes and stockings and chocolate and changing money. And I got caught up in it.

So that's how I got involved with the London gangsters, the Underworld, when I was still not much more than a young boy. I started to meet all the West End characters. I went to gambling clubs, which at that time were illegal. Around the West End, around Old Compton Street, everything was illegal: gambling, bookmakers, card parties, clubs, casinos, everything was illegal.

To my delight there were many prostitutes around. Being a young kid and seeing them standing on street corners, it was just too much. Of course, it was a different era. I used to look and I used to touch. They outnumbered the rest of the population. They used to line up, four abreast, to walk down the streets. Curzon Street, Park Lane, Wardour Street, that was their territory. At that time the Maltese ruled Soho and all the girls were out for the Maltese. They were the heavies.

Anyway, I had now got my introduction to a club. It was in Denman Street, which is by the side of the Regent Palace, and was called the Mazurka. In the Mazurka I met many characters: Kid Ash, Benny the Kid, Hymie Mince, Twitty Mitchell, One-Armed Lou, Crutchy Jock, Clubfoot Pat, Fagash Lil, and many more.

This was London's Runyonesque group. I also turned myself into a very good snooker player. At the age of seventeen or eighteen I was going to the Windmill Club in Windmill Street where all the top snooker players were playing. In fact, I played two of them. I played two amateur champions, Tommy Gordon and Patsy Hoolahan. I thought I was good until one day when I came up against Crutchy Jock, who played with a crutch while balancing on one leg, and he smacked my bum.

I was Albert's man. He lived at The Angel in Islington. I got very, very friendly with him and other underworld characters. I knew them all including Bert Rossi, who they called Battles, whom I liked very much, and Ray Rosa, who committed suicide. I got involved as a youngster with all the heavy people.

One of my idols was a character called Italian Major, who was very friendly with Dimes and he was all that I looked up to. He was a gambler and a good dresser. I was a boy trying to copy men.

The Astor was the nightclub of London and I fell in love with one of the dancers. The whole lifestyle fascinated me. A fellow called Sulky was the host. Bertie Green owned it but Sulky was the host. Everybody from all sorts of life came there. MPs, criminals, lawyers, doctors, you name it, used to go to The Astor.

I was Jack the Lad about town in those days. Every night was a club and life was all right. I suppose you would have termed me as a West End face. I was around. But there's an old saying: 'Out of sight, out of mind.' Now I haven't been in London for ages and when you don't see anybody you forget all about them. If there was anything to do: 'Oh, Morry will do that. He's the right man for that.' But now I'm not around I'm not needed, no one sees you any more.

Of course my parents got to know about my doings. My mother found me a job in Argyll Street, next to the Palladium, working as an odd-job man for a silk manufacturers. That was doomed from the start although I did try to make it work for a few weeks until the boss put a roll of silk on my shoulder and said: 'Take this downstairs.'

I hefted it onto my back and nearly fell down the stairs, it was so heavy. I thought, 'This is not for me' and so I turned around and told him: '*You* take the roll of silk. Give *me* my cards and my money.'

5

Brighton – University of Crime

After I had dismissed myself from the job the family decided to make a fresh start in Brighton. A time by the seaside and away from the badly war-damaged Tottenham and Haringey was the tonic my parents wanted. It also got me away from the bad crowd I had been mixing with. At least they thought it might serve that purpose.

Of course, Brighton was the worst place we could have gone to. For an eighteen year old rapidly becoming hooked on gambling and mixing with crooks, who were offering him an insight into how to get money without earning it, Brighton was the Oxford University of crime.

In 1946 we moved into a beautiful flat overlooking the sea in a place called Brunswick Terrace. It was a bad time for us all. My mother had lost her share in her uncle's business when it closed down. I had been stealing the wages and my uncle decided it was time to call it a day. Maybe he thought if he gave me long enough I would have bankrupted him. My father still had a good job in London. He was the manager of a floor in Moss Brothers in London. As soon as we arrived my mother took the job of manageress at Constable's dress shop in Brighton.

I soon started getting into trouble with cheque fraud. I was using the old gambler's trick of cashing cheques with friends for half their value hoping I would back a winner and then being able to meet the cheques when they came in. Of course I never did back a winner and was never able to pay my debts. We call it 'One Giant Snowball'. I would cash the cheques on a Monday knowing they wouldn't be in the bank until the Wednesday or the Thursday, giving me three extra days' grace to play with. By then I had cashed even more cheques and was facing even more trouble.

I'd been ordered to do my national service in the Air Force. It didn't seem a good idea so I became an absentee. One day we answered the door in Hove and the Redcaps were there, the Military Police, and they said: 'Your son is an absconder. He should be in the Air Force.' So, I made my way up to Padgate in Lancashire to do my RAF training.

To my delight, on my arrival they told me to go over to the pay office. I thought I'd died and gone to heaven. The man called out my name, told me to sign a form and then gave me some back pay, which was, I suppose, about £60, which in 1946 was an absolute fortune. This seemed a good start to service life. I didn't know what I'd been doing missing out for so many months.

That night I crawled under the barbed wire surrounding the RAF camp, went to Warrington Dogs and crawled back stony broke. Gambling had now taken preference over anything else in the world. The RAF didn't last long. I was soon to be released on medical grounds. You might well wonder what medical grounds there were for a healthy eighteen year old to be excused military training. There is a simple and short answer to that question: none at all. I stayed about three or four months in the RAF. They transferred me to RAF Lindholm in Doncaster, which is now a prison, but was then under Bomber Command.

I wanted to get out of there so fast it wasn't true. I did everything wrong. There was no future in being in the Services so I started acting soppy and got thrown out. I played about, let them think I was a headcase or something. They sent me down to Ely in Cambridgeshire which was where they had the psychiatric unit. The squadron leader said: 'Look, Spurling. Don't mess me about. You're no good to us. We're no good to you. Get out.'

Then one day back in Brighton I fell in love. June Breskal was a glamorous dark-haired woman married to the owner of an off-licence who was always so drunk he must have cleaned his teeth in the morning with John Bell's whisky. He never caught on that I was having an affair with his wife. She had a couple of children by him but they had nothing in common. We did. It was just one of those things. She was about my age and he was twice as old as her and drunk all the time. All of Brighton knew but he was too drunk to know or care.

I had moved out of my parents' place to get a flat of my own so I could conduct this love affair with June. She used to arrive at seven o'clock in the morning and slide into bed. Later she'd run a bath and make breakfast for me. I was infatuated with this girl, I didn't want to leave her, I didn't want to go anywhere. If I had a fiver or a tenner or twenty quid I was happy.

After June had gone home in the morning I would go off to a gambling club about eleven o'clock and spend my time there until late afternoon or early evening. They were just dives. I was stuck.

Brighton was a very nice place to live at that time. I lived in the better part, in Hove. I might add it's completely changed today. Apparently now it's the heart of the drug business, which is not my scene.

I became friendly with a feller called Sammy Bellson, who owned the Burlesque Club in Brighton. Sammy Bellson illegally ran the town. He was quite a nice fellow, a lunatic gambler. He had the run of the town and he had quite a few policemen in his pocket.

Sammy was into all the gambling in Brighton, although he made a mess of himself, finished up with no money and went back to Forest Gate in London where he originally came from. Brighton was a gambling hive. He had a club which they called The Iron Lung. It was all iron going down into the basement. Life was gambling and fraud and cars and cheques and this and that. It was where I met all sorts of people.

Once I had got into the Brighton Underworld as such, life became easy. It was just a case of wasting weeks and months by doing nothing. I always got money somehow.

I was into the boxing game. My uncle was a promoter and I used to go with him and I got up to a lot of things. I can remember how audacious I was. There was a fight at Earl's Court between Joe Erskine and Nino Valdez, the Cuban. I was sitting in Brighton without a shilling in the world. I got a phone call. It was about three o'clock in the afternoon. This phone call came from a man called Eddie Fleischer who was with another man called Natie KiKi, a bookmaker, very well known in London, both of them.

'We've got a move for you, Morry. A chance for you to get some money.'

'What is it?'

'Well, get to London and we'll meet you at Victoria Station.'

'I haven't got a penny.'

The Brighton Belle used to leave at 5.25 in the afternoon and took one hour to get to London.

'Borrow a pound to get to London and we'll take care of you.'

'I can't borrow a shilling.'

'Borrow a pound.'

They put the phone down on me.

At that time the Brighton Belle was 7s.6d return from Brighton to London. I had two hours to borrow one pound, which I finally managed to do. When I got to London they were there and they bought me a cup of tea and sat me down.

'Look, Morry, we've got you a ringside ticket for this fight.'

They had told me on the phone to get suited and booted. So I was dressed well.

'Yes.'

'There will be a million Welshmen there who want to back Erskine.'

'You can take all the bets for the Welshman.'

I thought to myself: 'Well, there's a chance here.'

They were sitting behind me and they had moody bets with me, imaginative bets with me, loudly, so that all the Welshmen round me could hear. I was sitting in the middle. It looked like the Rhondda Valley from where I was sitting, there were so many Welshmen. You couldn't see anyone else. Now they're all trying to have bets with me on Erskine to beat this big Cuban called Nino Valdez. I had hundreds and hundreds of pounds' worth of bets. I just took a chance, remember, with no money.

The bell rang after a matter of seconds and I heard the timekeeper counting, 'One, two, three . . .' I froze. I knew that one of the two was on the floor knocked out. To my great relief it was Erskine sprawled on the canvas. Apparently, which I hadn't seen, Valdez had hit him with the first punch of the fight and knocked him out. Of course, I said to myself 'Thank God for that' and all the money came into me. I proceeded to go out accompanied by these two henchmen, Fleischer and KiKi, and we split the money three ways. I had hundreds and hundreds of pounds. But if it had gone the other way I wouldn't have been here today because I'd very likely have been taken down the mines in Merthyr Tydfil and held hostage until the money was paid. But that's the type of thing that one got up to in those days.

The name 'Morry the Head' came about quite early on when I was living in Brighton because I had started losing my hair. I must have been about twenty when it began to fall out.

The name stuck. When the hair started to go I began wearing hats, the more stylish the better. Good hats from Lock's in St James's Street.

6

All at Sea

I joined the Merchant Navy, one of the few real jobs I've ever held in my life. Here I was, a young man just turned twenty, all set for a life on the ocean wave.

My mother and father, God rest their souls, thought it was going to be good for me. I was standing at the station waiting to make my way from Brighton to Southampton to pick up the boat. You needed a few quid to go away with. My parents realised I had done all my money and dug deep into their pockets to give me some cash. That was in 1948 and they found £20 to give me to use on the boat. That was a lot of money. By the time I'd got to Southampton I'd lost the money in the train. But it was a good game of cards.

Money's never had value for me. Never at all. When I tell one friend of my experiences, she trembles. She really trembles. Another thing about gambling is it teaches you about loaning money. It's the best way to lose friends. The worst thing you can do as a friend is lend money to your gambling friends. Sometimes I'm ashamed. I can't go round to some friends because I have borrowed thousands and can't repay it, even though I've repaid money in the past. I'm ashamed of myself.

So at the age of twenty, in 1948, I sailed to Cape Town on the *Caernarvon Castle*. I was employed by the Royal Mail on the Castle Line. It seemed a good idea at the time. I had got tangled up with some boys who were in the Merchant Navy and who were going backwards and forwards to Africa. I got so entangled at an early age I thought I'd go myself. It came as a bit of a shock. Two days out at sea there was a burial. The baker died. Obviously, I was seasick and I looked so ill as I was standing beside the coffin that when the captain said those words, 'We will now commit his body to the deep', I looked so bad I thought they were going to throw me in instead of the coffin.

I was a hospital orderly. There were two on every boat and I got to hear about a vacancy. I was in charge of the ill and the dying and was supposed to feed them and look after them. I didn't know the first thing about hospitals. I did the first trip, then I went back and I lingered and I went back again. You could call me at that time a juggler. I was into every little bit of skulduggery that was going. I was learning fast; at the age of twenty I knew most of the moves in the book. I only went on two cruises, in 1948 and 1953, and the rest of the time I was living in the Brighton area.

Anyway, there I was at age twenty aboard this huge cruise ship sailing to South Africa.

Although my first job was as a hospital orderly they got me out of that job quick enough. I think someone thought I'd be better off spilling wine down customers' white suits than killing them with my incompetency. After working as a wine waiter for some months I became what was known as a cowboy, a waiter in the restaurant. I knew nothing about wine, I knew nothing about waiting. I had forged my references. I had gone into the Norfolk Hotel in Brighton and taken out some sheets of paper.

I wrote down: 'Morris Spurling has been in our employ for a number of years. We find him very good, efficient . . .' and such nonsense. The truth was I didn't know which side the knife and fork went. All the complaints on the boat were made by the people I was serving.

It took two weeks to get to South Africa. There was a woman who used to phone down, an hour or two before the evening meal, to find out what soup was on. This went on for a few nights and one night the chief steward said to her: 'Excuse me, Madam. May I ask why you keep phoning down every night to find out what soup is on?'

'Well, I want to know the colour of the soup because this waiter upsets the soup over me every night. I might as well wear a dress to match.'

I was a disaster. Everybody was in uproar with me.

I put the wrong knives with the wrong spoons and the wrong forks with the wrong knives. So much so that when I got discharged the chief steward said to me: 'Spurling. I wanna tell you in fifty-odd years on the boats I've never seen a man make such a mess of a meal as you do.'

We stopped at Las Palmas and we went to a dog track where we all laughed because we discovered the hare was being pulled along by a rope.

There wasn't a cigarette to be bought on the boat because I had stolen them all. There were thousands and thousands of cigarettes locked away in a potato locker. I came off the ship with no money but all these cigarettes, thousands and thousands and thousands of them.

I was gambling, cheating, lying, anything to have a bet. Even on the high seas I lost my money because there was a bookmaker on the boat and we used to get the bulletins of the racing. At twelve noon, there used to be the midday bulletin with the leading horse race of the day and that was my delight.

I found an engineer who fancied himself as a bookmaker. I recall the Grand National in 1948 when Russian Hero won it, Roimond was second and Royal Mount was third. The three Rs.

The round trip took about four and a half weeks and I didn't back one winner in all that time on the 'Race of the Day' with the engineer. When we got back to Southampton I owed him more than the ship was worth.

7

First Brush with the Law

I had my first brush with the law when I was in the West End. It was 1950 and I had reached the age of twenty-two. I was in the Mazurka Club one night. The police came in and took us all down to West End Central station. I came up in court at Bow Street Magistrates the next morning and I was fined 7s.6d for being in a common gaming house. It didn't have a licence. This particular evening nobody had any money or at least purported to have any money. I had a few quid on me but I wasn't going to declare what I had. The police raided the club and when we got to West End Central Police Station (my first time in a police station) the police said: 'Turn your pockets out.' No one wanted to, but eventually thousands came on the table: the money came out their socks, out their boots, out their trousers, out their shirts and everyone was laughing because 'nobody had any money'. No one had declared any money at the gaming house and here was thousands in cash along with dozens of diamonds and jewels and watches. That was my introduction to just how crooked the criminal classes were. The table was heaped up with money. Lying bastards.

In those days I had no responsibility. It's no different to now. I've blotted every copybook now, but back then I was just beginning.

So it wasn't a big surprise when my gambling debts forced me to make a hurried exit from Brighton to the only place I knew would be safe. I was still friendly with quite a lot of Brightonians who were in the Merchant Navy and they convinced me it was worth a second try.

My sailing days ended in 1953 after my second and last trip. I sailed on the Royal Mail ship the *Bloemfontein Castle*. I didn't spend long in South Africa, a couple of days there in Port Elizabeth and East London. We were told not to go to a place called District Six on our own, which was like the Haarlem of Cape Town but of course we went. I found a lovely Cape coloured girl in this notorious district, in The Navigator's Den which was on Adderley Street. I just walked in and I think all the coloureds and all the blacks and all the people there were amazed at my bravado. But I did, and I got back to the ship and I got seen and I got a bollocking for it.

I wasn't cheeky. I was quite a mild-mannered type of fellow but it was a case of two avenues to take and I took the wrong one. Like that old saying, 'Tall Oaks from Little Acorns Grow'. Everything that I did led up to more skulduggery.

When I came home in 1953 I had the cunning and the ability to get a pound very, very quickly – only to gamble with though. My parents were never really sick of me because they loved me dearly, but they got angry with me. The shopping money I'd lose, the rent money I'd lose, the 'this' money I'd lose, the 'that' money I'd lose. Just lose, lose, lose. Of course, I wasn't into major crime, which unfortunately landed on my doorstep later on. But I was headed that way. I couldn't have earned the amount of money I needed to gamble.

In Brighton I fell foul of two policemen who eventually got five years each for bribery and corruption. I got blackmailed by the two corrupt policemen, Detective Inspector John Hammersley and Detective Sergeant Trevor Ernest Heath of Brighton CID. They entrapped me and were getting bribes from me knowing full well that I was involved in false pretences and cheque frauds and stuff like that. They went to Wormwood Scrubs and when I got sent to the Scrubs for my first offence I saw them in there.

Brighton was the most corrupt town in the country. Some people remark that it bore a lot of similarity to Graham Greene's book *Brighton Rock*. When they were filming that down in Brighton in the forties I was also there, just stopping with friends. I was one of the extras.

The first time I was sent to prison was in 1958 when I was still living in Brighton. I was signing away my own cheques and selling the goods half price to get money to gamble with. I was travelling up to London and one day the inevitable happened. I got arrested.

I was in Burlington Arcade in N. Peal's the sweater people. I was trying to buy alpaca sweaters which I would have sold to meet the cheques when they came in three days later.

I was arrested by a detective who worked his way up the ranks and finished up as a Commander. His name was Kenneth Etheridge. I got taken to Bow Street Magistrates' Court. My uncle, who was practically a millionaire in those days, came to court and tried to save me. The total amount was only a couple of hundred pounds which he offered to pay to the shopkeepers.

I was not happy with my solicitors. My uncle got up and

said, 'I've got the money to repay this', and the magistrate replied, 'No. The damage has been done, you'll go to prison for nine months.'

I even served the full two-thirds that you were required to do then. In today's age you serve half, up to four years. Then you're on some licence for a little while, I don't know, it all changes every day.

Of course in prison I learned every trick of the trade. I served six months out of the nine and when I came out I looked upon myself as a hardened criminal at the age of twenty-two.

I got friendly with one of the Great Train Robbers, as he would become, Bobby Welch. A very nice fellow. I met all sorts of people in Eastchurch: hoodlums, racketeers, gangsters, all sorts.

I think it's like when you hear discussions today with do-gooders on the radio or on the television, it's true when they say the first prison sentence can do a lot of harm. It did *me* a lot of harm. I think that it contributed to more prison sentences. The environment, the gossip, the talk, the people all helped shape me as a hardened criminal.

There's no getting away from it, prison breeds prison. I mean, if you cage a person the person begins to think and act like an animal. Nothing good comes out of sending a person to prison.

This is what it's like. Someone says to me: 'Right, Morris. You'll go and work in Spitalfields food market for six months.' When I come from there I know everything about Spitalfields. By sending me to prison I knew everything about prison. It's commonsense, isn't it? Which an old fuddy duddy magistrate didn't realise, or did realise but didn't want to do anything about.

Instead of learning a job I was learning all there was to know about crime.

That is exactly what happened to me and, unfortunately,

and I'm not speaking for myself, I'm speaking about life in general right now, that is what's happening today as well. I don't say they shouldn't go to prison, I'm not clever enough, but people go to prison these days for drinking crimes, driving crimes, rowing on the bus or tube crimes, for crimes that are not actually criminal as such. A fellow drives on the wrong side of the road or crashes his car, he goes to jail. I don't say he should go to jail or he should not go to jail, I'm not the expert on such matters, but if he does go to jail he'll come out knowing more things about crime than if he didn't go to jail.

Well, that happened to me and I got a buzz while I was in jail listening to the conversation. 'You get cheques here . . .' 'You do this . . .' 'You get building society cheques here . . .' I was hooked, I was gone. That magistrate contributed to my present state. There is no question, no shadow of a doubt that he, whoever he was, was largely responsible for my present state. There's nobody in the world who could convince me that I'm wrong on that issue.

I was tossed into Wormwood Scrubs, which is an abominable place. Getting a packet of five Woodbines and a packet of Spangles for my pay, 1s.3d I think it was, and then after a couple of days of stench and filth a coach came and took us down to the Isle of Sheppey to Eastchurch.

In my heart of hearts I knew there were more prison sentences to come. I knew it.

When the time came to leave Eastchurch after six months of being trained to go from being a silly kid to an experienced villain, June picked me up by car at the prison gate and we went back to Brighton. That was in 1959. We were met by my friend Charlie Mendoza and we had a reunion. He couldn't understand how I was sent to jail. No one could. My parents were very emotional. Those were very emotional times. Charlie was my best friend. He was the one who opened a London bookmaker's with the former Tic Tac man called Benno Miller, and it became very successful. Charlie was a fine man and we lived next door to each other. He died a relatively young man, at the age of fifty-five. Very tragic. I was broken-hearted. He had become my best friend and my buddy. He was a hundred per cent straight fellow and he could see me going the other way. He was annoyed because we were the best of buddies.

So, I came home from the prison sentence to Brighton and got into a rut. I was doing nothing but just gambling, going to the races and seeing June. I stayed away from the West End for a while. The romance with June had to end sometime, it just died away. She had two children and she could see there was no future for us. She wanted me but she wanted the comforts of a secure home. It was quite obvious what she was going to choose, she wasn't a fool.

8

Gambling with a Beauty Queen

It was while I was in Brighton that I had the unique experience of going out with a Miss United Kingdom. Her name was Joyce Cook and she held the title some time in the 1950s.

Joyce lived in Brighton not far from my home in Brunswick Terrace near the promenade at Hove. She was tall, she was blonde, she had beautiful legs, a beautiful figure, and most of all she was a beauty queen. She was a lovely, lovely girl who reminded me of Veronica Lake, the peek-a-boo starlet of those days. She had won Miss Brighton or Miss Portslade and she then became Miss United Kingdom. I was in my thirties and I wooed and won her. All Brighton was talking about it.

There were no casinos at that stage but I took her everywhere, nightclubs, restaurants, wherever. There was a feller in Brighton, Horace Martin, who had a drinking club called The Cottage and in the back of the drinking club was a gambling set up where you could back horses, or dogs, or play cards. This club was in Brunswick Terrace in Hove. Joyce and I used to go out every day and night and we'd invariably go to The Cottage Club.

During the day I used to back horses in there and during the evening I used to have a drink. Horace loved the girl as much as I did. And when I used to walk into the club with Joyce on my arm, Horace used to say 'Oh, she's gorgeous. I wish I had a girl like that. I'd give you anything for her.'

I said: 'Horace. Nothing would separate me from Joyce.'

I was with her for quite some time and as the weeks and months went by Horace kept asking me about her.

One thing about Joyce I'll always remember was that she had a lilting voice and an infectious laugh, something like a giggle. Every time Horace Martin used to say, 'I'd give you anything for her. Anything at all,' I would reply: 'Money wouldn't buy her.'

But unfortunately, in the end, money did buy her. I was in trouble, as usual. I walked into the club one night with not a penny to buy a drink and there was the same old song from Horace. 'I'd give you anything for her. Anything.' She was giggling and looking just lovely and again he said: 'Morry. I'd give you anything for her.' On the way from our home in Brunswick Terrace, with the bracing sea wind whipping into our faces I had come to a decision. My pockets flapped in the breeze, they were so empty. So I turned to Horace and said: 'Come 'ere.' I walked him across to a corner of the club where I asked him: 'How much would you really give me?'

'Anything. Anything.'

'Would you give a hundred pounds for her?' Well, a hundred pounds in 1950 was quite a few quid. 'Would you give a hundred quid for her?'

Instantly he said yes. So we walked back to where Joyce was standing and I got hold of her, lifted her up, put her on the counter and sold her to Horace for the hundred pounds.

She didn't know what to make of it. She started giggling.

'Joyce,' I said, 'it's been lovely knowing you. But you realise I haven't got a dollar.' I held Horace's hundred pounds in my hands and said, 'You now belong to him. Joyce Cook, you are sold.'

'I'm not a slave,' she told me.

'Well, you are sold.' I got his hundred pounds and walked out. I think there might have been a tear in my eye. Behind me as I reached the street I could hear that attractive infectious laughter giggling away for its new owner.

The sequel to this story came many years later up in London. For years I'd been going to a fish restaurant called Grahames in Poland Street off Oxford Street, opposite the old Bourne and Hollingsworth. It has always been reputed, and correctly so, to be the best fish restaurant in London. They do especially lovely grilled fish. Expensive, I know, but I've always gone there when I could scratch together enough money. On this occasion I hadn't seen Joyce Cook for twenty-five years. It was about five years ago round about seven o'clock in the evening. I sat down on my own with the *Evening Standard* looking at the next day's race meetings, and behind me I heard a giggle. An infectious giggle. And I thought to myself, 'I know that giggle,' and lo and behold who do you think was there? Joyce Cook. After twenty-five or thirty years I'd bumped into my old sweetheart. She was sitting right behind me and when she saw me she couldn't believe it. Joyce has finished up living in Fulham working as an estate agent. I thought that was the most incredible thing in the world to bump into her after all those years. Unbelievable.

9

Coming Home

I was a bum from 1953 to 1960. Wasted years, until I was thirty-two and I came back to London permanently after getting fed up with Brighton.

The first night back I went to a dice game in Notting Hill where I met a family called Cronk who used to run the area.

I had a flat in Notting Hill, in Pembridge Gardens. Soon as I got there I found a young woman, an attractive girl called Penny, who was a hairdresser.

So now I'm living in Pembridge Gardens, hoisting and gambling and I'm starting to get my act together.

Soon I moved into Stuart Tower. It was a new block of flats built in 1961 beside the Edgware Road. My parents moved in there as well. I lived at 4M and they lived at 3C or something, which was on a different floor. I recall meeting Ann Sydney who was Miss World. I used to try and chat her up every day, though I never got anywhere with her.

By that time Penny was living with me. The rent was only

£11 a week – now it's about £200 a week. It was Church Commissioners' property.

I believe the Victoria Casino opened up at about that time and I was starting to fraternise there. The son of a Dutch diamond dealer by the name of George Winberg owned it.

Nothing in my life was legal. I was betting at a Point-to-Point for Albert Dimes: I got a bit of chalk, a lump of wood and a box and I became a bookmaker, with no licence or anything. People used to come up for their money and I had none to pay them, so I got pinched.

There were loads of us doing the same thing, the whole of the fraternity from Frith Street and the Albert Dimes' mob who were all bookmakers. None of us was legit. When people came up asking for money I used to say: 'I'll send it to you in the morning. It'll be with your toast and marmalade. Don't worry about it.'

I used to give them the spiel and that was it. But on one occasion in 1963 a couple of plainclothes policemen arrested me. I ended up in Lexden and Winstree Magistrates' Court where I was fined £2 for failing to produce a written authorisation to act as a bookmaker.

Dice was the main attraction. The Cronks' place in Clarendon Road attracted many famous names. Of course, these games were still illegal. But already I was having more fun than I recalled from my days in Brighton.

I started to spend a lot of time over that way, gambling at dice, which I love. This was all downstairs in the basement run by the Cronks. Many years later I was to run into old man Cronk's daughter, Maureen, a lovely girl who later became a Page Three model who went under the name of Polly Dillon.

10

The Head Teams Up with the Swan

It was around this time I started hanging out regularly with The Swan. Most of my life has been taken up with the company and the help of this ex-partner of mine called The Swan.

Having met up with him many years ago in a gambling environment I discovered he is the only man in the world that I know who treats money with less value than I do. I have had millions, he has had millions plus. He is exactly my double. When I look in the mirror I see him.

He comes from Golders Green and is the son of a well-to-do Jewish family. Brian Kutner is his name. His brother is a multi-millionaire and won't have anything to do with him.

He has burnt more bridges than I have and I've burnt every one. I've got no friends, no family, he's got no-no friends and no-no family. We're birds of a feather.

His life is obsessed with gambling, perhaps even more than mine. When I used to gamble I used to love live society, girls, sex, clothes. He doesn't like anything but gambling.

If he was to win £10,000 at the races he would put an elastic band round it, take it home, go back the next day without taking a pound out of it, because he doesn't believe it's his money, he thinks it belongs to the races. He's that type of man. He used to wake up at two o'clock in the morning and go to gamble.

I've branched out on other ventures but he didn't. He's called The Swan because he's got a very long neck. So the partnership became The Swan and The Head.

We earned more money together with my fingers than any two men in the world. He was the 'distraction'. At this game, the game that I was at, stealing jewellery, distraction is eighty or ninety per cent of it. For me to beat a person without distraction is difficult.

We've had more rows than anybody you can think of. It's impossible to just get on with the job. If this was now October and I said it's October he would say it's December. If I said it was light he would say it was dark. We can never ever agree on anything. And, as I say, he's the most ferocious gambler I've ever seen in my life. Mainly because he just has no value at all for a pound note. I am very, very bad, he is worse. That is my description.

We started with the hoist. Women from South London used to go into stores wearing a big pair of knickers and they put everything down, pots and pans, knives and forks, shirts and suits, mink coats and umbrella stands, you name it they got it down their oversized drawers. That was a well-known game; today it's played out because of the technology, the buzzers, the metallic buzzers, although the tags can still be taken off.

He and I, when we were broke, we'd go into the West End. We used to wake up at nine o'clock, yawn, have a coffee and by midday we'd earned four, five, six hundred pounds each, simply by the hoist. Ties, shirts, shoes, you name it, we got it.

We knew everybody at the racetracks and elsewhere in London to sell them to, bank robbers, anybody.

Every shilling we got we lost.

Everybody in London was talking about The Swan and The Head. A typical day would go like this:

'You got any money, Brian?'

'No. You got any money, Morry?'

'No.'

Take twenty-five years ago in Hatton Garden. In Hatton Garden there are hundreds and hundreds of offices, wholesale jewellers, diamond dealers. We have robbed nearly every one. We'd pose as a couple of businessmen opening a shop somewhere. They'd bring out their diamonds and their rings and their bangles, baubles and beads and it became a 'Help Yourself'. They put them on the table and messed them about and that's that. The same as someone bringing out a jigsaw puzzle with all the pieces all over the place. If I take five or six pieces no one's going to miss them. But at that time we weren't aware of the real value of the stuff we were stealing.

Years ago, by the old *Daily Mirror* offices, there was a firm of diamond investors. We went up there posing.

'Oh. Good morning.'

'The boss is away at the moment. I'm the accountant.'

'Well, can't you help us?'

'Yes. I'll show you.'

The accountant brought out a box of diamonds and we helped ourselves.

11

International Jewel Thief

In 1963 we got fed up with the hoisting and went for bigger money. We decided we'd get into a higher echelon of crime by going to Switzerland. Well, why not be adventurous?

We went to Zurich to steal watches. Our first foreign trip as criminals. We didn't consciously set out to become international jewel thieves. It just happened that way. This was our first taste of crime on the Continent. We were after top-class watches, the Rolls Royce of watches, the Vacheron Constantin, the Piagets, the Patek Philippes, the Longines, the Cartiers.

The Bahnhofstrasse is the Bond Street of Zurich where nearly every shop is a jeweller's shop. We robbed them all. But we robbed them all of watches instead of diamonds. Later we would return for the diamonds. But this was a learning curve for both of us young scallywags. This marked the moment of another great change in my life. I was living bigger, gambling bigger, eating and drinking bigger, womanising bigger. I was playing the top. I was going from Cricklewood to Hollywood.

I was thinking bigger in all sorts of ways. My appetite for life was bigger. Life is all about units, really, isn't it? If you're on the dole and you've got no money, you'll go to Asda. If you're getting money you'll go to Waitrose. I was going from a 'Piss in the Bucket' club in Frith Street in Soho to the finest casino in the world in Monte Carlo, The Sporting Club.

I was stealing hundreds of thousands of pounds' worth of diamonds as opposed to ties and scarves and it was easier.

It didn't make me stop stealing scarves, because, for the moment, the scarf put food in my mouth. Everything was easy. About that time I was also putting hundreds of thousands of pounds' worth of cheques all around the Continent for ordinary goods which I could resell with ease to give me ready cash.

What happened was this. I had started off shoplifting and discovered I had a special talent. I could stretch out my two hands and lift a diamond so quickly the shopkeeper didn't know it had gone from his tray into my hand, whence it would disappear into my pocket. This trick is known in the trade as 'Palming'. When my friends in the underworld realised how good I was at this, it became my special skill for which I was often employed until I decided to branch out on my own. The second trick, similar to palming, is 'Switching' which is when you have eyed up a jeweller's wares and gone away to get a Cubic Zirconia, a paste diamond, of the same shape and size which you then take back to the shop and swap for the real thing. What I need to do this successfully is for someone else to distract the shopkeeper or assistant, either a man talking to him, in those days all the assistants were male, or a woman with a see-through blouse to thrust her breasts at him so his mind's not on the action.

So with these skills The Swan and I flew to Zurich and later we went to Italy, to Rome. We went to the South of France, we went everywhere getting money. It was relatively easy. The thing that stopped us in France was the OAS. We were getting lots of money in top-class jewellers all over the South of France. But all that came to an end when the OAS started robbing jewellery shops. They didn't have our style. They just marched in wielding automatic rifles and pistols and took whatever they wanted. In my trade the jeweller is often unaware I've been to his shop and stolen a diamond, so there's no general alert. But it's a dead giveaway when half a dozen people march in wearing balaclava masks and leather jackets, pointing machine guns and threatening to explode bombs. The jewellers started taking serious precautions and that made it difficult to work in the South of France for a while. We were performing in Cannes and each day the security became stronger, which was a bit of a killer since we had been raking in lots and lots of money.

We had gone to Zurich at the time when you could take only £30 pounds in cash out of the country. Cheque-book fraud was a useful back-up when I couldn't get money from the straightforward stealing of diamonds and watches. The £30 limit helped me with the cheque books I was using because all the European shops knew that if you were British you couldn't pay for anything in cash. For example, in Geneva they were so naive I didn't even have to use a cheque. There was a shop in Geneva called Le Maison de Piaget where the owner was a very charming middle-aged French lady who spoke good English. After looking at two or three of her watches, which were very expensive, I said that I'd like to buy two but unfortunately the British government allowed me to bring out only £30 in cash. She was aware of this. I said: 'I would like to give you my private cheque for this.'

'Don't bother, sir, take them.'

I was flabbergasted.

'My two sons are at school in Holland Park.' Which was next to Notting Hill Gate where I had a flat. 'They will come round and collect the money for the watches. Do take the watches.'

Well, obviously I took the watches, flew home and moved

out of the flat as fast as I could. By nightfall of the afternoon I had arrived back in London I was living in a new flat. At the same time I was giving cheques all over Europe for jewellery and clothes because I looked immaculate, spoke immaculately and presented myself as the perfect Englishman.

Why I never got prosecuted was, I think, because it was illegal to accept the cheques in the first place, so they couldn't call the police or the law. They would have been putting themselves in trouble. It was what we call 'A Straight Pros,' meaning that the shopkeeper in his wisdom was committing an illegal act and therefore couldn't do anything about it. It happened all over Europe. People suddenly twigged, like I had twigged.

12

The Perfect Englishman

Strangely enough I finished up in a French newspaper all because of my arguments with Brian, The Swan. As I say, he's the world's most argumentative man but he would disagree and say *I* was the world's most argumentative man. So that'd be another argument. Sometimes I get fed up arguing so on this occasion I decided to branch out on my own. I went to Nice where I was giving out dud cheques and stealing diamonds and not long after I got busted in a jeweller's shop in Nice. They recognised me from somewhere else because my description had been circulated. And so I'm busted in 1964. The *Nice Matin*, the local newspaper, described me as 'Un Anglais Très Comme Il Faut', which means 'The Perfect Englishman'. The defence lawyer, who was a Corsican called Pierre Pasquini, described me not as a villain but as an artist. 'He makes things disappear.' Pierre Pasquini was the leading lawyer in France and when he told the judge that I'm not a villain I'm an artist, the judge laughed. The newspapers described me as a magician because the shopkeepers couldn't account for the jewellery disappearing while I was talking to them.

I was thrown into the Rue de la Gendarmerie, the prison in Nice. Everybody goes to Nice for a holiday. I went there to go into prison.

Then it transpired that my first trip to Zurich in 1963 was also going to pay for a free return ride after the French judicial system had been satisfied I had paid the price for robbing the country of some of its plentiful supply of diamonds. In 1964 I was extradited from the Rue de la Gendarmerie in Nice in France to Switzerland when I had completed my sentence of six months in a French jail. I went to Marseilles, from Marseilles they put me on a train and sent me overnight to Geneva. There were warrants out for me from all these countries in Europe owing to these cheques.

If I could have got home to Britain it wouldn't have mattered because you can't be extradited out of your own country for false pretences. I didn't know that when I started but en route I was told it. However, I was in the painful process of discovering that you can be extradited from one foreign country to another.

So I was put on the train at Marseilles and transferred to Geneva, where I got two years under very tough conditions. From Geneva they sent me to Zurich from where I was led out by the police to the Bahnhofstrasse and asked which jewellers I did. I didn't tell them I did every one. I looked dumb and pointed, rather sadly, at one jewellers. I was trying to remember which one had got me the least amount of money.

I got two years' imprisonment in September of 1965 at the Supreme Court, Canton of Zurich, for professional fraud, an incompleted attempt at professional fraud and theft committed with associates. The sentence was reduced by the 363 days I had already spent in custody. They ordered that I lose five years of civil rights and be banished for fifteen years.

I remember being housed in a cell next to Donald Hume, the man who was convicted of being an accessory after the fact in the shooting of Stanley Setty, the brother of the man who owned the Mayfair nightclub, The Blue Angel. He was doing life for two murders in Zurich. When he heard I was English he went completely bananas, off his head. He was singing 'It's a Long Way to Tipperary' every day. I think now he's in Rampton or Broadmoor or something.

13

The Australian Gang

In September 1966 I came back from Switzerland after spending two years of my life in a dungeon. Switzerland deported me, banishing me from the country.

When I came home the biggest gambling club in London was called The Mount and run by a man call Franny Daniels who's now dead and who was Albert Dimes' right hand man. It was about this time that Albert Dimes introduced me to the Australians as the best of my kind or ilk or whatever you like to put it. I was to get fortunes with the Australians. They knew more stings and scams than I'd ever imagined.

One took place in the bank in Marble Arch where six of us walked in and kept the assistants talking while one relieved himself against the wall. Everybody in the bank left their positions to see what he was doing and so all the drawers were open and all the money was taken.

Another method was like a football team, ten or eleven strong, including three or four girls, who would all go into a jewellery shop. As they were all engaging the assistants in talk and distractions one of them would get into the windows of the shop and take every piece of jewellery that was in it. Every day in the newspapers it said: 'Australian Gang Strikes Again.' They cleared out shops in Bond Street in broad daylight.

Years ago the West End was a gift. It was an absolute pension. You used to go out broke in the morning at nine o'clock and get whatever money you needed until you wanted to stop. It was 'Help Yourself'. There was no technology then but the arrival of the Australians changed all that.

The Aussies set London alight back in the Sixties. Jack the Fib, who never told the truth in his life, lovely man; Pat Burns, Billy Hill, Australian Danny, Terry the Kid, Wee Willy, Wee Jimmy, Broken Nose Hughie, The Duke, who's dead now, his real name was Arthur Delaney, although Arthur wasn't much of a gambler. There was Black Nick, Peanut, The Lisp, Jim the Postman, Hollywood George, Punch, Verbal Barry; they were all working in London. Most of them were ferocious gamblers and amazing money getters. As a group they were very staunch people, not like now. If one of them happened to get arrested and it cost some money to get him out, to pay lawyers or to bribe police, immediately they chipped in and put in what they considered was their share. If it was three grand someone would put up a monkey (five hundred pounds), someone would put up four hundred quid, there was never any trouble about putting the money in. Even though they gambled they still always kept quite a bit of money safe. They would look after each other. Money wasn't their abiding thing in life. They'd always help anyone who was broke or in trouble. They were what we call 'Good People' and you don't see the likes of them nowadays in this drug-related society. Even in the criminal society everybody's thinking about the next snort of cocaine or the next shot of heroin.

They had some great characters. Jack the Fib was a larger

edition of me. He was a bald-headed man, about six foot, fattish face, smooth skin and smooth head. He's still alive in Australia and he became a millionaire at one time and lots of us used to go over and see him. His son Barry was also a big fat boy. He was over here, he was only sixteen at the time and he was out working with Jack and the Australians. Unfortunately he died in Bangkok when he was about twenty-five. The last time I saw Jack was at Wembley at the boxing and Jack was just going over to Bangkok to see his son, about twenty years ago. About a year or so later we heard he died from some out-of-the-way disease.

Arthur Delaney – the Duke – was like a young edition of Robert Redford. Blondish hair, very smart, always immaculately dressed, medium height, medium built, he was very good-looking and he was actually the governor, what they called 'The General'. He was in charge of the whole Australian shoplifting gang. He used to go to any town where they were going to work the next day, walk the streets, prepare everything. He was really an extraordinarily good planner.

Hughie Hairlip was a farmer's boy. He had a hairlip, quite obviously, and he was a typical farmer's boy from the outback. His people had a big farm somewhere up in the north of Queensland. He looked and dressed like a farmer just come off the train from the outback. He always looked the same.

Black Nick, he looked like a Greek. He was quite tall, fattish, quite well built with very swarthy skin and very black sleek hair. He looked like someone from a Mediterranean country.

Most of the others were nondescript people, you wouldn't have picked them out in a crowd. Maybe that is why they had such success. But they were the crème-de-la-crème of all the shoplifting and hoisting gangs that ever worked in Britain. Then again, in those days it was very easy, there was no security, no technology, no video cameras, no buzzers on the doors, the staff weren't conscious of stealing from shops. In fact, the crime was different in every way in those days. There were no burglar alarms in private homes, private people scarcely had any locks on their doors. This is going back thirty to thirty-five years ago. As times changed things got much harder. It's never the same. On the Continent, it's still much easier than England because they haven't had the terrible going over that the British shops have had. All right, they've suffered a few people coming over from England and perhaps from Australia, but on the whole they haven't really had the seeing-to that the British shops have had to go through.

They wanted me because of my demeanour, because of my style. Half of why they needed me was the distraction, I was good at drawing the attention away from the gang. Plus the fact that I knew of a lot of work for them – jewellery. Hotels, that was our strength. We got fortunes in the Grosvenor, in the Hilton, in the Ritz. All jewellers used to display their goods in showcases. Well, we took the lot. We used to know where the keys were – in the cloakroom. We'd watch the jeweller open up and then we'd get him out on some excuse, open the cabinet after taking the keys and get the lot. Every hotel in London we must have done. The Dorchester, we had all the cabinets open in the Dorchester. Took the lot.

During those years I had run into all the top gangsters and thieves through meeting them at these gambling clubs. But the Australians were the weirdest bunch of crooks I ever came across. They elevated shoplifting to an art form.

There were loads of scams I learnt from the Australians. Here's another game for a Monday morning. What we used to do was take an old car, go into a garage.

'I've broken down.'

The man would come out. As he comes out another one goes in and takes all the money.

That was the Garage Trick. Can't do it today because of the technology.

False money. There's always been false money. There's false

money about today. You know, forgeries, counterfeit stuff. I mean for twenty quid you go into a tobacconist's shop, get two sticks of licorice or chewing gum or something and get nineteen pounds in change from the false money. That's been going around for ages, everybody does that. I'm adaptable; I can go into any scam.

One day, we were in a shop in King's Street in Hammersmith, on a very busy Saturday afternoon, when Saturday afternoon in Hammersmith was like a Cup Final. This shop had a double-fronted window with the entrance in the middle. The name of the shop was Hinds. In both windows there were hundreds and hundreds of rings and watches and bracelets and chains, everything packed into two windows and one of them, one of the Aussies, who was like an Indian scout, went off and reconnoitred and came back and said: 'Right. There's eight of them.'

So there was going to be nine of us. One man is called The Taker. So it's eight against eight which leaves The Taker to furtively get in without being seen, which wasn't hard. Anyway we swooped. Before I went in I noticed that on every bit of the two windows there wasn't an inch to spare on which you could have placed another piece of jewellery.

After about five minutes, out of the corner of my eye, I saw The Taker, whose name was Keith, come in. And as we were distracting the staff he was in the process of putting everything into something like a bin liner in broad daylight with people going by, normal shoppers on a Saturday afternoon. He always used to say to me: 'Morry, don't worry about the mugs.' The mugs were the straight shoppers. Because he was in his blue suit and white shirt anyone looking in from outside would think he was one of the staff taking the goods out of the window.

Anyway, when he'd left with two suitcases full of jewellery, I started to laugh because I couldn't believe it. As I walked out the shop I noticed the windows were bare, not a single piece of jewellery left in the windows.

I was with a little fellow, Peter, in my car and the rest were in other cars and we had a rendezvous nearby. I said to Peter: 'Look. I just want to see what happens next.' This wasn't a one-off, this had been done hundreds of times. Obviously the police knew about the Australian gang but they didn't know where they were going to swoop. So we drove round and I parked my car opposite the shop and this is what I saw, something like a pantomime. I couldn't hear what was going on but why I started to laugh was because of the two empty windows. I could see all the staff including the manager standing outside the shop looking at the windows and just wondering what had happened. No one had thrown a brick in there or a bomb. It had just been cleaned out in broad daylight at three o'clock on a sunny Saturday afternoon. What I imagined being said was this:

'Rose. Did you take the goods out of the window?'

'No, sir.'

'Jim. Did you take them out?'

'No, sir.'

'Roger. Did you take them out?'

'No.'

'Well. All the jewellery has disappeared.'

I worked with the Australians for many years. I worked with them all over the world including their own country in 1980. I worked with them in Paris, Zurich, Geneva, Antwerp, and Baden-Baden, my favourite town. I worked with them in Canada, oh, dozens of different countries.

The first bit of work I did with the Aussies was the one I laugh about most. It happened one day when, due to my gambling, I was in a psychiatric hospital called The Belmont in Surrey. The man in the next bed to me was a real weirdo. He thought he was Hitler.

A crime reporter from the *News of the World* came to see me to propose writing a story. He knew all about me. So we went up to London for the day. I had to be back in the hospital by a certain time of night.

I had got on the train to Victoria and picked up the *Evening News* and in the paper it said that Lady Selina Jones, who still owns a shop in Beauchamp Place in Knightsbridge, was opening with a champagne party in the Brompton Arcade just off Sloane Square. And I thought, 'I wonder . . .' So I got in touch with the Aussies and told them.

The Duke, Arthur Delaney, was staying with the gang at The White House in Regent's Park. He was a very dapper little man. He used to boast of his exploits and call himself 'The World's Raffles', the best in the world, which has been attributed to me in the past, but anyway that's another matter.

About ten of us invited ourselves into this champagne party and there were millions of pounds' worth of diamonds and jewels on show. There were all sorts of Aussies there including Aussie girls and Aussie wives but they were all workers. Shortly after their arrival at the champagne party not a jewel or a diamond remained in sight. Not one. All the showcases, which were open, all the rolls of diamonds and jewels, everything had gone whilst the champagne party was going on.

When I left I got in a taxi and went back to The White House to see Arthur. I knocked on his suite door.

'Come in.'

And as I came in, I saw a sight I'll never forget. There was the Duke with a girl, both of them in the nude, lying on the bed and in between them was every bit of jewellery and diamonds this lord's daughter had put on show in her shop.

The Australians used to come over in batches, ten at a time, do a couple of months' work, send their money back to Australia and go back home.

As ever I was still gambling. In an evening I would be given money for my day's work, a thousand, fifteen hundred, two thousand, three thousand, whatever it was. Remember, I was only an eighth or a tenth of the group so you can imagine the sort of money we were cleaning up. Everybody got this every day. The next morning I used to roll up without my cab fare.

'Where's your money?' they used to ask.

'I lost it in the casino.'

At that time I was going into The Colony Club casino in London every night without fail. It was the best casino in the whole of London. There'll never be another one like it.

I was known as one of the smartest men in the West End. When I wasn't Morry the Head they used to call me Mayfair Morry.

I was a top Mayfair jetsetter. I would be walking about in Pinet shoes, Turnbull and Asser shirts and Huntsman suits. They were the best tailors in the whole of London, you had to wait ten months to have a suit made there.

There were occasional breaks in the style. For example, I once found myself wearing a boiler suit, with bin liners wrapped round me, pushing a barrow and emptying dustbins at Leyhill Prison for nine months. My Mayfair Morry nickname was changed there for a while to that of Morry the Womble. I had gone from mixing with the playboy set and the jet set at the Ritz Casino and the Carlton Casino and the Baden-Baden Casino to pulling a dustbin dressed in bin liners.

14

Bailed Out by the Mafia's Top Man

When I was living well I used to go Simpson's in the Strand for meat, Scott's for fish and the best casinos. During this time I became friendly with the actor George Raft, who was the 'front man', the host at The Colony Club. The Club was run by Dino Cellini who was the Mafia's gambling boss in Britain.

George Raft was the American film star who was once refused entry to Britain because he was accused of fronting for the Mafia. We were very friendly. I was in The Colony six or seven nights a week. The food was the best in London.

All the famous faces of the time would be there. I used to play dice with the likes of Jerry Lewis the comedian, Cubby Broccoli the Bond film producer, he was there every night, Roger Moore was there, Tony Curtis was there, Michael Caine was there. It was a high-class meeting area in Berkeley Square. The in-place to gamble, eat and meet top people.

Dino Cellini was the loveliest man I have ever met in my life. Elegant, smart, knowledgeable. Although Dino was the Mafia's number one man in Britain, a number one gangster, he never

ever showed it. Actually, I wouldn't really call him a gangster, he was too smooth. A man you would only expect to read about in books. You wouldn't see many Dinos in this world. He was everything that Hollywood could dream up. He was the brains, the legal man, not the hustler or the muscle. Dino was the man the Americans put there because The Colony was all American-style, the finest casino in London.

One night I wanted to borrow some money from Dino. I had gone broke. Night after night I was doing thousands and thousands. I used to have dinner with Dino and Raft and Freddie and Whitey. It was staffed by Americans, it was run in an American atmosphere and run in a meticulous American way. It was the place to see and be seen.

This night I was broke and I had decided to make my first move as such in there. I knew it would be hard and I had walked up to Dino and said: 'Can I have a word with you?'

'Sure,' the lovely way he said it. 'Whatdya want?'

'I need some money.'

'You can't borrow any money.' Just like that.

I was downcast. Then he looked me straight in the eyes.

'But, you can *have* some money.'

I was flabbergasted.

'I'm gonna give you some money and I don't want you to give it back to me. Because, number one, if you give it back to me you can ask me again and you can ask me for more, and then you can ask me for more and more and more.' He knew every move in the book. 'Eventually we'll lose your custom because you won't be able to pay me back and I don't want that.'

He spoke to me very quietly in the corner of the casino. 'You go over to the cash desk, to the cashier, and you'll get some money. I don't want to hear any more about either that money or any money in the future. I don't want to lose you as a friend, I don't want to lose you as a customer, I never want to lose you.' Which was very well put and very clever.

Now we've established that, and he's made me feel better, because he's gonna give me some money. He's not going to put his hand in his pocket, the casino is gonna give me the money.

'Well, how much can I have?'

'How much do you want?'

To be truthful I don't remember the amount but I think it was in the region of three or four thousand pounds, maybe five thousand. That must have been in the late Sixties, an absolute fortune. We both walked over, I signed a bit of paper and I got the money. I never repaid it because he wouldn't have taken it, whatever it was and that was it and that was Dino.

I always feel proud of the fact that through an intermediary, when he was dying in Rome, he asked for me. He asked for me to fly out there which I didn't do because he died even before I'd been told about it. That's the second man on his deathbed who's asked to see me. The other man was Moshe Cohen, a Jewish bookmaker who had his offices in Greek Street, who I was friendly with.

15

A Brief Acquaintance With
a Diamond Necklace in Rome

Albert Dimes had a friend in Rome, Dave Crowley, an ex-British lightweight boxing champion, who's now dead.

Dave had a bar in Rome under the Hotel Savoy. I went to Rome with The Swan. It was the year the Pope went to bless the waters, I can't remember exactly where. There were visitors from all over the world.

We arrived there on a Sunday and I'd made arrangements to go to see Dave Crowley in his bar to find out where the best jewellery shops were so I could visit them.

Dave sent me to a very expensive jeweller's shop. Before we went to the shop we checked in to the Hotel Excelsior on the Via Veneto which was one of the best hotels in Rome.

Brian had recently broken his leg and was hobbling about with a walking stick.

At that time on a Sunday in the summer in Italy it was

the custom for all the families to go out walking in the late afternoon.

We both went into this jeweller's shop and there was the most magnificent diamond necklace in the window. There were also several people in the shop. To my amazement the window was opened and while Brian distracted the owner of the shop I took the necklace. I had my back to the window, slid my hand in and got it. I then made my way back to the Hotel Excelsior and on leaving the shop I could hear whistles and screams and shouting, knowing full well that the owner realised the necklace had gone and that Brian was having a bit of difficulty getting out of the shop. I had gone ahead because I had the goods and Brian was limping.

We had to go up a hill and there were hundreds of people out walking, particularly since this was the actual day the Pope was blessing the waters.

Brian and I had parted near the Spanish Steps as he couldn't keep up with me because of his broken leg. He was only able to hobble around with the aid of a walking stick. Suddenly he was alone and at that moment a man came up from behind him and said 'Hold it there.' It was the man from the shop where we had just stolen the necklace.

Swan's heart sank as he knew he was well and truly 'nicked'. The man spoke good English and asked him to accompany him back to the shop. Just at that moment a policeman came past. They conducted a hurried conversation in Italian which Swan did not understand. The outcome was that he had to go with them to the police station.

Now I had the necklace but Swan had four valuable watches on him that we had stolen earlier in the day. He realised if he was searched and these were found he was going to be in a lot of trouble. As they walked along he had them in one hand looking for a way to get rid of them. They were walking with him on the inside, the man from the shop right next to him and the policeman just in front.

As they passed some hoardings The Swan saw a gap in them and threw the watches through this space. Miraculously, no one noticed.

When they were inside the police station, which was no bigger than the average living room, the man from the shop said he must call his brother-in-law who was the owner.

When he arrived he spoke perfect English and didn't seem very perturbed about the theft. All he said was he wanted the item of jewellery given back. Eventually, The Swan had to take a chance on their word being good.

I was safely back in the hotel with a necklace worth thirty or forty grand in those days. I was in the foyer, sat on a big armchair. I had put the necklace under the cushion of the chair and was waiting for Brian.

After about two hours he still hadn't arrived. So my instinct told me that he'd been 'buckled' as we describe being arrested, stopped or held.

I phoned Crowley and told him all about it. He said he'd try to get to the hotel to see me. A couple of hours passed before the revolving doors of the hotel opened and I saw Brian coming towards me with his stick. Behind him were two or three quite large Italian gentlemen.

'They know that you've had the necklace.' Turning to point out the Italians, he added: 'This is the owner, his brother-in-law and the top policeman. What they're prepared to do is if you give them back the necklace they'll take us to the airport and we can go and no charges will be made against us.'

'Look. Number one, I haven't got the necklace. Number two, the Mafia couldn't get the necklace off me if I had it.'

So we dallied and dillied, hummed and hawed and eventually Crowley arrived. After listening to the story, Crowley pulled me aside – the necklace is still under the cushion of the seat I was sitting on – and said: 'I think you'd better give it back to them.'

To my surprise, the owner of the shop said: 'We'll give you a couple of thousand pounds. Give us back the necklace and you can go.'

Which I thought was a wonderful deal considering that we had been in trouble. They wouldn't even be frogmarching us to the airport. After thinking about it for a few minutes I said to Crowley: 'Can I trust them?'

'Yes. Implicitly.'

They took out the money, all in lira, the equivalent of about two thousand English pounds. I went to the cushion of the chair, produced the necklace.

We would have been arrested and we would have been in a lot of trouble if we hadn't taken the offer. It was a gentlemen's agreement. They were prepared to give a sort of reward and on the spur of the moment I decided it was the best thing to do. When I lifted the cover of the seat they were amazed and I thought: 'Here come the guns.'

But they handed over the money. They were as good as their word. They were prepared to lose the money to get the necklace back.

Later that evening I set off with The Swan to tramp the streets looking for the hoarding. Eventually, after a long time, we found it. By this time it was pitch black. We managed to borrow a torch from the bistro at the corner. The Swan proceeded to jemmy away the wood with his walking stick. When we had enough space to get through we discovered it was covering a bomb crater. Despite his bad leg, The Swan scrambled down into this hole with me holding the torch. Once again another miracle occurred. In the dust and rubble he found three of the watches. We searched and searched but couldn't find the fourth one. It had disappeared.

Anyhow, we left Rome that night for Nice and sold the watches to a bookmaker we knew from Blackpool who wintered every year in the South of France.

16

A Detective Inspector Fell
into my Pocket

I was introduced to a man in Hatton Garden who worked as a watch and diamond dealer. After considering the position for a while I could see there was a chance of getting a lump of money out of this man.

It was in the Seventies and I decided to go for him and his jewels by exploiting a well-used plan. I would spend a bit of money with him, in the hope that by losing a few quid for one or two weeks I would soon gain much more. I started buying watches. As long as I was paying him cash it was all right. Then one day I went in and said I would like to buy a watch here and a watch there and the whole amount came to much more than I had been spending. I spun him a story about how I did not have the cash on me at the time and I was also unsure whether or not the people I was buying for would want what I had chosen. I always had an aunt in Bournemouth or an uncle in Japan for these occasions. It went something like this:

'They've got peculiar tastes. I don't want to commit myself at this stage.'

'Oh. That's all right.'

'But you know something. I'm running short of cash.'

'Oh. That's no problem either.'

I knew he was going to say this and what was also coming.

'Settle up with me at the end of the week.'

So the exercise had proved fruitful. I had some tasty diamonds and watches on approval. There's something special about walking off with a lump of diamonds on appro. I mean, the shopkeeper's actually letting you walk out of his place knowing you have his diamonds and for him it's all above board, it's all legal. Except there's going to be a problem. The diamonds are making their last appearance in his shop and you don't want to go to prison.

I had taken half a dozen very good watches off this jeweller and also diamonds. The total value at that time was £43,000. This was ten o'clock in the morning and my next engagement was Sandown Park Races whereupon I sold all of his goods. Incidentally, the races have always been a good place to sell goods. The bookmakers like a bargain. On this day I had reached my usual state by the last race at Sandown. In other words, I was broke. I had lost my money and he had lost his jewellery. Of course, I got home with a sore head.

Now what you have to remember is this: in those days bribery was rife in the West End. Eventually, lots of crooked policemen got caught – Commander Ken Drury, Detective Chief Superintendent Bill Moody, they all got done. In the Sixties and Seventies London's police force contained some very crooked individuals. You could buy yourself out of anything, well, almost anything. Later I was personally to know certain police officers, two on the Flying Squad, who were corrupt and these were high ranking officers. When I say I knew them, I was introduced to them. Everybody in London had a policeman in their pocket. You could ring 'em up and say: 'Look, do this, do that.' For money, you could get out of almost anything.

After Sandown, when I had lost all the money, I was frantic. I spoke to a friend of mine who said he knew two crooked policemen.

This friend was one of the pickpockets who worked the underground every morning. They went to their jobs just like ordinary people going to work in offices and shops. Their best times were the rush hours. They used to buzz the commuters' wallets and all that business, which was a business I didn't like.

I knew this pickpocket really well. We used to meet in a popular bar in Jermyn Street called Jules.

'You don't have a problem,' he said. 'Get a few quid together and I'll speak to one of these policemen who can organise something for you. It'll cost you about a grand.'

Now that was a lot of money back then but I had to get hold of it to stay out of prison. So a few quid was got, my friend spoke to the policeman, and after a few days I met him at Hyde Park Corner. He said: 'Look, the only way to get out of this is to get yourself pickpocketed.'

I'm in the bent cop's hands right now. He's the expert and he's getting my five hundred quid. So I need to know how he's going to make this work. So I say to him: 'Where? Where do I get pickpocketed?'

'Go to Selfridges because I know a crooked policeman in Marylebone Police Station which Selfridges comes under.'

The plan is explained. I am supposed to be riding up and down the escalator at Selfridges and all of a sudden, poor old me, I've been robbed.

I should be in films, what with all the acting I've had to do in my life. So I set off for Oxford Street learning my most crucial line which is: 'Ah. My wallet!' To be said with feeling.

I'm in Selfridges and I rush down the escalator to the security people looking every bit the flustered innocent business-man.

'We can't do anything for you, you'll have to go round to Marylebone Police Station,' they tell me. I'm happy now because this is all in the script written by the crooked police-man. I got well into the part. Now I am playing the central character on stage. Oh, I was so distressed at my terrible loss.

'Oh, my wallet, my wallet. I've lost my wallet.'

'What was in it?' A kind caring security face stares me in the eyes.

'Thousands! Diamonds! Watches! I bumped into two Filipinos, I think they must've had it.'

I arrive there and I am not at all bothered because I know the governor of the police station has several hundred pounds to turn a blind eye. He was a Detective Inspector in the CID and he was one of the most senior people in the station. So the Desk Sergeant says: 'Yes, sir. What can I do for you?'

'I've lost forty-three thousand pounds worth of diamonds. They've been stolen off of me. I was pickpocketed on the escalator in Selfridges.'

'What!' he said and nearly fainted.

'Yes. Diamonds. I've lost them.'

'Oh. I'll get the CID.'

Well, I'm not bothered because I know the CID knows the strength, is crooked, and I'm going to get off.

He said: 'Will you wait in there, sir. The CID will be down in a minute.'

Down comes this man, who's been taken care of, along with a big rugby-looking type of fellow, a six-foot-six fellow, a young CID constable, as big as the Houses of Parliament. It frightened me to death just to look at him. 'Hallo Morry. I've heard about all this. X has been on with a complaint.'

'Come upstairs a minute.'

He slams the door and they sit me down and says to me:

'Don't you fuck me about. Are you coming across with some shit about being pickpocketed on the escalator in Selfridges with all these diamonds and watches? What is this load of bollocks that you're telling me?' I thought: 'This is funny, he's supposed to have been taken care of, he's supposed to be on my side.'

I was rather surprised because I thought he would be a lot kinder having pocketed five hundred pound to be on my side. He's supposed to be my pal. Well, he wasn't at that moment. Life was starting to look bleak.

He thumped the table and he said: 'Don't shoot the shit to me, Morry the Head. You've had the man's diamonds and you've done them and you've done the money. I wanna statement off you. I'll be back to see you in a minute.'

So he said to his pal the rugby player: 'Come on.'

After a while he comes back, bursting through the door.

'You made that statement yet?'

'I'll . . .'

'Don't you fuck me around. I've seen a lot of you. Don't you think we're mugs, us policemen. We know every trick in the book.'

'Oh dear,' I thought, 'what's happened here is he's doubled on me.' Everything's going through my mind. He's got the money. He's done a double on me. I was astounded. I was in trouble.

So they threw me into an empty cell and let me wait. In the background I can hear the jeweller's voice and I can hear them telling him that his property had gone and all I heard was: 'Where are my diamonds? Oh. My business, my wife, my children. Where's the money?'

I'm sitting in the room wondering what's happened to me here? This policeman's supposed to be on my side but now X is screaming for his diamonds and suddenly: crash, the door opens and he comes in again. 'I got X outside so you're going down for a long time. You tell us what happened.' Bang. He slams the door.

In comes the rugby player: 'I want that statement.' I was trembling, I was shaking.

Anyway I stewed and I stewed. The door opened and they threw me an old sandwich and put down a cup of water and I was told in no uncertain manner: 'You can fuck some people about but you can't fuck us about.' This is by the police. I'm not saying anything but I am getting concerned.

After about six hours they called me into the interrogation room where the DI was sitting at a table with the big rugby-player lookalike. And I was asked details and questions and after ten or fifteen minutes he said to the other one: 'Go and get me a cup of tea, will you.'

As soon as the feller went out the DI looked at me and winked. My whole stomach turned over. He leant across the table and whispered: 'I had to make an act of it.'

I now knew what he was doing and it was very clever. He couldn't afford to let me off the hook without making a show out of it.

And that's what happened. I was released on police bail and never heard any more about the affair.

17

A Sure Bet

At the same time as I was getting into diamond stealing I was working the racetracks. I've visited every major track in the world and been warned or frogmarched off most of them. In those days the crowd and the atmosphere and the opportunity for scams made it more fun than even the casinos.

I was up at the Ayr racecourse. The name of the man was Dan Flynn, the biggest bookmaker in Scotland. You see, most bookmakers are basically greedy men and years ago the likes of Brian and me and Bill Roper the Doper would go on a racecourse without a penny and do what we know as 'Call a Bet' with no money. We'd go up to a bookmaker and I'd say: 'Two thousand to one.'

'Who is it down to?'

'Mr Spurling,' and I'd walk away without paying my thousand pounds. If the horse wins I get my two thousand pounds, and if it got beat, it's not criminal, it comes under what they call The Gaming Act: I owe the bookie the thousand pounds. All we were doing, Bill Roper, The Swan, me and several other people, was going round the country with no money having bets with bookmakers. The only reason they took the bets was they thought that we were important men because we were dressed well. So Bill Roper knew every bookmaker in the country and I was his protégé. He loved me and he took me everywhere having bets with bookmakers. And bookmakers are the most naive people in the world, very naive. I could go up to a bookmaker years ago and say: 'Ten thousand pounds on this. What price is it?'

'Two to one.'

'Twenty thousand on it.'

'Who is it?'

'Lord Chottomley from Chottomley Village.'

So he'd turn round to his clerk and say: 'Twenty thousand pounds to ten? Lord Chottomley from Chottomley Village, Northants.' End of story.

We were fucking bookmakers. Bill Roper told me that whenever I wanted to have a bet with a bookmaker never ever let him see you coming towards him because the bookmaker will always prepare himself mentally for his answer. He'd either say 'Yes, sir. You're on.' Or 'No, sir. You've got no account with me.' So Bill used to teach me that whenever I wanted to have a bet I should always come up on the bookmaker's blind side. It's like when a policeman arrests you, he doesn't come from the front, he always comes from your back and puts his hand on your shoulder so that you've got shock, don't know what to say. He never walks straight up to you and says: 'You're arrested.'

One day we were at Ayr and there was a horse, whatever price whatever name it was I don't know, but on this day one man working for the bookmaker was one of our plants, like a spy, who used to get a few quid off us for his false recommendation. This was how clever Bill Roper was. He used to make sure that our ally was working for the bookmaker that we were gonna fuck. The only thing you had to do with that bookmaker was give your correct name. If you gave a wrong name then that's false pretences, which you could be pinched for. So one day this Dan Flynn was betting away at the biggest Scots meeting there was there.

'Och aye. Och aye. Twenty-one to . . .'

You know how bookmakers shout the odds. I was making a beeline on the blind side of Dan Flynn knowing full well that our ally the spy was working for him, in front of Dan Flynn. I walked up to him as he was in full flow. I can't remember what the odds were. The horse might've been evens, one to one, five for five, ten for ten. I said: 'Even, five thousand pounds.'

And he turned around and he said: 'And who is it?'

And I said: 'Mr Spurling.'

And before he could answer the ally pulled his sleeve and got hold of his ear and whispered: 'That is *Spurling*.'

Now Dan Flynn didn't know Spurling from O'Shaughnessy or Donald or Reginald but without wanting to appear ignorant he went: 'Ah. Och aye. Mr Spurling.'

Now even though he didn't know me from anybody, I had the bet, even five thousand pounds, with no money. The horse proceeded to win. I got my five thousand pounds. Later on in the bar we gave the ally three or four hundred pounds for his work.

If the horse hadn't won I would owe the bookmaker the stake. He couldn't do anything except 'Warn me off', meaning Tattersalls and The Jockey Club will not allow anybody of my repute on a racecourse. Eventually I got barred because I owed every bookmaker on the racecourse, everyone. I was reinstated after a while. There have been many people warned off for owing money but I bet not many owed what I did.

18

Plaintiff and Defendant

One day I was summoned to Tattersalls' Committee in Holborn. Once again I had been betting with Scotland's biggest bookie, Dan Flynn. He still didn't know who I was and he had been giving me credit like it was going out of fashion and I had been winning with him. The upshot was that he owed me quite a lot of money. Several thousand pounds. At the same time I owed a firm called Bowden and Cox in Wolverhampton a lot of money. When Dan Flynn found out who I was he said he was going to stop payment because I owed everybody else. So I was summoned to Tattersalls' Committee. I think there was a lord who was the Chairman, it may have been Lord Willoughby de Broke. Anyway, it was a funny situation.

Come the day of the hearing I found both cases were to be heard at the same time. It was me versus Dan Flynn to get my money. Bowden and Cox were against me to get their money. So I was the plaintiff and the defendant in one courtroom scene. There were two chairs – one the plaintiff's and one the defendant's chair. It was just like a trial.

I was waiting outside and after some minutes of preliminary procedure I was called in. Once inside I knew I was going to have to be on my best behaviour. When abroad I try to act like a good old-fashioned English gentleman and I reckon I do a pretty good impression for foreigners who've never met the real thing. But on walking into this room I was confronted with what seemed to be half the English aristocracy. No doubt here that they were the real thing. This group of old-established crusty Edwardian Englishmen headed by this lord sat facing poor little old Morry the Head as he was led in trying to look his best but feeling distinctly out of it despite the Savile Row suit and the handmade shirt and shoes. There was just something about them which said they'd been bred for generations to look like that and little Morry, despite his wealthy background, had not spent long enough in the breeding process.

'Mr Spurling. Sit there,' a voice boomed in my ear.

Spurling versus Dan Flynn was to be the first case and I was the plaintiff. It must have been in the early 1950s and Dan Flynn owed me something like £3,000. By today's standards it would be a hell of a lot of money. I sat on the plaintiff's chair and after a lengthy deliberation the lord in charge said: 'Right, Mr Spurling, will you sit on the other chair,' where I was now to be the accused.

Life got sorted out in that respect. After hearing the arguments for and against he said: 'Would you mind waiting outside?'

I went outside and I didn't know what was going to happen. After pacing up and down the corridor I was called in again.

The lord said: 'Sit on the chair, Mr Spurling. On the plaintiff's chair.' I thought he was playing musical chairs with me.

'We have carefully considered this case and we have decided to give Dan Flynn eight days to pay you the amount.' I thought, 'Ooh, lovely.' An ultimatum, you see. I was going to get my money. It was not as if Dan Flynn was a fly-by-night who could just up and go leaving me penniless.

The lord in charge then said: 'Sit on the defendant's chair.'

Up I got, down I got. The only words missing were, 'Are you sitting comfortably, Mr Spurling?' And now he said: 'We have carefully considered this case and our decision is this. We are going to give you sixteen days to pay Bowden and Cox what you owe them.' Which was about £2,500 or nearly the same as was owed to me. So I could see what was happening. They were not stupid men and they had realised that I had no money but they were giving me the chance to collect the money off Dan Flynn and pay it to Bowden and Cox. There was really no alternative.

I went outside and walked down the street to the first available telephone kiosk whereupon I got straight on the phone to Dan Flynn in Scotland and said: 'Oh hi, Mr Flynn. I've got news for you.'

'What's that, you scallywag?'

'I've won the case and you've got eight days to pay me.'

He started mumbling on the phone. I knew he could do nothing about it since if Tattersalls said he ought to pay me then he had no alternative. So the conversation flapped back and forth for a while with me standing in the kiosk with a smile on my face.

The talk went on until I decided to bring things to a head by saying: 'I'll tell you what I'll do with you, Mr Flynn. I'll take some off if you'll wire it to me now.'

'What will you take off?'

'Two or three hundred pounds.'

So the same day he wired it to Ship Street Post Office in Brighton. I let him off a few hundred quid.

So now I had the money. I didn't pay Bowden and Cox and I got what they call a 'Warning Off' notice, warned not to appear on the racetracks.

Of course this caused me problems but I did still manage to get on the racetracks. Racetracks are like much of the criminal world in that they have informants. I would get on a racetrack and start making bets but not much later on the stewards or the security people would turn up and hoik me off. There would be an informant who would get a few quid for going up to the authorities and saying, 'What do you know? Morry the Head's making a book.' Everywhere I went I was pointed out and thrown off: Ludlow, Ascot, Brighton, I was thrown off everywhere. There had to be a way round this problem and after a while I found it. I never knew who the informants were but I went one better than trying to buy them off. Instead I found some crooked 'throwers off'. People who worked for the security who saw me as the invisible man after I had walked in and said: 'Here's a fiver, or a tenner, forget you've seen me.' They would pay the informants when they came up to get their money for seeing me. So everyone was happy and I was able to continue racing before I was able to get the ban lifted.

I got reinstated after quite some while, although I cannot remember how that came about. I found ways and means of always getting credit at the races in those days. I made a book, I went all over. Invariably it resulted in a fast exit out of the dog track or the racetrack with the bookmakers sometimes chasing me.

19

Doping the One-Time Derby Favourite

I n between stealing diamonds and watches there were other ways a scallywag could earn a pretty penny. I was introduced to many of them at an early age back when I was learning my skills in the late Forties and early Fifties.

One of the best ways of earning money was fixing the races. At that time there was a lot of dog doping and horse doping. I was working with a gang who all ended up getting prison sentences. On this occasion, I was fortunate – I stayed out of jail.

My buddy was a man called Joe Lowry, who came from Forest Gate in the East End of London. He was the gang's principal operator and the man who introduced me to it. I used to like him very much.

Through him I had met the brains of the outfit, Bill Roper. There was another man involved called Charlie Mitchell, who got killed in Spain in Marbella in a brawl outside a nightclub.

Apart from the regular dog-doping team we used to go all over the country doping horses. It went on for a long, long while. There was a big scandal about it in the Fifties. We made a lot of money out of it, in fact we nearly killed the one-time Derby favourite, Pinturischio, which Lester Piggott rode. I'd given it too many tablets.

We used to tickle the horse's throat, then we'd open its mouth and drop the tablets down. 'Dopers Strike Again' were the newspaper headlines. We doped the favourite and backed the outsiders. There was no security around the horses when we started.

There was a French girl who used to go to the door of the owners of the stables and as she was distracting them, talking a lot of nonsense in a nice sexy friendly French way, we used to go round the back, jump over the wall and find the yards where the horses were.

We used to wear balaclava masks in case a stablehand saw us, give the horse its tablet and that was it.

When the horse came into the parade ring it was groggy, like a man who was drunk. I don't know what we were using because a chemist had the formula.

We had this chemist who provided all the tablets for the doping. He threw himself off the top floor of Lewes Prison. His name was Smith. He killed himself because of the shame and the scandal. He preferred to die rather than go to court.

Two of the other people involved in it are dead now, Mitchell and Lowry. There was a third who's still working at the races. I don't know what's happened to the rest, they'd be old men now. I think they got two years each for this doping scandal.

I was only on the periphery, called upon when they needed an extra distraction. They did it with dogs as well, at Wimbledon, White City, Wembley.

Bill Roper was one of the key figures in the doping scene.

He was a very clever man who was always a move ahead of everybody else, a genius on the racecourse, a very clever man, perhaps the cleverest man ever to walk on to any racecourse in Great Britain. He had more scams and stings than you could dream about and he used me, as a presentable young man, to get credit for him at the bookmakers. He was always a move in front, a walking wizard, a walking computer. I believe he eventually left this country and went to South Africa or Jamaica or somewhere after making his money.

I recall how devious his mind was, how well orchestrated he was as regards getting money. He would spend hours plotting and planning to get money off bookmakers. One day we were at Haydock Park and it was about four o'clock in the afternoon.

'Quickly, we're going.'

'Why?' I asked. 'There's another two races.'

'Don't worry. We're going.'

We got on the train.

'Could you tell me where we're going?'

'Yes. Hendon Dog Track.'

At that time Hendon was very upmarket, on the corner of the North Circular Road. There was loads of money at Hendon, lots of Jewish textile dealers and businessmen.

'May I ask you why we've left Haydock Park in Cheshire to come down here?'

'I'll tell you in a minute,' he tells me. 'Come with me.'

We had about five or six hundred quid on us, which was quite a bit of money in the Fifties.

'We're gonna back two dogs in one race,' he tells me. 'We can't lose our money.'

'OK.'

So we laid out our five or six hundred pounds on the two dogs in the one race. And as the dogs were going into the traps he walked me round to the last bend, what they call the Cheap Ring. I was sweating because we'd laid out all our money. On that day it was a six hundred and fifty yard race, a long distance race. Anyway, the traps opened up and both the dogs that we backed are absolutely last. Six dogs, one was fifth and one was last. And as they're going round I'm getting worried and he's looking at me with no compassion at all.

'Don't worry.'

So they're coming round the last bend as far behind as the distance between Buckingham Palace and Aldgate. I turned to Bill and glared at him. 'What another mess you've got me into.'

'Don't worry.'

'Don't worry. What do you mean "Don't worry"?'

'Look over there.'

And as I looked I saw a fellow jump on to the track wielding a big pair of bolt cutters which he used on the hare. The hare went up in the air, the stewards called it 'No Race' and we got our money back. He had organised this the day before. He did this all over the country. Even I did it once.

One time I went to Portsmouth Dogs with another friend and I didn't have a shilling.

It was forty-odd years ago and the dog in question was called Tiger Tim.

'If you hear me say 'ten to one bar Tiger Tim' you must throw the spring,' this friend told me.

I had a piece of bedspring and I'd bought some fur. If you put the fur round the bedspring it would bounce and the dogs would go for it. I was shitting myself. I was standing by a couple of tea stalls and it was this dark, murky, horrible night in Portsmouth.

'Ten to one bar Tiger Tim!'

The moment I heard these words I had to throw the spring. It wouldn't leave my hand I was so nervous. When I threw the spring on, all the dogs went for that, it was 'no race' and we got our money back.

20

Dropping the Coins

One of my favourite jobs used to be doing the turnstiles at racetracks. There was one racetrack where I saw the old boy behind the turnstile had all the money that he'd been taking just sitting in front of him. As I went to pay I dropped all the coins I had in my hand on the floor. He bent down to pick the coins up and I took the money sitting in front of him. He didn't notice it because I didn't take *all* the money. I left some sitting there so it looked as though nothing had been taken. It's called 'Dropping the Coins'.

We went all over the country doing this scam, two or three of us together. We would go to a shop, usually a big store, the ones which have a lot of money, and I would ask for change for a ten- or twenty-pound note. I would pick up a Mars Bar and with the Mars Bar I would give the girl a twenty-pound note. She would ring up the till and before she could put my twenty pounds in the till I would say: 'Oh, I've got the right change, miss.' And I'd drop the coins behind her. She would bend down and pick up the coins whereupon my associate would slide the money from the till. Normally there's a prong on the money which you can see. Well, he had quick fingers which would slide off a chunk of money while she was on the floor looking for the coins. He knew what he was doing. But he wouldn't take it all because when she got up and she looked and I said: 'Oh, I'm sorry, miss,' there would still be money in the till. Transaction finished with a Mars Bar.

Half a dozen other people used to work at this game. There are nice criminal businesses, there are not nice criminal businesses and this wasn't a very nice criminal business.

I've stolen the members' badges from Cheltenham, £25 a head, stolen thousands of them and sold them outside to the general public. Racegoers love it. Instead of having to pay £25 to go in you pay £10. Stealing the badges was done by distraction. One of us got talking to the feller and the other took the badges. At any big meeting, any racecourse meeting, that's always on. We've been up to everything.

'Dropping the Coins' took me from wet Wales to sunny Australia and on to the snows of Canada and membership of the 'Mile High Club'.

21

Sun, Sea, Sex, Sand and Snow

You wouldn't expect to find connections between the Mafia in Australia and the Welsh Valleys but I can provide you with one. Fairly indirectly but it got me into big trouble.

Together with two friends I had set off from London in 1980 for a race meeting in the West Country at Chepstow. We did our money at the races and were left with only petrol money and instead of coming back to London one of us must have said we should go into Wales and try and get some money.

'Good idea,' I said. 'I bet you didn't know that as a kid I was evacuated down there to a place called Barry Island. Let's go down that way and see what we can get.'

We were driving along when all of a sudden what comes into view but a garden centre. They were always good value for money. The third member of our party has a knack for the job of ringing up tills. As I say, the normal procedure is to attract the attention of the girl behind the till and then steal the contents by ringing it open and dipping your fingers inside. Some tills make quite a loud ringing sound when they're opened but there are ways of combating that noise.

Our friend is looking with greedy eyes at the till and the girl has gone down the other end of the garden centre to answer some daft query put to her by our other friend. It's a busy bank holiday and the place is fairly full, although we have waited for a time when the queue for the till is non-existent. The ringer does his job but he's not quick enough. A customer has spotted what's gone on and notified the owner who rushes outside into the car park and takes our number.

'It's on top,' says my friend. That means we're in dead trouble. I drop him off at the railway station because he has to get back to London quickly. We've divided up the money and got a few hundred quid. I think we dropped our friend off at Newport and then made straight for the motorway. It wasn't long before a police car flagged us down and me and the till ringer were arrested and taken to Cardiff Police Station and bailed to appear in court. I was then in serious trouble. In fact, I was in serious trouble all round and decided to pack my bags and go to Australia. Sod Cardiff.

I get like this every once in a while. Life in Britain starts to wear me down and I decide the best thing to do is go on the trot and get away from it all. I had a few friends in Australia and it seemed now was as good a time as any for taking up their offer of life in the sun.

I made my plans quickly, the court case was a few months off and I wanted to be long gone before they realised what had happened.

So within a matter of weeks I got enough money together to fly out there. I didn't take too many risks and so it took some effort to get the cash just to reach Australia.

I went to Victoria Railway Station with an old friend, now dead, and bid him goodbye.

'I'll be back,' I said. I sat on the old Golden Arrow train that went from Victoria to Paris wondering what life had in store for me. I got off at the Gare du Nord in Paris and made my way to the airport.

At the Charles de Gaulle Airport I looked around for a post box. I had a rather special letter which I wanted to post, but not too soon before I boarded the aircraft.

On the train I had written a letter to the judge at Cardiff Crown Court in which I said: 'After serious consideration of attending your court on a matter of theft I have decided that you will not have the pleasure of seeing me in person. When you read this letter I must tell you that I'll be lying on Bondi Beach, looking at the beautiful bare-breasted thong-bottomed Australian women in the glorious sun, having a barbecue. I trust that you enjoy the snow and wet that you get in your part of the country. Good day, my lord.'

It was read out by my counsel. According to my co-accused, who *was* in court, the judge absolutely fumed.

In my pocket at Charles de Gaulle Airport in Paris was a thousand pounds which I had got by going into stores where I was well known, all in the West End of London, and giving cheques for suits, jumpers, clothing, all to people who knew me. When I was regularly gambling I used to buy shoes, ties, shirts and suits from all the top shops. So I went into these stores again and got a lot of goods on credit. I sold them all, giving me the grand sum of £1,000.

After posting the letter I bought a return ticket to Sydney, which in 1980 cost £960. The man that sold me the ticket forgot to collect his £960 and I didn't remind him. When they called for embarkation on to the Qantas flight that was taking me to Sydney I was highly delighted because I thought I was going free of charge. All of a sudden, over the loudspeaker came this announcement: 'Would Mr Morris Spurling please announce his presence to an official.' The manager of the airways, accompanied by two or three gendarmes, came up to me and said: 'Mr Spurling. You haven't paid for your flight. If you pay me now you can board it. If you don't you'll have to come along with me.'

Well, naturally I paid it. I arrived in Australia with £40 in the world.

Within two weeks I had a penthouse flat in Rose Bay, a suburb of Sydney, a Mercedes car, a Japanese au pair and bundles of money in the bank.

I had bumped into an old friend who had become famous in the West End for holding mock auctions in the street. He was also a notorious gambler.

I was very good at mock auctions because I too am quite an extrovert character and can draw large crowds within minutes. I love being the centre of attention.

'You need money, Morry?' asked my friend. What a wise bloke he was.

'What's on offer?'

He told me about a scam that involved selling badges. We would get hold of these badges which cost about thirty cents to buy. They came from Taiwan but looked quite flash. We could sell them at auctions for a dollar each. Not a bad profit. Soon we were selling so many we started to get noticed and gained the reputation of 'The Dollar Boys'. We were selling thousands and thousands of badges every day in Sydney, from the tube station to the Opera House to the racetracks to the casinos. But as time wore on, all the gambling was starting to take its toll. Gambling is much more important in Australia than over here. We were going broke every night despite taking thousands of dollars every day. We were going to the races and the casinos and the trotting and spending every dollar. So, in between times, I started doing my jewellery act. I couldn't believe it. The job was just as easy as in Britain, perhaps easier. So I did a few more jewellery shops and life started to improve even more on what I had already gained in

Sydney. I could still afford the penthouse, Mercedes and the nightclubs.

Then I bumped into a friend of mine called Margo.

'Well, hallo Sheila,' I said, spotting her one day peering through the plate glass of a well-known jewellers. 'Fancy seeing you here.'

'Good God, it's Morry the Head. I heard you were in town. Are you planning to do this one?'

'And you?'

'Just looking, Morry. You know me.'

We went off for a coffee to catch up on life since our times together in London.

After a while we came to an arrangement. It would make life easier for me if I had a beautiful scantily dressed woman on my arm inside the jewellery shops and auction houses. The assistants would be paying more attention to Margo than to what I was doing with my ten little fingers. She agreed to come working with me.

Together we attacked every jewellers we could find. At lunchtime we would lie on the beach and work up a bit of a tan, then in the afternoon we would go to the races.

One morning I find myself in another of the many coffee houses I used to frequent, reading a newspaper. I have a couple of them in front of me. Finishing one, I pick up the second and shudder as I read the headlines.

'Smart Englishman walks into jewellery shop – diamond watches and rings missing after he walks out.'

The English accent had been of a great help to me in Sydney. The assistants were happy to see a polite well-dressed English gentleman with money to spend. They had been right off their guard. At that time I was something of a rarity in Australia, now all the jewellery shops would be on the look out for a smart Englishman.

Sydney was just too small to get away with such work for

any substantial length of time. It's the most beautiful place on earth but not much bigger than Cambridge, so I was stuffed. And the money was running out because as fast as I was making it the dough was going into the little slots in the casinos.

You don't have to be in a place long to get wind of who's who in the local crime network. Morry the Head had put out word of his talents and the result was I had become quite friendly with the local Mafia. They knew of me almost as soon as the local jewellers.

Stupidly I started having personal bets with an Australian and ended up owing him rather a lot of money. It turned out he was also in the local Mafia. One night I was in this club having a vodka and tonic and these four tough guys in suits walk across.

'Aye, aye, what's up here?' I thought.

'Morry, we want a word with you.'

'I'm all ears,' I joked, but none of them smiled.

'Word has it you're not much good at paying your debts.'

'I always pay my debts, friend,' I told them, getting a little angry.

'That's good, Morry, good to know. Because people who don't pay their debts get thrown in Sydney Harbour wearing a pair of concrete shoes.'

'No need for violence,' I replied. I got out of that bar as fast as I could and never went back. But it didn't stop me having a few more bets.

The days passed by and I found a jeweller or two who had not read the papers and not been warned off the Englishman with the smart accent who liked to steal diamonds. So it soon came to the end of the week and life in Australia was suiting me fine. It was hot and sunny and relaxed and seemingly carefree.

Early the following week I had just parked my Mercedes and gone up to the flat when there was a knock at the door.

You can tell how confident I had become because I took no precautions to check who was visiting me, just went straight ahead and opened the door.

Standing outside looking panicky was Margo. 'Quick, Morry, let me inside.'

'What's up?'

'You've got to go.'

'I'm not going, I'm enjoying myself. And I'm doing well.'

'You owe the local Mafia and you're apparently not bothering to pay them.'

'Everyone gets paid in the end.'

'Morry, you don't seem to understand. When these people say they want their money they mean now. Not in a month's time or whenever some smart Englishman deems it necessary to pay them.'

'Who cares? I've dealt with worse in my time.'

'Morry. Listen to me. There's a contract out on you. They're going to kill you. Get out now!'

'Where to, Melbourne?'

'No, Morry, get out of Australia. These people are not joking.'

I had run across the Lebanese Mafia and owed several bookmakers. The exact amount ran into hundreds of thousands of pounds. The Mafia in Australia is comprised of Lebanese, Yugoslavs and local Australians, and I didn't fancy being buried under Sydney Harbour Bridge.

It's even dangerous talking about someone they've got rid off. You wander around saying things like, 'Have you seen so and so? I haven't seen him for a couple of days', and you'll be next. That's just the way it is.

After Margo's warning I caught the plane from Sydney to Canada. I was out of the country within a matter of hours.

During that long flight I became a member of the 'Mile High

Club'. I was flying from Sydney to Toronto with a stop-over in Hawaii. Sydney, Hawaii, Los Angeles, Toronto.

The stop-over in Hawaii was just long enough to start chatting up this woman who was on the same flight. By the time we'd passed through Los Angeles and were on our way to the final destination in Toronto we had become firm friends.

'You know what I fancy?' I said to her.

'No, Morry, but I can have a damn good guess.' And with that we both went off to the rear of the aircraft and squeezed ourselves into the little toilet. It was barely big enough for one man to relieve himself in let alone for two people to screw. But we managed it, just.

After we'd finished the most uncomfortable lovemaking of my life we both looked out the window and noticed we'd been flying over the Rocky Mountains. We both said it together, 'Fucking over the Rockies'. Don't know why but we both burst into laughter.

I was met by my friend, Canadian Harry, who found me a flat in Toronto and invited me to his house where I met his girl, Tina. After some discussion I said to him: 'If Tina wants to work with me at my game we'll cut up the money.' He agreed. Tina has since bought a huge bungalow complete with swimming pool out of the proceeds of our work together.

Tina was a stunner. She was another Page Three Canadian girl, beautiful. She was twenty-three years old with legs as long as Bond Street, boobs like punchballs and a beautiful smile. I knew I'd be on a winner with her.

So I set about teaching her all I knew about the business of 'Palming' and 'Switching'. Tina was to distract the owner or assistant while I dipped my hand into his wares and pocketed the proceeds.

We were very successful and slaughtered the whole of Canada.

I had caught the plane from sun, sea, sex and sand to snow and polar bears, which was horrible. Absolutely horrible. Despite our success and my good friends over there I hated Canada. It's just not home for the likes of 'The Head'. I found it the most horribly depressing place on earth. There is nothing in Canada. The only lively place is Montreal, where the British are not very well liked.

One day I went into a jeweller's shop in Vancouver. I saw three black girls in the shop, mini skirts, long legs and sexy boots. They were the business. I thought it was the Three Degrees, they looked so attractive. They were fawning themselves over some jewellery and some nice stones, trying them on, showing off with their fur coats and diamond rings on their hands. All the time I was trying to get the attention of the man who was serving them.

Suddenly one of them whispers to one of her colleagues in a voice I can't help but hear: 'Look at that asshole, trying to get our man away.' I hadn't known they were also jewellery thieves. They were at it themselves.

22

Quick Thinking by a Girl in New York

One morning in 1982, with Tina in tow, I set out to blitz the United States of America. We decided to do three auction houses by lunchtime starting with Sotheby's on Madison Avenue in New York. Tina wore a see-through blouse which left nothing to the imagination. I had a pocket full of Cubic Zirconias of every shape, size, and colour. Rubies and emeralds, I'd got it.

We went inside the first house and it was surrounded by New York Police armed with machine guns. They're only there as security to keep out the armed robbers. They don't know anything about Morry the Head with the switching thing. They would never expect that a man like me, well dressed, with a lovely girl on his arm, would be at it.

It was one of the viewing days when you could pick up the goods and touch them. The goods were all on view, which is what you expect at auctions. What I saw was a pear-shaped diamond.

'Look at that,' I said to Tina. It was about fifty thousand pounds. It was a lovely pear shape but I did not have a Cubic Zirconia which was similar although I did have one which was round.

Well, the girl who was serving me knew absolutely nothing whatsoever about diamonds. We were dealing with stones with an estimated value back in the Eighties of about twenty to fifty thousand pounds each. I knew the place was shutting up at one o'clock and it was now about twelve o'clock, so time was running out.

I knew that in the Bronx was an area like Hatton Garden in London where you could buy all the Cubic Zirconias you wanted. So we left the auction as sharply as we could without attracting attention, dived into a yellow cab and raced off to buy the fake. I bought a pear-shaped piece of glass for about five dollars and we went back and prepared to switch it.

I went to the toilet, pulled out what I'd got and placed it in my palm, and as I went back Tina was doing her work with the young salesman.

'Isn't it lovely,' she's saying to him as she's showing him her nipples. And as she's doing that I put my bit of glass in place of the diamond. So now he's got a three-quid piece of glass and I've got his fifty-thousand-pound diamond. Moments later someone else asked if he could also take a look at the self-same diamond. Now this man was a dealer, what we call a Frum Jew, an Hasidic Jew, a dealer from East 47th Street. He asks for the same diamond, number 318. By this time the diamond is a piece of glass and since he's a dealer who knows his stuff he's going to notice.

Guards were all around the auction house with shooters. Well, that didn't worry me. Who would think that a dapper Englishman would switch a stone in broad daylight? But there'd be no getting away from them once the alarm had been sounded. The moment the short little fat man bumped into me I knew there could be trouble.

When the dealer is asked for the stone I don't know what to do. I was looking for a way out. So when the Hasidic Jew bumps into me I say: 'Excuse me, please.' What I was trying to do was make sure that he did not pick up my bit of glass.

Tina took over like the well-trained accomplice that she was. She could see what was going on. She leant across me wearing her see-through blouse and said to the guy: 'Excuse me, may I borrow your loupe? We don't have one.'

The loupe is the lens which magnifies the diamonds. Of course, he turned back to her and said: 'With pleasure, Madam.' He had his loupe ready to look at my bit of glass.

His hat had nearly blown off when she pushed her near naked breasts into his face and he said in broken English: 'Mit pleasure.' And she saved the day. She took her time and I slid out of the door and I'd gone.

She eventually made her way out and that was that. I'd got the diamond and they finished up with my bit of glass as a lot of places have finished up with my bits of glass all around the world. The thing that I've always wondered is what happens to those bits of glass, because they go back in the window or in the showcase. Now what happens to them? Somebody can come in, buy a bit of glass for fifty grand or a hundred grand and they've gone away thinking it's a Cartier piece or a Tiffany piece. In safes all around the world today they might have Morry the Head's twenty-pence bits of glass.

Another day we found ourselves inside a New York auction house, Sotheby's I think it was, where we noticed an American policeman sitting in the middle of the room fondling a big gun waiting in case of armed robberies. I switched a thirty-thousand-pound stone and he was sitting there chewing gum and I thought he might have seen me. So being a bit daring I held it up to him.

'Don't you think that's lovely?' I asked.

His face was set in a permanent scowl. He looked at me without moving a facial muscle and said: 'You're buying it, buster, not me.' By this I was assured that he didn't know I had switched it and I proceeded to walk out.

While we were in America we went to Washington, New York and Boston, among other places. In Boston I had one of the best things going for me because it's very anglified and they welcomed me like I was Tina's sugar daddy.

Harry Winston of New York is the world's biggest jeweller. He made Jackie Kennedy's jewels. I went all over his factory and as I was walking round the factory drinking champagne I was putting diamonds in my pocket at the same time.

'A glass of champagne, Mr Morris, certainly.'

As I picked up the champagne I also picked up a two or three carat emerald which would be worth thousands. And lo and behold that too fell into my pocket.

23

Head to Head

Germany is a better place to work than Britain. I can't work here because of the video and I don't want to work here. There's not the value here. The value is in Germany. First of all, all their gold and diamonds are eighteen carat as opposed to nine over here. So you can get double the money. Over there it's vast. The goods are better over there. If you go into the Northampton of Germany which is, say, Stuttgart, it's twenty, fifty times richer. The jewellers are bigger, the goods are better. Baden-Baden, where I used to operate, is for millionaires only. You get the equivalent to London, Berlin. A million times more jewellery than in London even. Plus the fact I can walk along the street without anyone knowing me. If you come outside London to the small towns and you are a diamond thief, you're going to get rubbish. Apart from London, where is there that they have money? Birmingham, Manchester, Chester, Harrogate? In Germany, there's a million places.

I never did Ratners, it's like Woolworths, it was all mass-produced high street goods. Diamonds are worth thirty or forty quid. You go into Garrard's or Asprey's or Kutchinsky's, places like that there's value. Stealing requires effort. In Milton Keynes, for example, it's rife with shop lifting. It's as hard, in fact harder, to steal a Parker pen worth thirty quid in W. H. Smith's than it is to get a thirty-thousand-pound diamond. It's the impression you give the shopkeeper. If you wander in looking rich you're already in with a chance. It's all about style and your approach. If I walked into Asprey's, Kutchinsky's, Harrods, top stores, I'd be made very welcome because I look and act the part. But if a feller dressed in jeans walked into Garrard's the security people would smell a rat. If I go into any top jewellery store in the world, anywhere in the finest streets, the Via Napoleone in Milan, the rue Fauboug St Honoré in Paris, I know every one there is, I'm made welcome. They think they've got a rich man because I dress impeccably and I know my capabilities.

I suppose it was my presence, my demeanour, my audacious-ness that allowed me to do this, because in every jeweller's shop all over the world, when I walk in I don't think Prince Charles would get a better welcome and I think that is the be-all and end-all of it. Sheer presence. I stand out, it's as simple as that. I also think women like me. I make a good impression on them even when it's not to their advantage.

On my travels I was passing through Cambridgeshire and stopped off in a place called March where the Lady Mayoress had a jewellery shop and a furniture shop.

I walked in there one day and discovered she was rather eccentric. As I walked in two customers went into the furniture shop and she asked me to look after her jewellery shop while she was serving the couple with furniture, which I thought was quite amusing. I don't think Cartier's would have left me in charge of their shop, or Tiffany's or Van Cleef and Arpels. If this woman had known who I was I don't suppose she would have let me in the shop, let alone look after it.

I've been known as 'Morry the Head' for half a century ever since my hair fell out. And the name of my game is sometimes referred to as going 'Head to Head'. That means I face a jeweller, man to man, face to face, as I'm stealing his diamonds. I'm the finest Head to Head operator in Europe, maybe in the world, who knows? It's been said in courts from the South of France to southern Britain that I'm an artist at the trick of 'Palming' or 'Switching'. One eminent lawyer said I was a magician, able to spirit away stones from under a jeweller's nose. My friend The Swan reckons I'm top of the premier division of our type of crime, others aren't even in the third division. I think I've only ever been caught red-handed once, 'bang to rights' as we put it; usually I've been nicked for stupidities at a later stage. Since 1950 I've been sentenced to more than forty years in prison, although I've actually served only about a third of that time.

Diamond thieving for me is a huge rush of adrenaline. I can't describe it without mentioning sex. For me, the rush of adrenaline when I enter a jeweller's shop or an auction or a fair or a warehouse intent on stealing a fine stone is identical to the rush I get on entering a casino. I really do walk into a casino with an erection, it is that exciting. Oddly enough, both rushes are greater than that of meeting a beautiful woman who makes it clear I can sleep with her. Not much better, but a more sudden, intense flow of blood around the system. After that everything else is a let down.

The thieving has made it possible for me to mix in the best circles in gambling. I've gambled with Captain Lemnos, the Greek millionaire, heck, I've even lent him money when we were both playing at the International Sporting Club in Park Lane.

I've gambled in Baden-Baden, in Monte Carlo, that James

Bond thing is nothing compared to what I've been through. I've been to Vegas, Atlantic City, Wiesbaden, all the top casinos in the world; Sun City, Bophuthatswana, Macao, been to every racetrack in the world, Belmont Park, Woodbine in Canada, every Australian racetrack.

It was easier to get big money than small. That may sound absurd but it really was easier to get a bigger stone because the person I robbed would be more cautious with the smaller stuff than the bigger stuff. Who would have the audacity to do what I have done? Who would have the cheek to go into Cartier in Paris and switch a £43,000 stone, who would have the cheek to go into Harry Winston's in New York and drink champagne and pocket his diamonds? No one would do it. Mafia people wouldn't do it. Gangsters wouldn't do it. The risk of getting caught never entered my mind.

I've stolen more with my ten little fingers than the Great Train Robbers. A million a finger and we're talking old values here. Work out what a million was thirty years ago and it might give you an idea of exactly how much has passed through my hands. I don't think many people who don't understand the ways of gambling and this sort of life would believe that a man could steal this amount of money and be penniless now. 'How can this feller be without a penny?' they might ask. 'How can he be living in a back room of a hostel on £65 a week?'

I look like a moneyed man. The last thing the jewellers think is that I am a thief. I speak well, I dress well, I look the part. Friends tell me I am quite a good actor. I change moods to cope with those of the people I am with. I can cheer up sad people and excite the already happy ones. I try to give off an aura of happiness. If I am enjoying life I want everyone around me to be experiencing the same.

So the first impression the jeweller gets is of a well-balanced, happy and wealthy buyer, especially when I have got a girl half my age hanging on my arm. The owner or the sales assistant doesn't find it hard to see why there's such a broad smile on my face. The girl is normally dressed in a see-through blouse, pretty and young. Then we go for the younger salesmen if there's one around. They're more concerned with the nipple than with the ten-thousand-pound ring.

There is no violence in the work I do. It's mainly a case of distracting the people I am trying to steal diamonds from. It's sleight of hand. I loved the description one lawyer gave when he called me the Paul Daniels of my trade. I am seen as the best in the business.

24

Romance with a Top Model Courtesy of Her Majesty's Government

Isabel was introduced to me by the British government. I can't thank them enough. This is how it all came about.

There was a regulation in force during the late Sixties or early Seventies which meant British citizens were only allowed to take abroad with them the measly sum of £30 in cash. Now, you couldn't buy many exotic pieces of jewellery for £30, not even in those days. And Gerald Ratner had not, as far as I was aware, started mass producing on the Continent. Anyway, I would've starved to death on the resale of jewellery items worth a few quid at their shop price.

One of the most picturesque cities in the world is the ancient Italian city of Florence, one of the main tourist attractions of Europe. It is my favourite haunt for jewel robbery. In the centre of the city is an old bridge which must be the most beautiful in the world. It is called the Ponte Vecchio and its name means 'Old Bridge'. The piers were originally of stone and the road was made of wood but it was destroyed in a flood, rebuilt and then destroyed again. The latest version dates from 1345 and it was built with the intention of having shops on either side. The first occupants were tradesmen such as butchers and shoemakers and grocers, but in 1591 Ferdinando I evicted them all. The shops went to the goldsmiths and since then the entire bridge has become a kind of gigantic supermarket for jewellery.

The goods sold here are among some of the most fabulous pieces ever made. I was staying at one of the finest hotels in the city, the five star Excelsior Italie on the Piazza Ognissanti. The Excelsior has branches all over Italy and I was one of their frequent customers.

This year I was a happy little scallywag, because my own government had given me one of the greatest opportunities of my life to make money. All the European shopkeepers knew the British were unable to take any money out of the country and all had made some sort of arrangement. It usually involved a shopowner coming to an agreement with a family member in Britain to cash the cheques back in this country. By law, a European shopkeeper was not supposed to take an English cheque. So I was doubly protected by the law. This all suited me just fine.

I think this might have been in the late Sixties. I was back once again on the Ponte Vecchio looking for a diamond bracelet. It would cost me many millions of lira but I would be paying with a cheque drawn on an English bank. There was no money in my account and since the shopkeeper should not be taking my cheque in any case I would be in the clear. I inspected the goods and quickly came to my decision.

'But I cannot pay by cash,' I told the shopkeeper. 'The British regulations, you know.' I shrugged my shoulders as if to say how stupid can a government become.

'I understand. I understand,' said the shopkeeper. 'Do not be embarrassed. I will accept a cheque.'

So to my satisfaction I just wrote out a cheque to him, an ordinary English cheque drawn on Lloyds Bank and then I proceeded to walk out with the diamond-encrusted bracelet worth about £25,000. I knew I could get at least £5,000 for it, probably a bit more.

Again, it was midsummer and I spent the rest of the afternoon walking around the town shopping for little things which I even paid for with my own money. In fact, it was such a beautiful day I stayed out most of the afternoon having decided in a pretty little outdoors café, over a coffee, to travel the following morning to Rome.

My mind was quite far away as I strolled back inside the Excelsior. I went straight to the lounge bar and ordered a drink. As I was doing this I glanced around and saw two or three people sitting at a table. I vaguely recognised one of them. I paid for the drink and as I turned to find a seat one of these men approached me and only then did I realise it was the man to whom I had given the cheque for the bracelet.

'Excuse me, sir,' he said, blocking my way, but in a most polite, Italian manner.

'Isn't that strange,' I said to him. 'We were together only a few hours ago.'

'Yes, sir. I have been looking for you ever since. I eventually discovered you were staying in this hotel and immediately came here to wait for you.'

'Why?'

'The cheque you gave me for the bracelet . . .'

'Well, what about it?'

He coughed, as if embarrassed to be bringing up such a delicate subject. 'It is no good.'

'What do you mean? No good?' I was getting angry. I was shouting, just a little.

'Please come over to the table, sir.'

'What do you mean by saying my cheque is no good? What

are you talking about, man? I've never heard such nonsense in my life.'

He took me by the shoulder and started to shovel me off towards the table where his two friends were sitting. 'Please. Just join us for a while.'

As we reached the table and while another of the men was pulling out a chair for me to sit at, he added: 'Please meet the Chief of Police. My brother-in-law.'

Immediately I was worried. 'Oh, my God. What have we here?' I thought.

They were all extremely polite but there was a clear sense of urgency about them. They meant business.

'We telexed your bank.' That didn't surprise me. I had been passing cheques all over the Continent and had got jewels in Belgium, Austria, Germany, France and Holland.

'There is no money in your account, sir. No money to meet the cheque. I'd like my bracelet back.'

Quick as a flash I replied: 'Of course there's no money in my bank. Your cheque will not be in my bank for another ten days.' At that time it took ten days to cash a cheque written out in one part of Europe and sent to a British bank. It wasn't supposed to take that long but I had discovered it did. It was a part of my planning for this operation. So I turned to the man I had given the cheque to and told him, 'There is no way I am travelling across Europe with money sitting in a bank account not earning any interest. I shall be back in England well in time to transfer funds into that account, ready to honour the cheque given to you by me this lunchtime.'

The trouble was the Chief of Police was having nothing to do with it.

'If there is any doubt in my brother-in-law's mind, he must insist upon getting back the bracelet.'

I reminded him of the rules governing the handing out of British cheques.

'We are all men of the world here,' he said. 'I know you may be entirely innocent, in which case no harm has been done if you just give back the bracelet. You will have spent no money and my relative will be the loser, he will have to sell to another customer. But if I leave this hotel and it turns out you are a criminal and you have relieved my brother-in-law of an extremely large sum of money, I am going to be the one to lose face amongst all my relatives. So I must insist the bracelet be returned.'

This went on for quite some time. But gradually he made it abundantly clear he was not going to let me out of the bar until he had got back that bracelet. If I had insisted on holding on to it he would know I was crooked. No threats were uttered but I decided it would be a wise move to shrug my shoulders once more and hand it over.

We shook hands and parted friends, or at least gave that impression to each other.

After that experience I needed a quick vodka and tonic to buck up my spirits. I sat thinking what to do. Money was not tight but I would have to go out to work again. I checked my wallet and found I had a lot of money in various denominations but very little of it in lira. I decided I would go to the post office to try and change some of it.

It was about four o'clock in the afternoon and I've been standing in the queue for quite some time. It's hot, a little dry and dusty and I am starting to feel fraught. When my turn arrives to face the woman at the counter I discover she doesn't speak a word of English. I knew a little Italian but not nearly enough to conduct a conversation with someone who could not speak any English. This argy-bargy goes on for a few minutes until behind me I hear the most exquisite English accent, the most beautiful tender voice. 'May I be of some assistance?'

Swivelling round to see who is the owner of this wonderful

voice I nearly fall flat on my face. Standing a couple of places behind me in the same queue is the most gorgeous, good-looking girl I have seen in my whole life. She was six feet tall and absolutely stunning. Long black raven hair.

'May I help you?' she says again. Well, I just could not talk. I was staring at her, drinking in her beauty, and I was so much in awe of her I could not make my mouth start to move.

She asked me once more if she could help and fortunately I now found my voice.

'You can help me in a million ways.'

'Let me help you right now.'

She took over from me after I explained what I wanted and then spoke fluent Italian to the girl behind the counter. When she'd finished I asked: 'May I wait and buy you a drink for doing that?'

'No, there's no need. Thank you.'

'No. Thank you for helping me out. At least let me say thank you in a proper manner.'

'OK,' she replied and we walked out of the post office together.

We strolled along until we found one of those delightful cafés you see dotted all over Florence. We sat down at a small iron table in a little square and we introduced ourselves. Her name was Isabel du Roi. She spoke six languages, she was elegant, beautiful and what I would describe as 'class'. She had been properly educated and was talking to me in the most perfect English. She explained she was Italian but her mother was French, which explained her name. She was working as a model for a big fashion house.

I invited her to dinner. 'I can't come out tonight. But I would like to go to dinner with you.'

I didn't want to lose her, so I explained I lived in London and worked in the textile business so frequently travelled abroad.

'I live in Munich, so perhaps we can meet up there.'

'I would dearly love that.'

We exchanged telephone numbers and went our separate ways. Why she wanted to stay in touch I do not know. She really did want to get to know me. Why? Who knows?

It took me about a week to return to London and the first thing I did on getting back to the flat was to telephone Isabel.

'When are you coming back?' she asked me. We exchanged thoughts and spoke for about an hour. The following morning she called me and that evening I rang her. This went on for a few weeks until I had got some money together. The thought of being apart from her was starting to drive me mad. For some unknown reason she also fancied me.

That night I told her I was coming over.

'I'll meet you at the airport.'

'No, don't drive in. Meet me at the Hotel Bayerischer Hof.'

'All right.'

The following evening we were drinking in the bar of the Hotel Bayerischer Hof. She was lovely. I had sat down for about three and three-quarter minutes when I plucked up courage.

'Look, Isabel,' I told her. 'We're wasting time here. Let's go and fuck.'

'What took you so long!' she replied.

And bang. That's precisely what happened. We went straight to bed and stayed there all of that night and the whole of the following day and the whole of the next night. She was so gorgeous I even stopped gambling to be in her company.

When we finally emerged, shattered, from the longest session of sex I have experienced in my life, she said she had a surprise in store for me.

'I'm going to take you to Jacob's Cove.' It's a splendid restaurant up in the mountains near Munich. We spent three or four days together soaking up the countryside, the fine food and wonderful wines and generally wallowing in the pleasure of each other's company.

But all good times must come to an end. One morning I wake up and I discover I have hardly got enough money to pay the bill and I don't want to do a runner with Isabel on my arm. It is time for us to leave. I must get some money.

Isabel is class, real special, as well as being an absolute stunner. I know that if I walk her into a top jewellers, Asprey's, Cartier's, Tiffany's, they'll take one look at her and offer me the shop. Everybody was looking at me and thinking 'What's a silly old man like him doing with her?'

So it is back into Munich we go with me desperately trying to make some plans in my head. Isabel still thinks I am a textile merchant and I realise from talking to her that she is not a crook. This presents me with a double difficulty. I am going to have to fool both the jeweller and Isabel if I want to use her to distract the attention of the jeweller and allow me to steal his goods.

Munich's equivalent to our Bond Street is Maximilian Strasse. 'Isabel,' I say, in just the right relaxed manner. 'My holiday here is nearly over. I must buy some presents to take back for my family and friends.'

'That's no problem.'

'I want a Piaget watch and maybe a Rolex and the odd diamond ring.'

'Well, let's get on with it,' she says and off we go walking down the Maximilian Strasse into shops where the staff all know her by name and by reputation. She must have been on the front pages of *Vogue* or some other fashion magazine. Once I entered the shop with her on my arm the world was open to me. It must have been like going into a shop with the Queen. I decided to use the cheque book. Just an ordinary customer on holiday from England with his beautiful top model German girlfriend, half his age, buying her a special present. I took out the cheque book and signed away hundreds of thousands. We went from shop to shop to shop.

She was a little naive and had no idea what I was up to. 'My friend is here on holiday but his government . . .' And that would be as far as she would get before the shopkeeper brushed aside her protests and said, 'No problem. It's not a problem if you say so, Isabel.'

Out came the lovely gold Parker pen which I used to impress the shopkeepers and the cheques were filled in and thrown to the shops like confetti.

What happened to Isabel I never knew. I moved from Stuart Tower shortly afterwards and might well have mislaid her telephone number, or she mine. More likely, she discovered what had been going on and decided to have no more to do with me.

25

The Finest Jewellery in the World

A ndrew Grima is the finest jeweller designer in the world.
He was the Queen's jeweller and based in Switzerland.
London legend has it that Lord Snowdon opened his shop on
a Wednesday and Morry the Head closed it on a Thursday.
This was in the late Sixties.

Andrew Grima opened this massive jewellery shop in
Jermyn Street, the most fashionable part of London, slap
in the heart of Mayfair. It is next to the Forte Crest Hotel,
opposite the rear entrance of Fortnum and Mason. Well,
this shop looked like Fort Knox and he had the most
expensive jewellery in London. The manager's name was
Mr Tuson. What happened was, I browsed into the shop
at a time when I was living at Stuart Tower in Maida
Vale.

I walked into this shop and selected a couple of very
expensive pieces. A bracelet, a necklace, both diamond. All
his own design. After debating with Mr Tuson for a little while
he, to my astonishment, said: 'Why don't you take them, sir,

and show them to your aunt and let me know at a later stage whether you want them or not.'

As soon as he said that I said: 'Yes, I'll do that.' I was going to Bournemouth to an aunt or some other fictional relative. The usual story.

Well, I got the two pieces on appro, on approval, and went straight to Hatton Garden and cashed them in, which was a criminal act. As soon as I cashed them in I went gambling at The Mount in Mount Street and by the time that night was over I was broke and I'd done Mr Grima's pieces. I must have spent twenty grand that night. The jewels were worth about eighty or a hundred grand.

After two or three days of headaches and wondering where to get the money for Grima I got a phone call. It was Mr Tuson.

'Ah. Good morning, Mr Spurling. Have you decided on what you want?'

I got the girl who was living with me, a girl called Paula, to say: 'He's still away.'

I thought of an idea. I thought, if I have my car stolen with his goods in them I can't be responsible. So I got someone that I knew who was a photographer who was broke. His name was Patsy the Kid.

I said: 'How would you like fifty quid just to steal my car and leave it miles and miles away?'

'All right,' he said.

I had a little Morris Minor at the time. He came round, took the car and left it, not miles away, the idiot, but in Regent's Park. He might as well have left it right outside West End Central Police Station. Anyway, to cut a long story short Tuson phones me up again and I said: 'Mr Tuson. I've got some news to tell you.'

'Oh, you've decided which of these two pieces you want?'

'No. I haven't decided at all, Mr Tuson, because my car was stolen.'

'What's that got to do with my jewellery?'

'The theft of my car has got everything to do with your jewellery because your two fine pieces were inside it when it was stolen.'

There was silence on the end of the phone.

Roughly the same thing had happened with £43,000 worth of diamonds in Hatton Garden.

Anyway, I was summoned to St John's Wood Police Station by Roy York, who was in charge of St John's Wood and also finished up, I think, as a Commander at Scotland Yard. He sat me down and said: 'Now look, we know what's happened. You've done the money.' He was no fool. He knew what I'd done but nothing could be proved.

26

Soup or Sex?

One woman who didn't help me with the stealing but who became a good friend was Margaret. Funnily enough she was only the second woman in my life I cuddled up with, the rest were chucked out in the morning. I got very attached to Maggie, she was all woman, knew how to cook, knew how to fuck, knew how to dress, and knew how to speak. Maggie was a nice woman and it's tragic that she was disfigured in a car accident.

I was living in Grove Court in St John's Wood, which is quite a well-to-do block of apartments. I was friendly with a fellow called Malcolm at that time and he was talking on the phone to a girl and he said: 'Do you mind if I give her your number, because she's gonna ring me up?'

'No. Not at all.'

The hours go by and the phone goes and I pick it up. She says in a very Roedean accent: 'Oh, hallo. Is Malcolm there please?'

'Yes, sure, I think he is.'

They had a conversation and to my surprise he turned round and said: 'She thinks you've got a lovely voice. Would you like to talk to her?'

'All right. What's she like?'

'She's got the best pair of boobs in London.' And being a boob-oriented man I said: 'Oh, hallo. How are you?'

'You sound rather nice.'

'I am nice.'

From then on she said: 'I thought Malcolm was going to take me out. But he's a married man. Are you?'

'No. I'm available any time of day.'

'Jolly good. Would you care to take me to dinner?'

So I said to this Malcolm, 'What's she like?'

'She's gorgeous. And does she fuck!'

So I said: 'Certainly.' And we made a date. She, strangely enough, was living in Stuart Tower where I originally lived. At that time I was doing quite well. I had a lovely Daimler 66 and I did have a few quid. I was living in this lovely furnished apartment which belonged to a Canadian publisher, David Courtney.

We had a blind date. I arrive at Stuart Tower with a lovely bunch of red roses and I proceed to the fifth floor whereupon she's standing at the front door of her flat with a little poodle dog. She wore a black dress, which showed off a wonderful fig-ure. She was no youngster, she must have been about thirty-five to thirty-eight, but she was a stunner. Straightaway we clicked.

'Oh what nice roses,' she said, 'they're for me?'

I'd told her on the phone: 'Don't expect Robert Redford. I'm bald and not the world's most handsome man.'

'I don't mind,' she'd said in reply, 'the vibes sound good.'

I took her to the most fashionable restaurant in London which was Mario and Franco's The Trattoria in West Halkin Arcade off Sloane Street. It was a club restaurant the other side of the Carlton Tower.

Mario and Franco's was the doyen of restaurants in London. I'd already phoned and booked a table. We got in the car and straightaway she put her hand on my leg. As she was sitting in the front seat of my Jag her skirt was up round her bum and I thought to myself 'Oh my God, this is it'.

We got to Mario and Franco's.

'Good evening, Mr Spurling . . . How are you, Mr Spurling?' I loved all that. We had champagne and then we went down to dinner.

She wore the most ideal outfit I've ever seen. A black see-through dress with just one row of pearls around her neck. She looked extremely alluring and attractive.

We sat down at a table at this exclusive restaurant. 'Ooh,' she says to the waiter, 'I'll have the smoked salmon.'

I ordered some soup.

After we'd ordered she said things like: 'Well, we've been in each other's company for about an hour,' in this Roedean sort of voice. I kept looking at her because she had a dress on where I could see everything that she wore. Black panties, black bra. She was looking at me and her eyes were sparkling. I was suited and booted like the Mayfair man I was.

The soup and smoked salmon arrived and as she put the sliver of smoked salmon in her mouth she said to me: 'Darling. You look rather concerned. Is it that you want to fuck me straightaway or may we finish the meal?'

The soup slid all down my Sulka tie. 'Yes, I had been giving it some thought, to be honest,' I replied.

And that was it. She moved in the same night. After we got back to my place and we'd been in a sex encounter for hours she said: 'I won't be long. I'm just gonna pop home.' We only lived ten minutes away from each other. She popped home in her car or my car, and came back with a wardrobe full of clothes. 'I'm staying.' And that's it.

She was insatiable, she had to be bonked every ten minutes

of the day. I remember driving to a racecourse in Nottingham with her and took a shortcut and she said: 'Stop.'

'What's wrong?'

'Give it to me now. Please.'

When the Ritz casino opened I was playing blackjack for big money at the table. So gorgeous, gorgeous Roedean-educated Margaret, speaking like the Queen, was watching me play and she said: 'You need some luck, darling.' She unzipped my trousers and started playing with me.

'What are you doing?' I asked her.

'No one would dream of guessing what we are doing, darling,' she replies. 'This will bring you some luck.'

'But Maggie . . .'

'No one will look,' she told me in that Queen-like confident voice. 'Just carry on with your cards and I'll carry on doing what I'm doing.'

She was a complete nymphomaniac, in the car, in the kitchen, when the things were on the cooking stove.

'Come here, darling, I want you. Lift my skirt up. Give it to me.' As she's cooking the eggs and bacon. A complete and utter nymphomaniac. It was impossible to satisfy her. But we had some good times together.

Unfortunately the poor girl had a terrible accident on the M4 in which the pal of mine that was driving her got killed. He was a jeweller in Hatton Garden. His name was Gerry Satin and he got killed and she got badly disfigured. I have seen her once since then and she suffered through the accident. And that was the encounter with the marvellous Maggie.

27

Love at First Sight

In 1969 I really fell in love. Her name was Bridget Hallahan and I first encountered her in the coffee shop of the Hilton Hotel in Park Lane. She was enormously attractive and looked like a woman in her young twenties. Long dark hair, beautiful face, sexy legs, well dressed, sexy all over. It was love at first sight. I chatted her up, made a date with her. It happened like this.

The Hilton coffee shop was *the* place to be at that time. Everybody was there. If I wanted to meet someone I'd know they'd be there. The Hilton coffee shop at eleven o'clock in the morning was the gathering place of the set. You'd see the whole of London go by. The Hilton every morning and the Grosvenor on Sunday mornings. It was just like brushing your teeth. Used to get in my Daimler 66 Vanden Plas and it would take me to the Hilton.

One morning I saw a pair of attractive legs under the table which I couldn't help looking at. The owner had a paper and every time I looked the paper went that way and I looked that way and the paper went the other way and I looked the other way. This went on for ages until I said: 'Look, let's cut it out.' She lowered the paper and there was Bridget and she was laughing and I was laughing.

I was on form and had a bit of money at the time. We hit it off – it was a mutual thing.

'Do you like coffee?'

'No.'

'Do you like dinner?'

'No.'

'Would you like me?'

'Yes.'

Something like that. A bit of banter.

Little did I know she was seventeen. *Seventeen*. She looked like twenty-five. She was seventeen with a head of thirty. Later I was to discover she knew every move in the book. Oh dear, she was a 'gangster' in her own right, but she was a good-looking 'gangster'.

She lived in Adams Mews behind the Connaught Hotel in Haven Street near Berkeley Square. I had already robbed the Connaught Hotel. I did all the jewellery showcases of the hotels in London: the Dorchester, the Ritz, the Grosvenor, the Connaught and the Royal Lancaster when it first opened.

After a sex session on the first or second night in her Mayfair flat she leaned over to me and said: 'Do you know I'm seventeen?' Her slim beautiful naked body was half poised above me, her breasts firmer than the rocks from which my diamonds had been cut. I nearly fell through the floor.

This was towards the end of 1969. In 1970 the age of consent was lowered to eighteen so we had to wait just a few weeks or a couple of months until that law came into being.

Her parents were bound to find out about our relationship and of course the father just had to be a Colonel Hallahan who was a mercenary based in Zambia who had been decorated by

President Kaunda. I think he was Colonel-in-Chief of Kaunda's forces. He would be outraged and so would her mother.

Bridget had a Mayfair flat rented by her father. She moved in with me where I lived in Hertford Court in Hertford Street beside the London Hilton. At that time the Pair of Shoes casino was two or three doors up from me. It was London's top casino and of course it was legal by then. It was owned by Eric Steiner, a Swedish entrepreneur, and we used to go broke in there every night with regularity.

28

King of Diamonds

I wooed her in bed, in the casinos, in the nightclubs and the fancy restaurants but the best place I took her 'a-wooing' was down Regent Street.

Just picture this. Bridget is seventeen with lovely long dark hair and slim with a beautiful smile. She lights up every time we pass a jeweller's shop. At first she had no idea what I was doing, I had introduced myself to her as a textile merchant. That's my normal cover. But she's come to realise I am not quite what I seem, so today we are going on a foray into the world in which I am most at home.

It's an ordinary day in London in the late Sixties. Bridget and I have come into town by taxi from our flat in Mayfair. It had dropped us off at Oxford Circus. There was a small shop I wanted to have a quick look at before engaging in the business of the day. Now we are walking down the street towards Piccadilly Circus, arm in arm just like a pair of young lovers. I notice some people giving me odd looks, some in admiration. You see, having just turned forty-two and being almost completely bald I don't look like the classic description of a lady killer. So, I'm not surprised some people wondered what was going on.

One of my dreams had been to do Garrard's – it's the swankiest jewellers in town and of course an added attraction is the fact it's the Queen's jewellers. Like most top jewellery houses of the day it had an imposing doorman watching the customers coming and going. They were on the lookout for thieves. But if you turned up dressed like a wealthy man with a gorgeous woman on your arm no one bothered to link you with the criminal classes.

'Good morning, sir,' said the doorman as we entered.

Bridget is clearly impressed with the goods on offer. Nothing in Garrard's is cheap. They sell only the best which just happens to include some of the finest diamond and emerald brooches in the world. I fancy looking over one or two with Bridget. We go upstairs and are met by an extremely pleasant, amiable man called Mr Leary, who's the managing director of the jewellery department. He makes it a point to serve us, I think he must fancy Bridget.

'We're looking for a brooch,' I tell him.

'I see, sir, let's see what we can do.' He turns away and goes to one corner where he picks out a few boxes of jewels. He sets these down in front of us.

'What do you think of these, sir and madam?'

'Dazzling,' breathes Bridget. 'How much are they worth?'

'Does sir want to know?' asks Mr Leary.

'I'd better,' I said, managing to summon up all the confidence of a businessman well able to afford any item in the shop.

'That one you're holding at the moment is a diamond and emerald of particular quality. It most takes my fancy amongst all these pieces. It's nearly forty thousand pounds.'

'Gracious,' gasps Bridget beside me. 'Do you think you can afford it, darling?'

I peer at it more closely. 'I'm not sure. I certainly like it. But what about you, Bridget? Is this what you want?'

We ask Mr Leary to show us some more jewels. We stay there about an hour before telling him we can't make up our minds. But, we assure him, we'll be back tomorrow.

'Some store,' she gulps as we walk down towards Piccadilly.

We take lunch in the Café Royal and chatter away pleasantly until we finish the dessert. Over coffee I slip my hand into my pocket, after first ensuring there are no prying eyes, and carefully bring out the diamond and emerald brooch. I move my hand across the white linen tablecloth and catch Bridget's eye.

She pants as she sees the brooch.

'You little devil,' she cries out in amazement, 'that's the forty thousand pounds one.'

'Oh, is it?'

'Well, that's put paid to going back there again, now hasn't it. And I was rather looking forward to seeing that opal once more.'

'Not necessarily,' I tell her, leaning towards her side of the table in a conspiratorial manner. I whisper across the inch from my mouth to her face: 'He didn't notice it had gone.'

'Well, he will once he wants to show it to another customer.'

That night in bed after a long session at The Colony Club we lay back shattered. I really had not intended going back to Garrard's again so soon. Bridget was right. They would soon notice their prize piece had been stolen. But, since we had got the money for the brooch and spent it gambling, there was no alternative. The sooner I went back the safer it would be. Either that or we would have to scratch the Queen's jewellers from the list for quite a while. The sight of Bridget's naked breasts gently stirring in her sleep gave me confidence beyond what I normally possess, though my friends say that would be almost impossible.

Needless to say, by nine the following morning we were back in Garrard's. Mr Leary again served us and this time I walked away with a couple of the most beautiful brooches you've ever seen in your life. One was an antique which belonged to a Lady Zia Werner, whose husband was a big racecourse owner. As we walked out the doorman bid me a good day and very politely said almost as an aside, 'I see you're a racing man.'

'Indeed, I am.'

'I couldn't help noticing the *Sporting Life* under your arm.'

Bridget gave him one of her lovely all-embracing smiles.

'I wondered, sir, could you tell me a winner?'

Now there was a horse running that day at Southwell trained by George Vergette. He trained horses around the Nottingham area and had a horse running called 'King of Diamonds'. It seemed a most appropriate name for a horse for a doorman at Garrard's. I patted my pocket as I advised him to back that one.

'You'd better have a couple of bob on that, old chap, it'll win today.'

That night the proceeds of the theft went down the slot in the Victoria Club Casino. And the following morning I awoke with Bridget beside me in bed. I went to the kitchen and found we were not only out of milk, but had neither orange nor even lemonade.

'Bugger,' I whispered, 'no food in the house. Again.'

Something startled me. I jumped back and saw Bridget standing in the doorway staring at me. She was propped up against the open door, stark naked, and as she yawned she stretched out both arms and arched herself back on her heels. I stood there speechless.

'What's up?' she asked.

'We're out of everything.'

'Not possible,' she confidently replied. 'I've got a thousand in my handbag.'

'No you haven't,' I replied.

'You didn't use that as well, surely?'

'Don't you remember?'

'I was too drunk to remember anything after eleven last night.'

'We'd better go back to Garrard's.'

'Not again. It's too dangerous.'

'But Mr Leary's keen to sell me something.'

'But you're not going to buy. He's going to start questioning what we're doing.'

'Once more. They haven't noticed anything's gone yet, I'm sure of that.'

So there we are, back in Regent's Street for the third time in three days strolling arm in arm, as if desperately unable to make up our minds about a present to seal our love. I wasn't frightened of going back into the same jewellers three times in a row but all the same, I was on edge. As we crossed the threshold I concentrated everything on the job in hand. I felt a tug on the arm. Turning sharply, I faced the doorman. I momentarily shuddered.

'Thank you very much for the tip, sir.'

My mind was a blank. A lot had happened since yesterday and our earlier conversation had quite slipped out of my mind.

'King of Diamonds won at Southwell, ten to one. I had two bob on it. Thank you very much.'

'Oh right. Good horse. Good horse. I'm glad you took my advice and had a win.'

Bridget wore an even shorter skirt and an even more see-through blouse and we walked out of there with even more diamonds.

'I see how you do it,' she told me, once outside.

'Do you,' I said, 'I hope not.'

'I don't mean the actual moment of taking the stuff, I

mean how you're able to get away with it without being seen.'

'Oh, do you,' I replied, quickly bringing the conversation to a halt by hailing a cab which was slowly approaching us.

'Jump in,' I told her, 'we're going somewhere special.'

The staff at Garrard's had bent over backwards to help us with no knowledge of what happened due to the presence of Bridget, because everybody had been in awe of her, she looked so beautiful.

It didn't end there, because Garrard's display at all the international fairs. I used to go to Garrard's at these fairs and I would mentioned that I knew Mr Leary, telling them he used to serve me. That meant I was well thought of because although he'd retired he was held in great esteem throughout the jewellery world. They would bring out brooches, rings and loads of good stuff. So Garrard's became a 'Help Yourself'.

Bridget loved this life. She was over the moon and she was still only seventeen. It was a thrill for her. She was the perfect decoy. Whatever fashionable Mayfair jewellery shop I used to take her into the staff were all head over heels to serve her.

It amazes me to think of the cheek and audacity that I used at that time. I had a lot of confidence because of her presence – it would be like walking into a hotel with Madonna on your arm.

At night we'd go and gamble in the best casinos in London: the Colony, the Ritz, the Hilton, the Playboy, the Palm Beach in Berkeley Street.

The average day would begin with us waking up and me going straight to my trousers. There was never any money in them.

An average day before we got married would be like this. We would wake up broke. One day we woke up in a fleapit hotel in Paddington without a pound.

'Bridget. Come on. Dress yourself. Off we go.'

'Where are we today?' She loved it. Oh, she loved it. The cheek and audacity of it all.

The sun always shone when we had diamonds. Then we'd go home, go to bed for a couple of hours, have a bath and then go to the Ritz Casino or the Victoria Club Casino.

'Good evening, sir. How are you?'

'Hallo, madam.'

We both loved this life of crime. The Daimler 66 Vanden Plas was the apple of my eye and driving around with Bridget was just like being in heaven. I was on cloud nine. I didn't take any notice of the world outside because I was so thrilled to have her on my arm with money in my pocket to gamble with. I didn't worry for the next day. I was dressed immaculately, Sulka tie, Jermyn Street shirt, Italian suit, crocodile shoes. She was dressed to match.

We ate at Wilton's, which is the finest restaurant in London, we ate at Scott's, at Simpson's. I took her to Ascot and Cheltenham; she loved it, she just loved every bit of it.

We'd wake up in the morning in the hotel and ask ourselves who were we gonna rob.

'Bridget, have you got any money?'

'No. Have you got any money?'

'Oh my God, where shall we go today?' So we'd have coffee, look at the map and decide where to go.

'I'd love to go to Cheltenham, there are some beautiful jewellers there.'

'OK. We'll go to Cheltenham.'

Or Chester, or York or Harrogate, the finest towns in the country. On a one-day trip we would go to Harrogate and have tea in Betty's. Typically, we'd have woken about nine or ten, had a bath and got in the car. I think we always used to have sex before we went out because it was a bit of luck. She needed it, I needed it, so that would be the ritual. Sex for breakfast and then we went out.

We would drive to Harrogate, go into a jewellers and I'd say: 'I'd like to buy my wife something.'

'Yes. What can we do for you, sir?'

One of the places we visited was Ogden's in Harrogate, where the manager was looking at her like she was a film star while I was putting my hand in the drawer. Always, she wore a see-through or a low-cut blouse, always, and always light pink. She'd cross her legs and the feller nearly fell over looking at her legs. No bra, of course. It was a scam that she loved doing – remember, she was only a teenager.

Once I'd got the diamonds I'd be off to sell them as quick as I could. I would sell them in Hatton Garden or Bayswater. Not legitimate diamond dealers. I used to work on roughly a third of the cost. So if a diamond cost a thousand pounds I used to get three or four hundred quid for it, if a diamond cost ten thousand pounds I would get three or four thousand pounds for it. I would get this from crooked buyers whom I cannot name.

We'd go back home, have some more sex, have some dinner and go to a casino. At that time we were frequenting the Ritz, the Victoria Club, the Palm Beach, Crockfords, the top casinos in London. I am barred from most of them now. I'm in the throes at the moment of reapplying for membership to a couple of casinos but I'm not bothered if I don't get back.

29

Marriage and the Missing Piggott

The time came for us to get married. I wanted her so much and she wanted me so nothing could stop us. Her father flew over to see me and we met at The White House in Regent's Park.

Colonel Hallahan was absolutely the biggest man I had ever seen in my life.

He said: 'So you're Morry the Head, the bastard that's run away with my lovely precious flower of a daughter.'

He picked up little me and carried me through the lounge bar into the swimming pool area and held me above the pool. All the time he was shouting and yelling like a man possessed. I thought I was going to die.

Little did he know that Bridget had more scams and stings and moves than I'd ever thought about. But I wasn't about to tell him.

His hands were like goalkeeper's hands. I was terrified of him. He dropped me beside the swimming pool and we returned to the bar. After buying him three large whiskies he became my friend because finally he said to me: 'If you love her, if you really love her, I'm not going to stop you.'

We were chatting away like close friends when all of a sudden the door flies open and in walks Bridget's mother screaming like Katharine Hepburn. 'Oh, my poor daughter.'

Now a change comes over the husband. He's no longer the brave soldier he was at the start of our encounter. He's browbeaten by this woman and there's nothing I can do to change her mind.

But he must have had some influence because they didn't try to stop us getting married.

I planned the wedding like a military affair. It was to be the talk of London. All the big names wanted to come and see The Head's marriage to this exotic beautiful teenager.

I had booked the Tower Suite of the Carlton Tower Hotel in Sloane Street overlooking Buckingham Palace for the afternoon reception, the cocktail party; and the Barracuda Restaurant in Baker Street for the wedding dinner. Everything booked for no money. The Barracuda had just opened and was the in-place at that time.

Hundreds of pounds' worth of flowers came from Moyses Stevens of Berkeley Square, the top London florist. I never did pay the bill.

I had a five-piece Italian band flown over and there must have been three or four hundred people at the wedding.

We got married at Harrow Road Register Office but the day before the wedding I had pawned the ring to have a bet with so when we arrived there was no ring. I had to borrow the money to get it out. From Harrow Road we went to the Carlton Tower where if you looked out of the window you saw the Queen's backyard.

Bridget looked lovely on the day. I was standing there with her and the toastmaster. As the people came in he called, 'Mr and Mrs So and So, Mr and Mrs So and So.' Many of the wedding presents were cash. An envelope, which I knew contained a cheque, was handed to me and it immediately went into my inside pocket. I had this blue silk suit, tailor-made with specially large pockets to hold the envelopes. I kept saying, 'I must do a wee,' and she said, 'Why?'

'I dunno. Must have a weak bladder. I'm drinking too much champagne.'

My excuse was to get to the toilet to open the envelope to see how much the cheque was for. I kept thinking: 'This is not a bad game, getting married, if you keep getting cheques. I'll get married every week.' After the first wedding I said to Bridget: 'Shall we do this again?'

I ordered the cake at the finest patisserie in London which was called Searcy's opposite Harrods. After ordering the cake, which was three tiers, Bridget said it would be nice to put something fixed on top of it. We were walking by Fortnum's when we passed the lovely shop called Swaine, Adeney Brigg, they did lovely leather and crocodile. They've since moved to Bond Street. We saw a statue of Lester Piggott in the window.

'Oh,' says Bridget, 'that'll be marvellous because all your friends are bookmakers, racegoers.' So we walked in and hired the statue with a £50 deposit, took the statue back to the cakemakers who fixed it on top of the cake. It must have been worth about a thousand pounds which was a lot of money in those days, back in 1970.

When I was called upon to make a speech by the toastmaster at the afternoon cocktail party, 'Piggott' was on display in the corner of the room. As I got to the microphone the lights went out. They came on a few seconds later and I noticed the cake was still there but the Piggott had gone. I couldn't believe it and instead of saying what a bridegroom normally says, 'Dear mother, dear father, dear family, dear friends, dear this, dear that . . .' I picked up the microphone and said: 'Would the dirty bastard who's nicked Lester Piggott please put him back.' Which brought a round of applause and laughs. A friend of mine had done it for a joke, he hadn't done it to steal it, so I got it back much to my relief. I put it in my pocket for the rest of the wedding celebrations.

We had a whole host of guests: George Raft, Dino Cellini, Freddie Ahab, they were all The Colony regulars.

The wedding was hilarious. But the wedding night was strange. When I should have been in bed with an eighteen year old glamorous young lady I was walking round Shepherd's Market, looking for a whore. Why? I don't know. I can never answer that, perhaps it's a kink, I don't know. Bridget thought I'd gone gambling, but she was too busy looking for the cheques to care that much.

Bridget and I went all around Britain hunting for jewellery, the eventual result of which I was arrested and once again sent to prison. Middlesex Sessions sent me down for seven years. A few days earlier Bridget had been bound over after pleading guilty to four charges of dishonestly obtaining jewellery and one further charge of attempting to dishonestly obtain jewellery, so she retained her freedom.

She left the court in tears. I've always had a sneaking feeling the mother gave us away because she never forgave me for marrying her little daughter. Anyway, she got what she wanted. During the time in prison we were divorced.

I was not free again until August 30, 1974, four and a half years later.

30

Murder at Mount Street

The Mount Street Club became famous because it was the scene of the Buggy murder. Somehow I happened to get involved and it led to the last ever meeting I had with my former wife, Bridget.

The Mount was a favourite haunt of mine and I got on well with the people who ran it, Eddie Fleischer and Franny Daniels, Albert Dimes' right hand man, who is now dead.

What happened was this guy Buggy had a car which was left in Mount Street. After a few days when Buggy's girlfriend reported him missing they found this car and discovered it had been there for several days. At that time there were no traffic wardens or parking meters or yellow lines. Eventually there was speculation throughout London's West End that he'd been shot in The Mount Street Club. No one had actually been in the room, but they'd been in the ante rooms and they'd heard the shots and eventually rumours began circulating and it was known he had gone.

He was found just off Brighton beach. They'd dumped his

body in the sea and it had surfaced. They hadn't put enough weights on it and it came back up.

Eventually Franny Daniels and his right hand man, Alf Lewis, were charged with the murder. Franny was on remand for quite some time but eventually he was acquitted, as was Alf Lewis. To this day nobody has ever been convicted of Buggy's murder, but most people have a very good idea of exactly what happened. He tried to muscle in on the club and the people there wouldn't stand for it. They were tough guys themselves.

I think they roughed Buggy up before shooting him because when his body was found he had a broken jaw. Buggy had come a bit late to try and get any money because the club at that time was not doing so well. The big money had gone. He had come at the wrong time. He was put up to it by another gang whose name I won't mention, they were trying to muscle in. He was a bully and a pseudo-gangster. He shot somebody outside The Pigalle, and there was some connection with Shirley Bassey, I don't know what, but he got nine years for it. I didn't like Buggy. He was a Scots gangster and a bully. The person who was friendly with him and used to go and visit him in Leicester Prison was a guy called Sulky who ran The Astor Nightclub.

I had parked my car by the side of the Connaught Hotel which was opposite The Mount. This was one afternoon about two or three o'clock. As I went to go in the club I saw two or three fellers coming out of the club with a carpet in their hands and one of them was the driver, a little feller called Alf, who used to work for Franny.

'Oh hallo, Morry, we're not open this afternoon, we're changing the carpet and doing some decorations.'

'OK.' I drove away and never thought any more about it. Afterwards I found out that in the carpet was the dead feller, Buggy, who'd been shot about an hour previously. He was rolled up in the carpet which was why they weren't open for business. And then I heard there was a confrontation about money, Buggy pulled out a gun, someone else pulled out a gun, whether it was Franny, whether it was his nephew Waggy, whether it was this one or whether it was that one, I don't suppose anybody'll ever know and it wasn't my business, I didn't want to enquire. But all of a sudden I get a message that West End Central Police Station want me. I was seen that afternoon going towards the club by a plainclothes policeman who took a note of my car number. Of course they asked me all about the shooting. I told them all I saw was a carpet, I didn't see any bodies or anything. I never went in the club.

It was in association with this Buggy thing that I last saw Bridget. She was in a solicitor's office, as she was a witness to the Buggy murder.

When Franny was arrested for the murder he wanted to see me in Brixton jail where he was on remand. I went to see him and I volunteered to be a witness. I can't remember how I was going to be a witness or what I was going to be a witness for. I went to his solicitor who was Harry Stevens of Baldwin, Mellor and Co. of Bouverie, EC something or other, and Bridget was sitting there. We'd split up but she was sitting there and we sort of smiled at each other. What happened was neither of us were used in court as Franny got out of the charge.

31

The Underworld Takes its Revenge

Now, as I say, I'm not a violent man and I don't like violence. Most of my life I have avoided it. But there have been one or two occasions when violence has come my way.

I was with a friend of mine from Fulham called Gary who took me to a jewellers in Wimbledon one Saturday morning.

After lifting three diamonds I said to him: 'Where are we going to sell these on a Saturday morning?'

'I know a guy called the Monk.'

I'd heard about this fellow who lived in Wandsworth, so we proceeded to this address, walked in, sat down, and I sold him the diamonds. Now he bought these diamonds without even looking at them through a glass or through a tester. He bought them on face value. Instantly, I knew he was a bit of a mug because nobody buys anything without checking, because there are so many false stones about. And especially you don't buy off a feller like me without checking.

So when this feller bought them straightaway I instantly knew he was a mug. And whenever you find a mug in life you have got to rob him, because if you don't rob him there's a big queue behind you. If you can sell a painting as a Picasso, you sell it, because if you don't there are other people behind you trying to sell it. In life, if you're a villain like I've become, unfortunately, and I find a mug, I've got to rob him. A mug's a source of ready cash.

As we walked out the door with the money Gary says: 'Oh, good, we got some money.'

'I got news for you,' I say, 'we're gonna get a lotta money off this feller.'

'What do you mean?'

I explained what I was planning to do.

'Oh yes, you're right.'

On leaving after the first occasion this Monk had turned round to me and said: 'Morry. I'm always here, I'll always buy from you. I've heard good news about you, you get the best in the world.'

That did my ego a lot of good and taught me that I was gonna do him at the end of the day.

Anyway a week or five days went by, I arrive, knock on the door.

'Come in.'

'I've got something for you.'

Down in the basement we go and I sell him these bits of glass to the tune of three, four, five grand. He bought them straightaway, never put the tester on them, what we call 'The Testing Machine', never put the eyeglass on, just bought them.

'Morry. I'm here every day.'

'OK. Lovely.' Bang. Get upstairs, give my friend his money, do the money, skint again.

Three days later. Down in the basement, more bits of glass.

'Fucking 'ell,' I thought, 'what's going on here?'

Do every dollar again. Only lasts me ten minutes. In the betting shop, done the money.

The third time I phone him he says: 'Yeah. Come round.'

Unbeknown to me he'd found out about the glass bits.

I've got back with my Fulham friend to do him a third time. Normally he answers the door. His wife answers the door that day.

'Is he waiting for me?'

'Yeah, of course,' she replies, 'he's downstairs waiting for you.'

I get downstairs with my next lot of false diamonds and there's a big fellow in there I know but I didn't know the connection with the Monk.

Monk said to me in a funny sort of supercilious way: 'What have you got for me *this* time, Morry?'

I thought, 'Aye aye, something wrong here.'

He turned round to my friend and said: 'We won't be needing you today.' Then I smelled a rat. As I turned round to try and get out the big feller blocked the staircase. I thought, 'Oh fuck me.'

He said: 'Morry. There's your so-called diamonds on the table. You've fucked us, haven't you?'

I didn't know what to say. He said to my friend: 'You go out, we'll have a few words with Morry.' Now I knew I was in trouble. This was the first time in my life that I really, really shat myself.

This guy was big and I'm really worried now. I'm in the basement of a cellar. A cellar! No one can hear me and I thought, 'Oh, fucking hell, my D-Day's come here.' Worse was to come. He turned round and said to someone: 'You can come out now.' And a little feller walked out and he was built like a tank. He was a Turk and in his hand was a baseball bat.

'Where's the money for the diamonds that we gave you, because you sold us all glass.'

157

I felt like I was in the middle of a gangster film. I'm walking backwards and the guy's walking towards me with a baseball bat. All manner of things are going round in my head. And he's pinned me against a dressing table and when I look up there's all knives on the dressing table, big thick knives. I thought, 'Fucking hell, it's on me here. I'm going. This is the end of The Head'.

'Where's the money?'

'I haven't got no money,' I reply.

'Oh. You haven't got it. But you took a liberty with us, Morry, didn't you?'

'Well, that's life,' I told him.

'Oh, *is* it?' Whereupon his hand went up to get one of these big knives. I thought he was gonna cut my head off or cut me down the face, last thing I wanted. The little Turk then got into the act.

'Leave him to me,' in broken English.

The Monk steps back and says, 'All right.'

Now the Turk is standing in front of me holding this baseball bat. He whacks me right over the arm. I thought it had come off. It nearly knocked me unconscious. He whacked me again and I fell over. I just could not move my arm. The big feller picked me up and sat me down on the table.

'We want our money.'

I said: 'Look, you can kill me but I got no money. If you give me a chance to go out and get some money I'll give you a few quid. But get this guy off my back, this Turk.'

After some discussion they said: 'All right, we'll let you go but we want our money.' Which was a miracle.

I stumbled up the stairs and my friend was waiting for me in the car. He took me home, put me into bed at his place. I was in pain, pain like I've never experienced. You couldn't imagine it. You hit someone with a baseball bat and catch 'em on the nerve, on the elbow or something, you break the arm. And that's how it was. And I'm not a very big fellow.

It took weeks to get my arm together. I was in terrible, terrible pain, but I couldn't go to hospital with it.

To cut a long story short, Johnny Bindon was the governor of Fulham. He was the number one man in Fulham. I didn't know him, but I knew of him. When my friends heard the story about what happened to me they went to him and asked him to help, to go round and see this guy and tell him to lay off me.

He did it on merit, that's what life's all about.

I met Bindon in the pub in Chelsea. He was a big feller, a man to be feared. He was going out with Vicki Hodge, daughter of a baronet. When I told him what happened he said: 'Oh. We'll go pay Monk a visit.'

Next thing I heard, he's gone to Monk's house, smashed all the windows in, got hold of Monk and said: 'Now where's the Turk? If Morry gets touched any more you got me to contend with.'

That was it, the end of the story.

Johnny Bindon was a character. He was on the verge of breaking through into the Royal Family. He was very friendly with this daughter of a baronet and he was a well-known character.

That was the only time in my life that I was in a situation that was really bordering on danger. My arm wouldn't straighten up for weeks and weeks. I've never felt so much pain in my life. I was frightened of the knife but it was the baseball bat that did the damage.

So my life has incorporated murder, gambling, sex, humour – what else? Good friends. Well, I am a lovable chap, no harm intended to anyone. I don't steal private diamonds off beautiful women, I don't break into houses, scaring people to death, in fact, I don't ever want to frighten people at all. I'm not that sort of criminal. I'm a scallywag. But there are times when even a harmless scallywag needs a bit of muscle behind him to help him out of difficulties, just as I did with Johnny Bindon in South London.

32

Champagne, Chips and Fish

Paris is one of my favourite cities.

What happened on this occasion in 1984 concerned two people, one I knew well and one who was well known in Britain at the time.

The first was my friend Alfie Haines, who died recently, who resembled Alfie Hinds, the famous escaper. Alfie Haines was the one responsible for a scam I concocted with a Brazilian using false diamonds – a switch. He was a master at making up copies of all the diamonds in the world.

I was on the run and couldn't come back to this country. I used to phone Alf every day because he was a dear and trusted friend. I'd travelled to Europe with Tina, the girl from Canada, with a lot of gear on me: diamonds, gold, this, that and the other. I trusted Alf to sell it on. So I phoned him around the time of the Prix de L'Arc de Triomphe which is held every October at Longchamp. You get the finest racing people in the world at this race – the Aga Khan, people like that. A lot of British bookmakers go there and operate illegally, because there are no bookmakers in France; it's all Tote odds.

So near the day of the race, the Arc, I ring Alf.

'I'll meet you in the Hôtel George Cinque. I've got a lot of gear for you to take back to London and sell for me and we'll go to the races.' So I arrive in Paris that Sunday morning.

'You got any money?' I ask him, giving him the gear.

'Very little. Have you?'

'No. I ain't got no money. I'll wait for you to sell the gear.'

'Shall we go to the races? There might be a move at Longchamp.'

So we went to Longchamp and had a drink when all of a sudden somebody that we knew from the races in England came up to us and said: 'Listen, you got a chance today to get some money. There's a feller from Leeds called Graham, who's in the bar with a few girls. He's buying champagne and he's looking for people to have bets with him.'

'Oh,' I said. As usual, I was dressed to perfection with a button-hole and generally looking extremely smart, the very picture of a wealthy businessman. Alf and I walk into the bar and order a drink. He came up and he was a very big man, bigger than Bruno.

'Ah, I know thee,' he says to Alf. 'You're Alfie Hinds.'

Alf and I went to the toilet a few moments later. 'Oh,' he says to me, 'he thinks I'm Alfie Hinds, not Alfie Haines.'

Back in the bar, this man's going on about Alfie. 'I see thee on television t'other night. You're very good.'

Then Alf introduced me as the punter who wanted to have a bet. So I lit up one of my big cigars which have always been the come-on and he asked me, 'Would you like some champagne?'

'Yes, I'd love some. I'd like to have a few bets today but we'll settle up with each other, win or lose, in England.'

'Fine,' he says, 'perhaps Windsor tomorrow night.' Which

was on the Monday afternoon starting at two o'clock.

I said: 'If I've got any money to come you can give it to me at Windsor. If you've got any . . .'

'By 'eck, that's fine, no problem. Bring 'oop the champagne.'

Now I'm in the mood. The first race I might have had a thousand, two thousand bet with him. Gets beat.

'Don't worry,' he says, 'Windsor tomorrow.'

I went through six races and I did not back one winner. I must have drunk three bottles of champagne on my own. I drove Alf to the airport. He went back to London. I stayed in Paris, working, trying to get some money and arranged to meet Alf later in the week. As regards the bookmaker, I didn't give a toss. I owed him seventeen thousand pounds.

Windsor was the day after L'Arc and the first race was at two o'clock. This pal of mine who works at the races phones and says to me, 'I've just had the most hilarious five minutes with the bookmaker from Leeds.'

'What happened?'

'This is what happened. The first race was two o'clock. The bookmaker was there at ten o'clock in the morning, in the bar, eating.'

When my friend saw him he said to him: 'How did you get on in Paris, Graham?'

'Oh,' he says, 'I had a marvellous time. I was introduced to a man called Mr Morris who's coming here before the first race to give me seventeen thousand pounds.'

So my friend said to him: 'Really?'

'I had a wonderful day.'

And the feller said to him: 'Mr Morris, you said. What was he like?'

'Oh, he was lovely man. He smoked big cigars, wore the best suits. He's coming here, you'll meet him.'

So my friend said: 'What does he look like?'

'He was bald, he never had no hair, very smart. And I believe his second name was Head.'

Whereupon my friend started to laugh.

'What thee laughing at?'

'Head? Morris? That's Morris the Head. And he gonna give you seventeen thousand pounds?'

'Aye, he'll be here shortly.'

'Would you take seventeen pounds for the seventeen thousand pounds?'

'Are thee telling me that Mr Morris is not coming with my seventeen thousand pounds?'

'I wouldn't like to give you seventeen shillings for the bet.'

When I didn't appear and the penny dropped later in the afternoon he turned round to my friend and said: 'He's took right liberty with me. I'm not worried about the seventeen thousand pounds but he drunk all my fucking champagne.'

About four or five years later, I arrived at York Races for the big meeting in September called The Ebor. I stood talking to someone and all of a sudden, out of the blue, a huge man appeared alongside me. He'd got his arms crossed and as I turned I saw that it was Graham.

'Don't I know thee?'

I had a hat on and he was looking at me and I thought, 'Oh my God.'

'I know thee but I can't place where I know thee from.'

So I said in French: '*Je m'excuse, je suis Français,*' and hit the crowd faster than a four-minute miler. I went right through the crowds with him running after me. I lost him. He tumbled that it was me all right.

During the Seventies when I was living in Stuart Tower I was gambling at the Victoria Casino every night because I knew the two owners very well, Cyril Levan and John Ashton. The latter is dead now. I was penniless, in trouble, owing everybody.

Anyway, I had a brainwave of sub-letting the flat, so my girlfriend Paula and I put an advert in the newspaper. We thought we'd make a bit of money.

In the meantime, I kept on going up the Victoria Sporting Club every night and I bumped into a feller there, as one can do in a casino, who was having £500 and a £1,000 pound bets at roulette. We got to have a drink at the bar and I told this fellow, who was called Haslam, that I had a flat to let. Paula was with me and I knew immediately that he fancied her. He was an ex-air force pilot who loved backing horses. He had a fish business in Lowestoft. He came back to the flat and he liked it very much, so I told Paula to play up to him.

A little while later he gave me a deposit on the flat and was going to move in the week after. No sooner had he given me the deposit, which I think was a thousand pounds, but I was back at the Victoria Club, and I had soon lost the money.

He wanted to take Paula out to dinner so I told her to continue playing up to him. While talking to him I mentioned that I was very friendly with Scobie Breasley, who was the champion Australian jockey riding over here. I said I had got tips.

'Oh, will you tell me one of the tips?'

'No, not really.'

'Why not?'

'It's very confidential.'

I was having him on. I didn't even know Scobie Breasley. But I did have an Australian friend who I knew could speak like Scobie Breasley. This was a good sting.

I arranged with a friend to phone me up when I wasn't going to be there, Paula was in the bath and he was sitting in the front room. The phone went and this is what Paula told me happened.

When Haslam picked up the phone a voice said: 'Hallo Morry. It's Scobie.'

Of course Haslam thinks he's talking to Scobie Breasley. He said: 'Oh, Mr Morris is out. Can I take a message?'

'Oh yes. He's told me that it's all right for me to tell you. I'll win the first at Brighton on "The Rift".'

'Thanks very much,' said Haslam and then put down the phone.

Of course I came in about a quarter of an hour later and Haslam said: 'Scobie's been on. He's going to win the first at Brighton.'

I knew exactly what he was going to say.

'Let's go to Brighton,' he added.

We jumped into Haslam's Jag and went down to Piccadilly to the Cox and King's branch of Lloyds Bank, which was only for ex-servicemen, where he drew out three or four thousand pounds.

We went down to Brighton Races, arriving there about ten minutes before the first race in which Scobie was riding. I had picked out this horse, The Rift, thinking it would be a short price favourite but to my amazement it was ten to one.

We had about a thousand to fifteen hundred of his money on this horse. Again to my amazement, the horse won. We left Brighton in a mass of champagne and wonderful feelings and headed straight back.

'Morris,' he said. 'You are the bestest.'

'Well, I told you Scobie never lets me down!'

By the end of that night all the money had been lost in the Victoria Club Casino. That's what it all boils down to because I made him back black and it came red, I made him back odd and it came even, I made him back low and it came high. And all the money had gone. Now, he wants to move into the flat. Oh dear, I had to delay this move. So, it was a series of more Scobie Breasley calls. 'I'll win on this, I'll win on that, I'll win on this . . .'

After the first one, nothing ever won, so he was getting sadly disappointed with me and again he wanted to move in the flat or rather he wanted to move in with Paula, my girlfriend.

He started taking money out of his bank and eventually there was nothing left. There might have been a bit of fish left in there because the whole fish business went for sale, he lost that as well. I can't remember in detail what happened except that a couple of months later I went up the Victoria Club and there was Mr Haslam playing in shillings. He'd lost all his thousands, all his fish and he never ever got into my flat or into Paula's knickers.

33

Fortunes and Flukes

Garmisch-Partenkirchen is on the borders of Austria and Germany. It's one of the richest skiing towns in the world and where all the affluent Germans go. It's south of Munich, about half an hour away. On my travels in Germany I arrived in this extremely wealthy town at the height of the summer, went into a high-class jewellers, and obtained a few articles which came to quite a bit of money and I was highly delighted.

Six months later I was in Munich in January and I decided I would have another look at Garmisch-Partenkirchen. I knew there would be a lot of money there at this time of the year. I drove through the snow, the cold and the freezing weather, and didn't recognise the town because when I was there in the summer it looked totally different.

I trooped round in the snow and ice and the wet ruining my lovely Russell and Bromley shoes, looking for a jeweller's shop.

Eventually I found one and I walked in and thought to myself: 'This is a bit familiar.' I'd walked back into the same shop that I'd been in during the summer and didn't know it.

Of course when I asked the well-dressed German lady, 'Have you got a nice single stone diamond?' she looked at me and pressed the buzzer, calling her husband.

'Have you been here before? I think I know you.'

I started talking in French but realised I was in trouble. I had to get out, and fast.

There's only one way out of Garmisch-Partenkirchen – towards Munich. You can't go any further, unless you can ski.

I ran to the car, jumped inside and about half an hour later am driving as fast as I can when I look up and there's a police helicopter following me. I didn't fancy eating sauerkraut for the rest of my life entombed in a German jail, so I slowed down a little and tried to blend in with the rest of the traffic. Fortunately for me there were a lot of cars and trucks on the road that day and the police either lost me or didn't think it worth the hassle of stopping the traffic to catch me.

So to my relief I got back to Munich and lived to steal another day. What a stupid sod to go into the very jewellers I had robbed the previous summer.

One Saturday morning in London I had gone into Garrard's in Regent Street as a customer and had stolen a diamond and emerald ring which I quickly slipped into my pocket. But there was a man who was constantly looking at me and I thought I was being shadowed by a store detective. I thought, I've got to get rid of this ring, I've got to put it back. At times it's harder to put something back than it is to steal it. So I asked one of the staff if I could use a toilet I'd used previously in the week.

'Yes, sir,' he answered. 'You can just pop in here if you like.'

I'd told him that I thought I'd got a bit of diarrhoea, so he walked me over to the nearest toilet.

I decided to get rid of the ring, so I had a pee and much to my regret I threw this heavy diamond ring down the lavatory pan, pulled the lever and went out. I hated having to flush away such an expensive diamond. I left the toilet and returned to the store. After negotiating one or two things I thought, 'I'd better get out of this', and I fully expected this man to stop me. On my way out the man did in fact follow me and I thought, 'Oh, my God, here we go,' but to my sheer amazement and disbelief it turned out that he was a customer. He stopped to look in the window and I went. I was sick as a pig. I knew that Garrard's shut at one o'clock on those days and I was broke so I went straight to a friend of mine and told him what happened.

'You're a fool,' he said. 'If you put that ring down the toilet it will still be there. The flush doesn't move it. Like if you put a penny down the toilet.' I didn't know this. So I went and found a good friend, Roy Green, who's now dead. He worked for me on many occasions. I told him what happened.

'Look,' I told Roy, 'you can have half the proceeds. Get to Garrard's first thing Monday morning, ask them if you can use the toilet. Put your hand down the pan and you'll find a lovely, beautiful diamond and emerald ring worth quite a bit of money.'

Needless to see Garrard's opened at nine and he was there at a minute past nine.

After looking round he says, 'Can I use your toilet?'

'Yes, sir. It's upstairs.' But I'd told him it was on the ground floor.

'Haven't you got one nearer?'

'No, sir. Only the staff toilet on the ground floor.'

I suppose that having said I had a touch of diarrhoea the assistant had been kind to me and let me use a toilet that was not available to the general public.

So what happened was that anybody in the world could've found that ring, probably a cleaner, probably the woman that does the toilets out, or it could still be there twenty years later – who knows?

When I lived in Stuart Tower, if you looked over the road, you could see the bank where I had an account, the Midland Bank in Cropthorne Court.

If you drew the blinds from my window you looked across the Edgware Road and you could see the bank positioned right under a block of flats. As usual I was penniless, in trouble, owing just about everyone. I was wheeling, dealing, gambling, you name it. And every morning I used to ring up the bank to ask for my balance. It was just a habit.

'This is Mr Morris Spurling, could you tell me my balance, please?'

And the clerk used to say: 'Yes, Mr Spurling. You've got three pounds ten shillings.'

She was becoming quite a friend, 'Oo, Mr Spurling, you've got six pounds odd.' And one day I had eleven pounds. I wasn't overdrawn at the bank but I had never had any money in it. If I had eleven quid it was a fortune.

One morning a friend of mine who was in the antiques' business comes to me. He was another gambler. He knocked on my door and he said to me: 'Can you do me a favour?'

'I'm looking for someone to do *me* a favour.'

'Look. I want a cheque for about seven or eight thousand pounds.' About a million pounds at a time when you've got six quid in your pocket. But it's what they call an accommodation cheque.

He wanted a cheque off me for seven or eight thousand pounds and he would give me his cheque for the same amount of money or just a few quid more so that we both deposited the cheques at the same time in the relative bank accounts. He could use it in a business matter. He had to flash my cheque. But the cheques weren't to be banked respectively until two days hence. So if it was a Wednesday they would be banked on Friday. We both knew there wasn't a shilling in the accounts.

I gave the cheque to Paula and promptly forgot all about it.

Well, Paula, being the dumb blonde that she was, banked his cheque in my account on that very same day.

The usual procedure happened the next morning.

I got up out of bed, drew the blinds, wherupon I could see over the Edgware Road to the bank at Cropthorne Court, made myself a black coffee and telephoned the bank.

'Good morning. It's Mr Spurling,' which I'd been saying for months and months, 'of Stuart Tower. Could you tell me the balance of my account?'

'Yes, sir. Four pounds, six shillings.'

The following morning I phoned up while I was still in my pyjamas and dressing gown and said: 'Could you tell me how much is in my account?'

'Yes, sir. You've got seven thousand and four pounds, six shillings in your account.'

'I think you've made a mistake, Miss, this is Morris Spurling, Stuart Tower.'

'Yes, sir. You've got seven thousand and four pounds, six shillings.'

I was holding the phone and looking through the window at the bank where the voice was coming from. I said: 'Well, will you please put me on to the Head Clerk because I think you've made a mistake.'

He came on the line.

'Good morning, Mr Spurling, you're querying your balance.'

'Yes . . .'

'Is there anything you'd like?'

'Will you hold the line please?'

I put the phone down, got in the lift, ran over the Edgware Road, into the bank, still in my dressing gown and pyjamas. Everyone was looking at me. When I entered the bank the fellow still had the phone in his hand thinking he was talking to me back in the flat.

He kept looking at the phone and then looking at me. 'Ah, Mr Spurling. What would you like?'

'All of my money, please.'

I left about a fiver or a tenner, withdrew the rest, went back into the flat, got dressed, went to the races, did the money and that was that.

Now I'm sitting back waiting for my friend to come on the phone. He didn't ring, he came straight round. There was a bang on the door: 'You dirty bastard, what have you done to me, you've ruined me.'

Of course, what happened was the bank paid against an uncleared cheque. Both banks sued us. He got the sack from his bank, I got the sack from my bank. We owed them the money, no end results.

Antwerp always brought me the greatest prizes. I got fortunes in Antwerp. It's not surprising as it is the heart of the world diamond industry.

I used to just get in the car, put it on the ferry and drive from Calais to Antwerp. Antwerp is like a magnified Hatton Garden. Blocks and blocks of offices and in every office there's untold diamonds. In some of the escapades there I was even putting in my glass from Woolworths for their diamonds.

I would switch, steal or do whatever fate had in store for me. I got a quarter of a million pounds' worth of goods the last time I was in Antwerp which I turned into nearly fifty thousand pounds.

I had been introduced to a diamond wholesalers by another firm who didn't have my requirements and it was quite simple.

I just picked up two packets of diamonds in front of the feller's eyes and put one back. He closed the box and put it back in the safe. There lay the prize in my hand. This was not one diamond, this was a packet of them, roughly half the size of a pack of cigarettes. Once again I did a Paul Daniels. It was like picking up three sweets in Woolworths and putting two back, keeping one in your hand.

This tiny little packet was half the size of a cigarette packet and we sold it for £46,000, as a result of which the Belgian police would very much like to have an encounter with me which I'll avoid for the rest of my life. His £23,000 lasted three days, mine lasted perhaps three weeks.

When I was a young man in my teens I was a fairly good snooker player, the sign of a misspent youth. I played top players, amateur champions and I acquitted myself very well. My ego built up and I thought I was very good until I got mowed down by a young Welshman called Marcus Owen who turned out to be a professional.

In relation to this £23,000, I was doing my money as per usual and it was dwindling and dwindling. During this time I bought an Austin Montego car for nineteen hundred pounds. However, there is a snooker competition every year at Derby. So, after a couple of weeks, out of the twenty-three grand, all I had to show for it was a Montego car and about five grand left out of the money. I went to Derby in my Montego. On the first day of this tournament which lasts a week, I did the five grand. But remember, I'm a judge of snooker. Now I'm desperate. I haven't got a penny in the world except my Montego car. I found somebody I knew who was a bookmaker on the snooker matches.

'Do us a favour. I haven't got a dollar. Do you wanna buy a Montego car?'

'Let's have a look at it.'

I'd do anything, once I'm broke.

So he came downstairs.

'What do you want for it?'

'Sixteen.'

'I'll give you fourteen.'

'Fifteen.'

'Fourteen.'

I'd have taken anything. I sold the Montego car for fourteen hundred pounds. This is in Derby, the snooker tournament's in the second day. Rushed up the stairs. Had the fourteen hundred quid on a snooker player who got beat. I proceeded then to catch the train home, no car, no money. Broke.

And that was the tale of the £23,000 that I got in Antwerp. Where did the rest of it go? Horses, dogs, snooker, you name it.

Fancy having a car on a snooker player.

34

Bullets and Glass Under
the African Sun

In 1975 I decided to go to Johannesburg for one simple reason: DIAMONDS. It goes without saying that I was also desperate for money, so I had arranged to meet The Swan in London.

Sheets of rain swept across the city drowning everything in sight. I had spent my last few pounds on five Hilditch and Key handmade shirts from Jermyn Street and now had no money for a taxi. During the previous months I had built up quite a collection of debts. Money had been borrowed from friends as well as being owed at casinos and racetracks and shops and hotels. Some of these friends were fellow gamblers and they had also had strokes of bad luck and now they wanted their money back. The weather contributed to my feeling of misery.

As I looked at the faces around me I could see the same feeling of desperation reflected in them: the anxious looks, the tight grip around the mouth which distorted the skin and made the eyes look mean, the hunched shoulders and the hundreds of pairs of worn-out shoes slipping over the wet paving stones. Even the bright lights winking their neon message around the statue of Eros failed to lighten my mood. It was not too far to walk to the Ritz Hotel but it was certainly a new experience. When I arrived I felt like asking the commissionaire for a towel.

It was not too long before my mood started to change. The subdued lighting, the deep comfortable seats which buried you alive, the attentive staff and above all the warmth helped to halt my depression and buck up my spirits. Oh, and a vodka, 'ice and lemon please', had a helping hand in there somewhere.

I knew Brian was in the same situation as myself. He had worked with me on several good robberies and we had decided to meet up and look at new possibilities. We were both in trouble.

Brian was late. I sat in the comfort of the Ritz trying to work out how much I had already spent. I could feel the loose change slopping around in my pocket and knew it was not enough to buy me one block of ice in this charming hotel. Of course, I could easily do a runner but the thought of banning myself from the hallowed halls of one of the best hotels in London for the price of a few drinks was too cruel to consider. So I read the papers and ordered another drink. Time was slipping by deliciously slowly and I started to think.

Now my business is diamonds. I love them with the passion I feel for women and gambling. Diamonds are some of the most beautiful objects in the world. I had watched them being sold in jewellers' shops around the world, I had witnessed their effect on some of the most gracious necks in history and I had watched as dealers caressed hundreds of loose stones in the trading capital of the diamond business, Antwerp in Belgium. But one place is particularly special to those of us who love diamonds with such abandon: South Africa. A country built on its mineral wealth where diamonds come up out of the ground like potatoes in Ireland. The more I thought about South Africa the more I wondered why on earth I had not visited that country before. In the heart of the diamond business there had to be a few stones with my name on them.

Brian arrived and after a bit of a chat during which I confirmed he was almost as poor as me I put the thought into his head.

We had worked together, on and off, since 1963 and were now running out of countries. After visiting the restaurant, he paid the bill and we left in high spirits knowing we would soon be out of the miserable rain and in the warm sunshine of Africa.

We booked our flights the next day, totally unaware of the disaster that was going to be our African holiday.

The trip started to go wrong from the very beginning. We arrived in Johannesburg at the wrong time of the day. The races were about to begin. We were tempted. So we took a taxi and went straight there, not even bothering to check in at our hotel. We stayed until the very last race and then stood on the turf without a rand between us.

However, we knew there was someone living in the city called Manchester George. He's known as The Cheat. He got his name by cheating at cards all over the world. We hitched a lift to the Carlton Hotel in Johannesburg and arranged to meet with him.

The Cheat helped us out with a bit of cash so we were able to get back to our original plan which was to see what the diamond capital of the world had in store for us.

The following morning we had an early breakfast and set off for the Hatton Garden area of Johannesburg, which is called Jeppe. It was one of the most heavily fortified parts of the city. All the shops and dealers had huge steel grilles and solid iron

Morris Spurling

bars in the windows and on the doors. They knew the value of the stones they were selling in this country. We called on several diamond houses without getting a chance to take a single stone. They were just too well guarded. Our feet were sore from tramping around the streets and our mouths were worn out from talking with the owners, trying to establish a moment when the stones could be lifted.

I should explain that Brian is what in the trade is known as a 'Talker'. That is, he does the talking to distract the trader while I take the diamonds. We were known as 'Talker-Taker'.

As we turned the street corner I saw a shop which seemed to attract my attention for no rational reason. I felt pulled towards it, perhaps because we had to take a decision to stop work that day and it might be a good idea to look at just one more. Who knows?

Anyway, once inside our hearts lifted, our mood changed and we were firing on all six cylinders.

The reason being that the man who welcomed us had just returned from the Kimberley Mines after buying a big parcel of stones.

He was keen to show us what he had recently purchased. He was like a little child he was so happy. We in turn were dazzled by what he laid out in front of us. We were shown an enormous number of diamonds, worth hundreds of thousands of pounds – in fact, millions. Without a thought we had slipped into stage one of the robbery, the 'Dummy Run'. Without saying a word both of us were formulating a plan. I told the man we had other places to visit but had been more than a little impressed with the diamonds he had already shown us and we would certainly be returning the following day.

The car we were driving was something called a Ford Taunus. We found it at the double and headed back to the Carlton Hotel for a celebration drink.

I was in the best mood ever. Whereupon 'Brian the Talker' said to me: 'Why are you so happy?'

'We're sitting on a million pounds. The stones will bring us a fortune back in London.'

'Well, you can't get *those*!' he told me.

'I'm going to,' I replied and I went on to explain to him exactly how we would accomplish this job.

There is a street in Johannesburg called Commissioner Street. It is lined with shops which sell false diamonds, Cubic Zirconias, imitation diamonds.

A lot of people wear them instead of the real thing because they look so good and also they can sometimes be quite expensive. Some of the TV shopping channels have made a fortune selling them.

Anyway, while the dummy run was in progress I had taken good mental measurements of some of the diamonds we had been shown straight from the Kimberley Mines. The adrenalin was pumping through my body as I told The Swan I was going to switch the cubics for the real ones.

At this stage he had one of his famous bouts of bowel trouble. In short, he had a bad attack of the nerves and told me that he was not going to have any part in this theft.

So I said that was all right by me and told him he could catch the first plane home. 'I'm gonna do it,' I said, knowing full well he would not want to fly home alone and broke.

The sun was up early that morning but we were up even earlier. I was already looking forward to the damp, rain-drenched streets of the West End.

We drove down to Commissioner Street where with the last of our money I bought ten big carat stones, all of them paste. Then we phoned the jeweller we had visited the day before and made an appointment to see him at midday.

We drove to the airport and booked our seats on the aircraft in the afternoon knowing full well it would be a bit of a dash from his place to the airport.

Our card cheat friend was also in on the theft. He wanted to leave South Africa on account of the fact that he too was in debt.

'Which ones are you going to get?' The Swan asks me.

'I'm going to start with the big ones,' I told him.

'If you go for the big ones and he realises it we are going to be in serious trouble.'

'I can't help that,' I replied, 'I'm sitting on a million pounds here, I'm not going to go for the tiddlers.'

His face was a sight. I even imagined he really meant he was not prepared to take part in this theft and was going to take the flight home that morning.

'You've got to do it right,' he tells me, as if I would deliberately muck up the job and get us all caught.

'Of course I will.'

A huge surge of adrenaline rushed through my body as the two of us, 'The Talker' and 'The Taker', headed through the streets of Johannesburg for the Jeppe area.

The roads were far less crowded than in London and most of the vehicles we saw had experienced better days. Some of the shops were tatty and rundown as though the sun had been allowed to peel away the paint and gently work its way through to the dark interiors. The approach to the jewellery quarter seemed to be over in a trice. The car was parked and we became our old familiar personalities – two successful, wealthy businessmen buying a present for a good friend. The jeweller had one of the old-fashioned bells which we could hear echoing throughout the house as I pressed the bell push. Footsteps came across the hard wooden floor and then the door was opened by our new friend from yesterday, the jeweller from the Kimberley Mines.

'Come in, come in,' he implored us, as though the whole

street was waiting to jump through the door and steal his diamonds. He smiled and shook us both firmly by the hand.

We were the only people in the diamond house. Inside, it was lit so the goods would be shown off to their best ability. The walls were hidden behind sealed metal containers and old wooden cabinets, their shiny polished surfaces reflecting the stones we had come to see. He had them all in one big mahogany box which had seen better days. It looked like a treasure from his past, a bit like the Chancellor of the Exchequer's old briefcase he trundles out on Budget Day. At the front of this box were the fifteen-carat stones, then the twelves, followed by the tens, eights and tapering on down until you came to the very small ones at the back, the one-carats. This gradation of the diamonds was some impressive sight. They lay there, the big rich ones fat in all their glory, staring at me as if they were little puppies begging to be picked up and loved and taken home to be properly cared for. They picked up the light in the room and scattered it like rays of glittering fire every time he moved the box to demonstrate their quality.

I allowed myself a quick, surreptitious glance at my watch. The job was going according to plan. I checked the rear of the room. There was a curtain covering what I thought was a locked door. Once inside the place the owner had carefully locked the front door behind us and thrown a switch activating some sort of electronic alarm system. There would be no doing a runner from this diamond house. It was the most secure place I had seen outside the big diamond auction houses of Antwerp.

Brian and I had now manoeuvred ourselves into the classic position for 'The Switch'.

The jeweller was on the right of the box, the talker was in the middle and the taker, me, was on the other side of the box. I was as far away from the jeweller as I could get and all his attention was on Brian, the talker.

The Cheat was going to use a phone box between Jeppe and

the airport so he could get straight to the plane once he'd done his work. We had synchronised our watches and The Cheat was going to phone on the hour.

It was about an hour and a half before the plane left. So we all had our times sorted out.

I wait for the phone to ring, watching the minute hand of my watch approach the hour.

Outside we could hear the distant rumble of the traffic, horns hooting, a few kids yapping and fighting and the noise of car doors slamming as people came and went. Our senses were heightened as the moment approached. Our efforts had been successful so far and now we could do nothing but wait for the next stage of the plan to unfold.

I looked at my watch once more and as I did so the phone rung, breaking the polite chit-chat between the talker and the jeweller as effectively as it would have done had someone thrown a brick through the window.

The moment had arrived.

The telephone was half hidden behind some papers in the corner and the owner had to move them out of the way before answering it.

I switched the first stone.

The large piece of glass was now lying in its place in the dark mahogany box looking for all the world as though it was a real diamond among friends. Only an expert with a suspicious mind would know its true value. The big man on the telephone was an expert.

Having lifted the first of the huge diamonds I switched my concentration over to what was going on in the corner of the room, no more than a few yards away from us. To my concern the jeweller was going 'Hallo, hallo, hallo . . .' into the receiver. He looked at the telephone with a puzzled expression and put it down.

With a slight shrug of his big shoulders he turned and

walked back towards the desk on which was sitting the mahogany box and several million pounds' worth of diamonds.

The moment he reached us the telephone rang again. As he went back to the other part of the room to answer it I switched a second and third large stone. Two more bits of glass went into the box and the Talker-Taker team seemed like a million pounds better off. Funny how little a million pounds can weigh.

I relaxed just a fraction. As far as I was concerned I had not finished. There were several more stones just begging to join their two friends in my pocket. Again I switched my hearing over to listen to what was being said on the telephone. This time I started to worry. The jeweller was still going 'Hallo, hallo, hallo' into the handset. I looked at his expression and knew there was something wrong all round. From being a lovely nice kind man he looked as worried as a man can be when he is not sure what is really worrying him. I wanted to leave immediately. I had got an awful lot of money in three stones. They were his three largest in the batch he had shown us from the mine. We were also in a locked chamber which reminded me of Fort Knox, littered with locks and bars and alarms and odd gadgets stuck on the door to allow people in and out.

If you are sitting at home and the telephone goes and you say 'hallo, hallo' and there is no answer you are going to get suspicious, particularly if it goes again. And this man was a jeweller with an appointment with two strangers. He was reluctant to let us leave, but he had nothing on us. He could not have tried to search us since none of his diamonds appeared to be missing. He was talking as though he knew something was going on but was not sure what. Eventually I think he let us out hoping that he had seen the back of us and good riddance. If he had any evidence he would have kept us inside while he called the police. But the stones were all in place in their pretty little old box.

The street was full of people. Was this lunch hour Johannesburg-style? Where there had been one person outside the shop there were now twenty. Where there had been one car there were now two hundred. I turned to the talker and told him there was something clearly wrong with the job, adding: 'Quick, let's get out.'

At the entrance to the diamond house, which we were now exiting with all the speed we could manage with dignity, was a column of stone stairs. As we got to the bottom of these stairs I heard a shout. Turning round, I nearly died.

Standing behind me, framed in the wide open door of his diamond house, was the owner. Six feet tall, built like a fighter, holding a gun in his hand pointed right at me saying: 'Stop or I'll shoot.'

That was when I learnt that jewellers in Johannesburg were allowed to use guns to protect their products.

Now Brian is the worst driver in the world. He had managed to park this Ford Taunus in such a strange position it seemed it would take minutes to extricate it and put it on the open road, but we had no alternative method of escape. We leapt into the car, wasting precious seconds getting clear of the other parked cars and fled.

After about a hundred yards we thought we had got away. We changed our minds a moment later when a bullet smashed the rear window. The noise was terrifying. The realisation that we were being shot at and could die was also pretty frightening. In fact, I was petrified.

The Swan says I picked two lumps off the dashboard and asked him what they were.

'Those are bullets, Morry. He's firing them at us.'

Apparently I said something like: 'Oh, really.' I was well in shock by then.

The jeweller was not only pretty good with the gun but also a black belt karate champion. He must have locked up the shop before continuing his pursuit of us which gave us that little start on him. A black taxi driver had stopped and given him a lift enabling the car chase to get underway with a vengeance. Another bullet hit the smashed rear window, passing straight through and whizzing by my head. At least, it sounded as though that was what was happening.

Brian was in his element. The bowel trouble, which had mysteriously infected me all of a sudden, had completely left him and his mouth was full with a big Havana cigar. He smokes six big ones a day and he had lit this one the second we were going out of the door of the house. There was thick cigar smoke inside the car, bullets crashing through it and shards of shattered glass flying everywhere.

To this day I do not know whether Brian had any idea where he was going.

'Look behind us,' he yelled, 'has he gone?'

I looked back. Then I learnt that you cannot see out of a back window which has had bullets shot through it.

I was in deep shock by then. So instead of climbing into the back and punching out the glass I opened the car door to look back at our pursuer and as a consequence I nearly fell out. Another bullet whizzed past me; this time the hairs on the back of my neck stood to attention as the bullet appeared to come within millimetres of my flesh.

We were dimly aware of the sound of people honking their car horns. We were far too exposed and so we cut up a side road to get clear of the mess behind us, hoping the maddened jeweller would not spot us making the turn in time for him to follow. Moments later we were in a worse mess. The road we had turned into was a one-way street and we were going the wrong way up it at seventy miles an hour! It was one of those quiet side roads where cars bumble along at twenty miles an hour and shoppers dawdle, gazing at the wares in the windows. All hell broke loose. Cars were heading straight for us making no attempt to get out of the way so we were forced to leave the road and travel part of the distance on the pavement. Women and children were flinging themselves into shop doorways to avoid us. We made it to the other end without hitting anything and turned into a main road which we hoped was heading out of town.

By now we were driving aimlessly. The taxi was still behind us but there were no more shots. We could make out the sound of what seemed to be a couple of police sirens and the traffic was getting worse. We closed our eyes as we shot through junction after junction, cars squealing as we ignored their presence hoping to create a path through the steel nightmare we had ended up inside. Then, far too quickly for us to really take it in, there was a road block. Three cars stretched across the street completely blocking the road. They were ordinary cars, not police squad cars. A quick glance told us the only way through was to the left where a market stall was obstructing the pavement. We crunched into it at full speed, sixty or seventy miles an hour. Apples, oranges, bananas, plums, coconuts, pears and pieces of broken wood mixed with the bits of glass which had now smashed on impact. We came to rest at a crazy angle in the middle of the road not too far away from the road block.

The next thing I knew was the door being ripped open and there was this six-foot-six man whom I had just robbed standing over me with a face which could have killed at a thousand paces. Beside my shoulder was a bunch of bananas and approaching my neck was his hand and it was difficult to tell which was bigger. This hand wrapped itself around my neck and hauled me out of the car. I stared into his small angry eyes as I felt two fingers go under my chin and lift me up off the ground and into the air. I fell hard on my back in the road listening to the screams of the people who had witnessed the car chase.

Now there was something else to worry about. Something hard and nasty was stuck up my nose. I opened my eyes. It was his Luger. I lay on my back, aching from the fall, and he stood over me with one foot planted firmly on my chest. 'Give me back my diamonds,' he yelled over and over again. I did not understand at that time what he was saying since in his anger he had switched from English to Afrikaans. But I knew what he meant. I felt as though my back had been broken and I could hardly breathe. There was nothing for it.

'Here they are, old chap,' I said. 'Don't let's go that far, you know.'

I dipped my hand into my pocket and gave him back his diamonds.

Brian was running up the road doing his best to evade capture. Unbeknown to us the gun held only six bullets and he had fired them all, but we didn't know that. He took the gun from out of my nose and pointed it at Brian and yelled in English: 'Stop or I'll shoot.'

Whereupon Brian took his white handkerchief out of his pocket, held both arms up in the air, still with the cigar in his mouth, saying: 'I surrender.'

He kept us covered with the gun until the police appeared and took us to a wonderful place called John Vorster Square – that's the place where Steve Biko was held. Once there we were thrown into a dungeon, put in chains, handcuffed and tied to a toilet. Chains linked the cuffs on our hands and feet and were wound through the metal toilet. We could hardly move. Four days passed before we got out of there. The toilet was filthy like the dungeon in which it sat. We used it for the usual purposes, shaved in it, washed out of it and drank the water from it. It was not a pleasant experience.

Our solicitor was Maurice Zimmerman, a former wing

three-quarter with the Springboks, who later became chairman of the team's selectors.

We got to hear that the finest QC in South Africa was a Greek called George Bisos who was to defend Winnie Mandela. We were allowed to approach him and ask him to represent us.

Bisos agreed and came to see us. He did not seem unduly troubled by the crime. In fact, he found it humorous, telling us it was more of a comedy than a serious charge.

At this we felt relief. After washing, shaving and living out of the toilet for a couple more weeks we went on trial as two international jewel-thieving scallywags.

At this stage we learnt the true horror of our bad luck. The Cheat, who we had relied upon to distract the attention of the jeweller, had used a vandalised telephone box. He had not checked first to see whether the telephone was working. Of course he was on the aircraft setting off for Heathrow while we were lying in a main city street with a Luger pointed at us.

The jeweller was asked to give his evidence.

He stood in the witness box and let out the whole sorry story. The two telephone calls immediately made him suspicious. He knew something was wrong but not what. So the moment he had closed the door on us he checked his diamonds and discovered pieces of glass had been substituted. He told the court that he would never have done this had he simply had one ordinary enquiry on the telephone from an interested potential buyer.

If The Cheat had used a proper working telephone box we would have been safely back in Britain with the diamonds.

The judge added to what the jeweller had said when he told us that had it not been for the vandalised phone box: 'You two scallywags would have got away with our most precious commodity.' We had since discovered that the worst thing you could do in South Africa was to steal diamonds because you were robbing the government.

I had been called upon to give evidence in court and had looked over to where the judge was writing. I saw he wrote the figure of a nine. I now turned to Brian in the dock and said: 'We've got nine.'

'Nine months,' he said. 'What a good result.'

'No, nine years, you mug.'

He then collapsed in the dock – a nine-year sentence. End of the world.

We were sent to Pretoria Central for the first five months of our sentence where we slept on the floor of a cage with the lights on every night. Our third companion in the cage was another Englishman.

The cage was only as big as a toilet, so if you wanted to turn over during the night you had to notify your colleague that you were turning so that he would turn as well, otherwise you would get a foot in your face as you were sleeping. They fed us on millipop – which is the national diet – corn or uncooked rice or something. And you've got that three times a day, breakfast, midday and night-time. The trouble was you got the whole three meals in one lot at breakfast time.

Our five months in Pretoria Central were not very eventful. Nobody could understand how we had received such an incredibly long sentence. The psychiatrist who interviewed us, the social workers, the prison authorities, nobody could understand it.

We should have served six years out of the nine but we got out after three years and three months. During our time in prison both my parents died within six months of each other. Brian's father was also dying. Our relatives and friends contacted the Foreign Office who persuaded the South African government to release us early on humanitarian grounds.

Every couple of weeks they brought up people from all over

South Africa to hang. The night before that happened the prison would go deathly quiet. It was known they were going to hang them at dawn the following morning. They might do ten or fifteen in one morning. During the hanging season you could hear the rumble of the other prisoners from early in the morning.

In fact, one morning the footsteps stopped outside our door and I thought they'd made a mistake and come for us!

South Africa has the most judicial killings in the world. More people are killed there in prison than even in America where, though they sentence more people to death, most of them wait for many years before being executed, if at all.

During our time in prison a friend of mine, Brian Cook, who was filming, came to see me. He was there because Richard Harris and Ann Turkel were making a film called *The Golden Rendezvous*. It gave us some comfort, knowing there were people in the outside world aware of our plight.

After five months we were bundled into a wagon and sent down to the Cape to an open prison called Victor Verster where Mandela was held at the end of his long incarceration in South Africa's prison system.

We were told there was an up-and-coming barrister in Jo'burg who could get us out of the nine-year sentence, but he needed a lot of money. I didn't really want to get involved, but Brian insisted we send begging letters home to England for money to employ this top barrister.

In the open camp at Victor Verster, I was working in reception giving out clothes for the new people on arrival. We were told we had a visit from a man who had flown down from Jo'burg to see us and when he walked in and saw us I automatically knew there was something wrong. He wore a Savile Row suit, crocodile shoes, a diamond ring, Rolex watch and carried a Gucci briefcase, which was altogether out of place in Cape Town. After asking us how much money he could get for making an appeal on our behalf I thought he was trying to do a sting on me. I knew in my heart things weren't right.

But The Swan insisted we employ him and then followed days of furious arguments. I refused to believe this man could do us any good but The Swan was having none of it. In the end I just gave in and said 'let him help if he can'. So money was sent to him from our friends in England and we spent ages waiting for the appeal which was going to be held in three or four months. He'd had several thousand pounds for his work.

Time passed and I carried on with my job, handing out clothes for the new arrivals. It was the same monotonous drill for me. I used to say: 'What size shirt?'

'Sixteen.'

This would be a disembodied voice floating out from behind a screen.

'What size shoes?'

'Seven.'

'What size collar, what size this and that . . . ?'

Then one day I said: 'What size shoes?'

And a voice replied: 'Size seven shoes please.'

And I thought: 'That voice is quite familiar.'

When I walked round the screen, who do you think it was? None other than the lawyer who'd had the several thousand pounds to defend us: Sam Aarons. He'd got a five-year sentence for robbing his clients of their money.

I turned round to The Swan and said: 'That's another fine mess you got me into.'

Well, after the initial shock it was hilarious. He was disbarred from the Jo'burg Law Society and became one of us.

We had a hard time at the start of the prison sentence, but we met a hell of a lot of characters. It's quite unlike the British prison system. There were two Scottish boys, Donald and

Andy, who lived in Zambia and were caught trying to ship a carload of cannabis on the old *Windsor Castle*. They came back to Britain after finishing their sentence and since one was a Campbell he was fortunate enough to be able to go up to Campbeltown to claim an inheritance.

Another man we met was an Australian called Colin Bird. He escaped while on a visit to the dentist. I later bumped into him on a trip to Sydney.

It wasn't all bad humour over there. One glorious summer's evening we were playing cricket inside the grass square that comprised the prison. Suddenly a guard, known as Tronk Bewaarders, an Afrikaner name, came running up to me and said: 'Quickly, there's a phone call for you.'

The entire prison erupted in laughter. It was impossible to get a phone call inside that prison. But all the same, I went off and took my call. What had happened was that the exchange had blundered and a phone call from England *had* been allowed through. Anyway, I had a good long chat with a friend of ours from London.

The next day I was walking along the path which circles the grass centre of the prison chatting away to The Swan when up came the lieutenant who was in charge of the white section.

'Spurling,' he said, 'I understand somehow you had a telephone call last night.'

'Indeed I did.'

'I can't understand how this could have happened. I hope you haven't told anybody about it?'

'Well,' I say, 'I haven't told the kaffirs in the next door prison but everyone here knows and probably half of Cape Town by now.'

On another occasion there was a man in the white section of the prison called Pat who was determined to get out. He hit on the clever trick of concealing himself inside a rubbish bin. It was carried outside the jail and he was slung, along with the rubbish, into a truck and he managed to make his escape. But he wasn't to be free for long. He was captured later the same year and sent to the maximum security prison at Sonnerwater. Again, he got away from there and joined a couple of other escapees. They went on a rampage all over South Africa robbing banks and security vans. Eventually he was cornered near Germiston and was killed in a shoot-out with the police.

I felt terribly sorry for the poor blacks in the segregated section of the prison. Life was terribly harsh for them and conditions were awful. Every morning we saw a black body hurled out of their section into the walkway which separated them from us. They would be dead from knife wounds, beatings, even, in one case, a man's head had been severed from his body. It was the other blacks who were doing this to them.

We were extremely lucky to have avoided what in the business was known as a 'coat', that is to say the Draconian sentence handed out to habitual criminals. It consisted of a minimum of nine and a maximum of fifteen years. It was given its name because of the blue overcoat that was handed out to each recipient of this terrible sentence at the start of their confinement.

One of our friends in Victor Verster was a man called Shorty Lemensic, who was doing his third coat.

Shorty was a war hero, a fighter pilot trained and based in England. After the war, he just couldn't settle down and even though his family were well off he drifted into a life of crime. Naturally he was given more than enough chances before he was eventually sent to prison. A compulsive gambler, he was scarcely ever out for longer than a year.

When he came to Victor Verster he was perhaps sixty, but he still played football and could outrun people half his age.

He was the kind of person who made one believe prison life was a healthy one. Also, I have never met anyone who could do a crossword puzzle as quickly as he could. *The Times* and the *Daily Telegraph* puzzles were easy for him – he rarely took more than ten minutes to solve them.

As Jews, Brian and I were allowed special food for Passover. Among the items we got were packets of butter, which was an unknown quantity at Victor Verster. We were allowed to keep it in the hospital refrigerator. Shorty was the hospital orderly.

One evening The Swan was approaching the hospital and heard me shouting at someone.

'Where's my butter?' I was shouting, 'where's my butter gone?'

Although The Swan couldn't hear the reply he twigged straight away what had happened.

Earlier in the day Shorty had been moaning that although there was a poker game that evening he had no stake to play with.

In those poker games, any commodity was used instead of money. If you had money you played with money, if not then food, cigarettes, shoelaces, practically anything was acceptable including the shirt off your back. The Swan instinctively knew Shorty was playing with my butter.

I was furious and exploding and The Swan apparently stood in the door watching and listening to all of this. He told me later he decided to go off and sort it before things got worse. He wanted to save me from getting into more trouble.

He went off to the bungalow where the card game was taking place and true enough there was Shorty sitting at the table deeply engrossed in action. To one side he saw all the goodies piled up on a side table where the fellow who was running the game was sitting. In the midst of all the biscuits, coffee and tobacco was my little packet of butter. Shorty looked up and saw The Swan and knew he had spotted the butter. He smiled at The Swan and did nothing more than shrug his shoulders and went back to the game.

The Swan was looking after me well at this stage. He was wondering how on earth he was going to get the butter before I came charging in and screaming the place down.

The only way to do that was to hoist it. But how? Suddenly he thought of the trick we often used back in England – 'Dropping The Coins'.

The Swan produced a number of coins and said to the fellow who was running the game: 'Give me two rands' worth of chips.'

As he went to hand over the coins he lurched forwards as if he had slipped. All the coins dropped behind him. He looked at the poker table but no one had taken any notice. As the fellow in charge turned round to pick up the coins The Swan bent down and slipped the packet of butter into his pocket. No one had seen him take it.

The Swan then placed his chips on the table and seconds later says: 'Oh. I have forgotten my spectacles. I'll be back in a moment.'

He wanted to get the butter back to me before I came looking for Shorty. As he left the bungalow, I was coming over the grass towards him.

'Oh, Morry,' he says, 'I was just going to find you. I took your butter by mistake. Here it is.'

He says I looked puzzled for a few seconds then took it and went on my way to eat my evening meal. The Swan reckoned he had averted World War Three by his action.

There was something of a sequel to this. The Swan went back to the poker game and eventually Shorty cleaned out the game. The Swan pulled him just as he was going to cash in and told him what he had done. He laughed and said he would return The Swan's two rands which he had lost in the game. Like all gamblers he meant it at the time but The Swan's still waiting.

After three and a half years staying at the South African government's pleasure they sent us home.

The Cheat, who had caused all this trouble by not doing his work, met us at Heathrow and did nothing more than shrug his shoulders.

35

My Page Three Girls

Seven girls worked with me throughout my long, infamous career. I call them my Page Three girls, although only one was a real *Sun* Page Three model.

All the girls earned fortunes with me but not all of them wasted it the way I did.

There was a most exclusive wine bar in Curzon Street called Pips. I used to go there every lunchtime for a glass of wine. I always noticed a very attractive girl serving. She was called Jean and had previously worked as a British Airways hostess. After a couple of weeks of going in there to see her I asked her to come out for dinner and a drink one night. I fancied her like mad but I was twice her age. She agreed to go out a few nights later. Five minutes after having dinner we were in bed together.

Jean realised after a couple of days that I was broke, so I made a proposition to her. We both needed money.

There was a diamond show in Munich where I wanted her to wear a see-through blouse, short skirt and attract the man. She did.

With Jean's help I stole thirty-seven diamond rings off a man from Antwerp. It was a jewellery fair and all the man did was stare at Jean's titties. Jean had taken him off into another room so I was left all alone.

After the theft we got into a taxi, me, Jean and The Swan and he said to me: 'Did you get anything?'

'Well, I got this.'

'Oh,' he said looking at it. 'That's wonderful.'

I pulled another diamond out of my pocket and asked what he thought of that.

'Wonderful, Morry, just wonderful.'

'And this?'

'First rate.'

This went on for a few minutes until I said: 'I got this.' And I turned out of my pocket the remainder of these thirty-seven of the most wonderful diamond rings. By the time I'd brought out the thirty-seventh in the taxi Brian couldn't talk, he was so overwhelmed. This was nearly a quarter of a century ago. What was each one worth? I don't know. Thirty thousand quid? Five thousand quid? What's the whole lot worth today: half a million? A million? Who knows. It's all numbers anyway.

I was in the Brenner's Park Hotel in Baden-Baden in Germany, which is the finest hotel in the place. Glenda Jackson made a film there called *The Romantic Englishwoman*, most of it based in this hotel, the most beautiful hotel in the whole of Europe. I was with The Swan and Michelle.

We arrived there looking for money and we saw a showcase full of diamonds belonging to Harry Winston, *the* Harry Winston from New York. There were only half a dozen pieces in the showcase but they were exquisite, worth thousands and thousands of pounds. The Swan and I were looking at a square-cut emerald-shaped diamond worth quite a considerable amount of money, together with some earrings and a brooch.

'Do you know, you can switch this,' he said.

'Do you think so?'

'Yeah.'

'Let's have a dummy run.'

So I went over to the young concierge and Michelle was there with her see-through blouse. 'Could I have a look?'

'Yes, sir.'

He turned off the alarm bell, walked over to the window and opened it, all the while gazing at Michelle's tits.

The window lifted outwards, you had to take a step back otherwise it would hit you. I had a good look at the ring while Michelle was foisting her breasts upon the guy. He loved it.

The square-cut ring was approximately two carats and worth a lot of money. We returned to Britain with the prospect in mind to get a two-carat replica made up over here and then to go back there and switch the stone.

A couple of days later we set off to do it. We got on board British Airways. I said to Brian: 'Have you got the ring?'

'Yes,' and he's given me the ring and it's three times the size of the one we're going to switch it with.

'What's this?'

'It doesn't matter,' he says. Whereupon we have one of our international rows.

'It doesn't matter, you'll do it anyway.' Now, I've got to do it but it was like the difference between shopping at Harrods and shopping at Woolworths.

The trouble is we're now on board this aircraft and we're over Europe and I've got to do it. So I'm starting to worry. But when we arrive, thank God the young feller that was there before and took a fancy to Michelle's tits is still there.

So we're halfway towards our goal.

Anyway it came to D-Day. We were ready. Action stations. I approach the young concierge.

'Do you remember, I would like the ring for the young lady?'

'Oh yes, sir.'

I was wearing a lovely green Lock's hat and a cashmere overcoat, she was wearing her blouse which she made even more see-through and The Swan was lurking in the background ready to distract him by bumping into him as I switched the stone.

He opened the window. Now the window is perched over our heads. Michelle's pressed her tits up against him, he's looked at them and I've dived in the window, got that beautiful stone of Harry Winston's in my hand and put back my bit of glass. Unfortunately this guy has looked at what I've put back and he's gone absolutely white. He knows! He knows what I've done. Now I'm in shock. I don't know what to do.

'Michelle, move up,' I say. She knew what to do.

So she stuck her tits in his eyes to enable me to put the right one back. But as I put the right one back I've gone into the window and BANG, I've knocked my head against the top of the window and fallen on the floor. Now there's all commotion. The Swan's come by with his cigar and nearly knocked it into his face. The guy knows what I've done, I've knocked all the diamonds off the pedestal that they were on.

He's screaming, we're screaming and it was just a miracle to get out of there. We got a cab, got to Stuttgart and that was it.

'Next time, Brian, get me the right size.'

I've been back since. All the Kuwaitis and top Arabs stay there – it's a most wonderful hotel. It's near the casino where I used to go, the Baden-Baden Casino which is the most aristocratic place in the world. All the rich Germans go to Baden-Baden to take the Spa waters, mud and all that, to get healthy. It's a town for the elderly, the rich, the retired. Only millionaires need apply.

Back in Britain I was going out with a Bunny Girl called Dee

Dee Harris. She asked me to pick her up in my car. I had my lovely new Jag and I went to collect her in Brompton Square. I pressed the bell and a girl answered the door wearing nothing more than a little pair of knickers. It was Marilyn Cole, the Playmate of the Year.

'Oh,' she says, 'you've come for Dee Dee.' And I was mesmerised. 'Won't you come in?' she asks.

Fell over the doorstep.

She says: 'Do you mind if I walk about with nothing on because that's how I normally dress inside the flat?'

'Mind! I wish you had totally nothing on.' She just laughed and called Dee Dee to say I had arrived. And that's how I met Marilyn Cole. Oh what a woman she was. She was six feet six tall – statuesque. She married Victor Lowndes who owned Stocks and the Playboy Club.

36

Wrong Face, Wrong Place

B ack in the Sixties when the OAS started their campaign to kick the French out of Algeria, we got caught in the midst of that. We were performing, for want of another word, in the South of France. On the Côte d'Azur, on the Promenade des Anglais in Nice, lovely jewellers' shops we were thieving from with no trouble. Then the OAS came with their machine guns and bombs scaring off all the jewellers. This was when we ran into an old London friend called Sidney Ulman King.

I'd known Sid King for thirty or forty years. In the West End he was working as a confidence trickster. He ran a tipping agency, had got into trouble for fraud and deception, exactly like me, been in and out of prison, had thousands and thousands of pounds, had got into further trouble and fled to France. I hadn't seen him for a few years. It was a lovely mild January day when The Swan and I flew into Nice. A few hours later after checking into a hotel we were walking along the Promenade des Anglais, which is the main road in Nice with all the top jewellery shops. We were about to perform when, outside the Negresco Hotel, a voice said: 'Morry. Brian.'

We turned round and there was Sid King sitting with an attractive woman. He introduced us. 'This is Wanda, my girlfriend.'

I heard later that Wanda married Lord Boothby.

We had a few drinks.

'While we're here we want to do a couple of shops.'

'Listen,' says Sid, 'now you're here I'll take you to the Casino in Monte Carlo where you might be able to get a bit of credit.' Lovely.

We performed in a couple of shops there, got a bit of money, Sid King bought the goods and he took them to Monte Carlo. We didn't get any credit in Monte Carlo.

We nearly got killed going there in a Ford Anglia car, nearly went under a big French lorry driving on the Grande Corniche. I couldn't see because as I was driving The Swan was blowing cigar smoke in the car. Sid King walked with a limp and he had a big stick which he was using to hit me on the shoulder as a way of giving me driving instructions.

'Be careful,' he kept saying.

Anyway, we got to Monte Carlo and we got back.

The Swan left me with Sid. He went home and I stayed on and as a result of staying on I got arrested.

I lost sight of Sid King but eventually when I came back to London and was once again imprisoned in Wandsworth who did I see on the hourly exercise but Sid King. He had come home and given himself up and that was that. We were walking round and we said to ourselves, 'What are we doing in here?' because he was exactly like me. Whatever money he had in his pocket was for betting. And he'd had an awful lot of money as well.

When I got out of jail, I went to see him. We had a drink, and I said 'I'll see you again at the weekend'. On the weekend a pal of mine said to me: 'Morry, do you know what's happened? Sid King committed suicide in a back room in George Street off the Edgware Road.'

And it was all as a result of this sporting life. He was gambling, got into terrible trouble, in debt, owed money to gangsters, that sort of thing. Exactly the same as me. And he couldn't cope with it, so he committed suicide. Sometimes I think of him and I say, 'There, but for the Grace of God, go I,' as it could so easily have been me. Perhaps I was born with more resilience, get up and go. There are many people in life who if they'd gone through the traumas and tribulations that I've gone through would've taken their own lives, of that I'm sure. They couldn't cope with it. It's difficult to cope. Every day, to me, in the last many, many years, has been a Custer's Last Stand. Every day is a headache from the moment I open my eyes. I've learned to cope with it.

Every day I have a list. I've gotta pay this and I've gotta pay that. The Swan used to say to me: 'You got your Daily List?'

I digress. It wasn't all gloom in those days. The sun was out and we were again back in France on a glorious summer's afternoon.

The Swan and I were in Lille, which is a very big silk town. We went into a shop and we were talking to a man who was an ex-prisoner of war. This lovely elderly man showed us his tattoos, given him by the Germans when he'd been in a concentration camp. He said to me, when we asked for some jewellery: 'I don't have much stock here. I don't carry much but my partner, Mr Tannenbaum, has almost everything and he lives in a place called Vaucluse.' Now that is 'millionaires only need apply' territory in the South of France near Cannes.

So he referred us to this partner of his in the South of France who had millions of pounds' worth of diamonds in his possession.

Over the next few months The Swan and I travelled from country to country, robbing jewellers and selling the stuff and gambling and living it up and generally having a good time. We kept having rows, though.

After a reasonable but not spectacular trip we'd driven back to Britain and we'd been rowing all the way in the car until we got home. We sold what parcels we had for about £10,500 which wasn't a good trip for us. You might think £5,000 each was good but usually we came home with £20,000 or £30,000 because over there it's so easy compared to here.

I'd rowed with Brian all the way so I was pleased to get rid of him – and he was pleased to get rid of me. Then I got a telephone call.

'Do you want to go to work?'

'Yes.'

End of the row.

So we did some work in London but as soon as I got any money I gambled it and was back broke again and working on my own thanks to having another row with The Swan. Now, when I'm broke, as I can't stress enough, logic goes out the window.

I am lying in my flat in London thinking of this Mr Tannenbaum and his millions of pounds in diamonds as I worry about not having a penny and the latest breakdown in relations with The Swan, when all of a sudden the telephone rings. It's a friend, Terry.

So I went to see him.

'Terry. I don't even have a shilling. I'm flat broke.'

'Morry, you're always flat broke. So what's new?'

'Terry. Lend me a thousand pounds' expenses. I've got a good idea where I can get millions. I'll put you in the action and I'll get good stuff and you'll have a good deal with me. For your thousand pounds you'll be able to buy something very cheap.'

'Oh. If I lend you a thousand pounds you'll go into a betting shop and you'll be broke and you'll tell me a story and what can I do?'

'I promise you faithfully, I've got a move.'

It's obvious he doesn't believe me but we part friends.

A few days later the phone rings again and it's Terry with the thousand pounds for expenses. I grabbed my passport, bunged it in my inside pocket and flew to Nice.

On arrival, I arrange to meet Mr Tannenbaum. At this point I should explain something. I have stolen diamonds all over the world and know how to tell a real one from a fraud. But that is about the limit of my knowledge. Much of the time I relied on The Swan to provide the knowledge. He has learnt all there is to know about the diamond business. I am always in too much of a hurry to bother. The Swan often complains I will not take the time to plan a robbery and once I've got the stones I will sell them at any old price rather than wait until the following day to get a better one. So together, when we go into a shop or warehouse, people really do believe we are jewellers about to go into business ourselves or are just looking for some new goods. On my own, the joker of the pack starts to come to life.

So I am on the phone to this bloke and he's all keen to see me. I have been well recommended and at this stage can do nothing wrong. I am not worrying since lacking confidence is not one of my problems.

'Yes, come to my house,' he tells me.

'I'm on my way,' I tell him.

I take a taxi from Nice Airport up into the most wonderful part of God's world, called Vaucluse, high in the mountains above Cannes. It was like being in another world. When I stop I see a mansion such as you might expect to find in Beverly Hills. Outside, in a car park bigger than the one at Wembley Stadium, there's a Rolls, a BMW, a Porsche and two Bentleys – and they all belong to the staff of Mr Tannenbaum, who hasn't arrived yet. The gardener owns a Bentley, the maid owns a Porsche, the butler owns a Ferrari, the cleaner owns a Corvette.

I was welcomed in. It was like Hollywood, perhaps better, and the wife came out. She was a most beautiful woman.

'You're Mr Morris. My husband is on the way back. Will you sit down? Will you have a brandy?'

She had more gold on her than there is in Fort Knox. That was the type of woman I like and I was thinking to myself, 'This is going to be easy', when in walks Mr Tannenbaum. Now, he's a young, smart, good-looking Frenchman about thirty years of age. He steps out of the latest Aston Martin and, through the windows of his mansion, I see the forecourt of the house is starting to resemble the Motor Show.

'Mr Morris.'

'Yes. Mr Tannenbaum, pleased to meet you.'

I said I'm a dealer and I've been all over the world. I mention Harry Winston, the biggest jeweller in New York. I mention this and that fellow dealer and as I do so I am rather like an amateur card player sitting down bullshitting with the high rollers. So he was engrossed in me. I looked quite smart. I had a silk suit on, crocodile shoes, smart tie, the best shirt. Impression is everything in this game.

'I won't be a minute, please sit down.'

He came back into the room with a box as big as a box of Cadbury's Milk Tray. And in that box were more diamonds than I've ever seen in my whole life. In fact, there were more millions in that box than one could describe. Bigger than the Lottery, bigger than anything I'd ever seen in all my thirty, forty, fifty years of this game. More at any one time than even in Antwerp where boxes of the best had been brought out to show me.

'Sit down and we'll have a look and see what you want.'

Let me just describe this diamond stealing business. It's all to do with psychology and having the correct mental approach and having enough knowledge to get by. The longer I am in a shop or with a dealer or with anybody that I want to steal from, the less relaxed I become. At the very start with Mr Tannenbaum things were beautiful. He saw an English customer. But unfortunately I was on my own and despite being the best in the world at the game of palming and switching, my lack of knowledge of the diamond business is starting to show. I could have done with The Swan's help.

He began by showing me a two-carat worth twenty thousand pounds, a four-carat worth fifty thousand pounds, equivalent to Baroness Von Thyssen's which I'd had, and I can see and I can feel that his initial friendliness was beginning to wear off. A cloud came into his mind, perhaps a question mark, 'Who is this man? What am I doing showing him millions?' Quite quickly the situation had reversed itself and I am starting to become anxious. Under normal circumstances after ten or fifteen minutes I've got the prize. I should've already stolen two or three by now but I haven't despite one feeble attempt to do the job.

And let me tell you, after twenty minutes of talking to him I learnt he was no fool. So after twenty minutes he had the hump and wanted to get rid of me. He may even have known what I was at. And that's very strange. He might have thought I'd got a gun on me or something. After all, he's showing me tens of millions of pounds' worth of diamonds.

Five more minutes of me bullshitting and he no longer wanted to know. In fact, he shut up his box.

'I'll come back to you, Mr Morris.'

He put the box back in what I think was his safe, I couldn't see as it was in another room. He came back into the room with a serious look on his face.

'Look. I'm going to drop you down at the airport.'

I had told him I was going back to Paris.

211

'See here,' he says, before setting off, 'we're not going to do any business.' He had sussed me out.

The drive from his house took us through the most wonderful part of the South of France. It was about a twenty-minute journey and it was now pouring with rain. The heavens had opened. He never said one word from getting in the car at his house to the airport. In fact, I was relieved to get out of the car the tension was so bad. He emphatically knew what I was at and it was a miracle he didn't call the police because I was wanted in France. In fact, I've always been wanted all over Europe. He drove off and I caught the plane to Paris.

Now, I had borrowed a thousand pounds off my friend to do this job and promised my friend lots and lots of money.

I arrived in Paris from Nice, not knowing what to do, not knowing where to go. The thousand pounds is now about seven hundred quid after the plane fare. I thought to myself, 'Well. What I've got to do is look for some money in Paris.' And I've slaughtered Paris, all of Paris. I once stole one object in Cartier's worth £40,000 – a diamond and emerald brooch, the best I've ever seen, but that was another matter. At the airport I phoned up my friend Terry.

'Terry. You're not gonna believe this.'

'Oh, you've done the money. I know what you're gonna tell me. Don't tell me no stories. You've done it to me before.' He never gave me a chance to finish.

'I'm phoning from Paris. It went boss-eyed.'

He didn't believe me and put the phone down.

So now the thousand pounds is about six hundred quid. So I get a cab from the airport to an hotel which I've stayed in many, many times before. And thank God I had stayed in it before because when I walked into the foyer the manageress knew me.

'Ah. Monsieur Maurice. *Comment allez vous?* How are you? You've come back.' The sweetest voice from the sweetest woman. She brought a glow to my heart.

'Yeah.'

'Ah. It is so good to see you.'

'I'm gonna have a drink in the bar. There's my passport. Take the number.'

'OK.'

All of a sudden. 'Monsieur Maurice.'

'Yes?'

'This is not your passport.'

Whereupon I started to laugh. 'What are you talking about?'

I'd gone through British immigration and customs on the way out to Nice.

'It's not your passport.'

'What are you talking about? Not my passport?'

'Come here.'

Well. I opened the passport. Staring me in the face was this man with bushy eyebrows and a head full of hair – The Swan. I nearly collapsed.

'Oh my—'

I instantly realised what had happened. On our previous journey we had arrived back in the dark at Dover. After we'd handed in our passports to be checked he'd given me back the wrong passport. I'd just put it in my pocket and he'd put his in his and we never looked at them again. I didn't even look at it catching the plane from Heathrow and it all hit me then.

My God. I've gone through British customs and immigration and they've let me go through – he's full of hair and I'm bald – it's like me trying to go through with a woman's passport. It's impossible. You wouldn't do it. No man in his right mind would go through on another man's passport, intentionally. It's impossible. I didn't know whether to laugh or cry.

When I'd had time to calm down a minute I said to her: 'Ah. It's like this . . .'

I explained the situation to her.

'It's all right. Let's have a drink.'

And then it hit me. How am I going to get back?

I woke up in the morning and phoned my friend Terry to say: 'You're not gonna believe this?'

'You what? What's wrong now?' He was pissed off with me.

I muttered something.

'You've done the money.'

'I've not, Terry. I said you dunno what's happened now. I've accidentally switched passports with The Swan and now I don't talk to The Swan. We've had a row.'

All of a sudden from being angry about the money he starts laughing.

'Well. What are you gonna do?'

'I dunno. I don't know. You can't get The Swan to bring me over my passport because when he shows it it's the wrong one.'

My head's splitting. I keep opening this passport and looking at this man with all his bushy eyebrows and lovely head full of hair, grey hair. So I don't know what to do.

And I've got to get some money. It was pouring heavens' hard with rain. I'd got a lovely suit on and I was getting it and my shoes ruined.

There was an antiques gallery that had just opened. The thousand pounds is now four hundred quid but within five minutes I've stolen a ten-thousand pound ruby and diamond ring which made things just a little better. Now I'm walking down the Avenue des Champs-Elysees and things are starting to brighten up.

I've got the diamond ring and I get a taxi to Charles de Gaulle Airport. At Charles de Gaulle I've got about a hundred quid left out of the thousand pounds.

I had a look at the barrier where you've got to walk through to show your passport. There must have been half a dozen

214

policemen there. I thought: 'How the hell am I gonna get through here?'

Not only have I got a crooked ring on me which is worth about ten thousand pounds but I have this useless passport.

Anyway, I walked up to the bar because I needed a vodka to save my life. When I've got a vodka in me, strangely enough, I see things more clearly. I'm a bit more audacious. Before every big jewel theft I've done in my life I normally have a vodka first. Then I don't care. When I'm stone-cold sober I have my doubts but once I've had a vodka I'm not worried about the IRA, the Red Brigade, the Mafia or anyone. What comes, comes after.

As I order the vodka, who happens to be standing by the side of me but David Owen, the MP. Now, when I've had a vodka the world is my friend, I'm audacious. I'm very, very audacious.

So I said to the barman in French: 'Excuse me. That is David Owen standing there reading the paper. Would you give our next Prime Minister a drink, please.'

And David Owen liked that.

'That's charming of you.'

'Mr Owen, I've been a fan of yours for years.' I didn't care if it was Owen, or Sschnowing or Rowing or whatever. But I gave him the crap that I've been a fan of his for years because now I want to get my mind round what I'm going to do with this ring and this passport. So, we are engaged in conversation. David Owen, the MP, a very eminent politician, and Morry the Head, one of the world's leading jewel thieves, with a crooked passport on him and a crooked ring. More large vodkas pass between us. I keep looking at the gate because I'm going to be showing someone else's passport.

The next plane was due to fly out to London City Airport. My car is at Heathrow, which is a long, long way away. He tells me he is going to have one more drink with me, that it's been a pleasure knowing me, we were talking about rugby or whatever and he's going to take leave of me. I thought to myself, 'If I can latch on to him I'll get through,' because I had an idea they use their diplomatic passports, an assumption I now know was wrong, but back then in the panic of the moment every idea was coming to me and I'd had three or four large vodkas and I'm trembling at the thought of going through customs.

'. . . been very nice to meet you.' Blah, blah, blah. And he's gone. So, quick as I can, I rush after him and start nattering just as we reach the bit where we're showing our passports. He's being all friendly towards me and I'm looking like a smart Englishman and they don't take a second glance at the passport, I'm not sure they even looked at it. I'm through and on my way back to England.

Once through British immigration I got out of the airport, bent down and kissed the ground. If it was good enough for the Pope it was good enough for Morry the Head.

37

A Sticky Business

Back in London the months go by and all of a sudden the usual thing happens and in a little while comes the moment when I wake up realising I'm due in court the next morning. Along with a friend I start chewing over this problem, thinking of a way I can get out of this trouble I'm in.

So he said: 'Look. I've got an idea. A pal of mine saved his kid from drowning the other day and the judge wouldn't send him to prison.'

It was a cold winter's day.

'What am I gonna do?'

'Look. We'll go to H.M.S. *Belfast* that's moored on the Thames.'

It was on a Sunday.

He said: 'I'll phone up the *Sunday Mirror* and *The People*. I'll get all the reporters down and you're gonna dive in the water and save my two children. They're both gonna fall over into the water.'

'Are you joking?'

'No.'

'They're both gonna slip. They're gonna fall into the water and you're gonna jump in and save them.'

'Are you mad, Harry?'

The kids were only about four or five years old.

Anyway, he convinced me because he wanted to save me from going to jail.

We had all the reporters down ready to take photos and everything because my pal knew some journalists and photographers.

It comes to the morning and I've had a look at the river. Oh dear. No man alive would've willingly jumped into the Thames. I wouldn't have jumped in for a thousand pounds let alone to save two kids' lives.

But he was ready with his kids in his arms. He was going to drop them both into the Thames.

'Harry,' I told him. 'I'd rather go to court and get four years than jump into the water to save them two kids.'

All the reporters were round with flashbulbs and everything. They'd already had the story 'cos they were crooked reporters and so the story was ready before it had even happened.

'Here they go,' said Harry.

'Hold up,' I yelled. 'Don't, I'll go to court.'

Of course all the newspapermen were disgusted. They were livid that I didn't jump in.

Anyway, they wrote some story about how I stopped some lunatic throwing the kids in the Thames. The judge heard about it.

'I commend you,' he said, 'but you're still going to jail.'

You could call into the Victoria Sporting Club and find me there almost every night some years back.

It was a place where time stood still. You arrived in a limousine, tipped the driver a few notes and entered another world for almost as long as you liked. Many people came along purely for the company. I was there to gamble.

My day would already have been longer than that of most working people. I would have woken at about six in the morning. Usually there would be a pretty tangle of long hair lying across the pillow beside me. Inevitably, my new friend would be sleeping while I was almost instantly awake. I have always got up early. It seems a waste of life to lie in bed, thinking or worrying about the day ahead. Nobody ever achieved anything by staying in bed all day.

Sometimes I would wake up in a West End flat, a place costing me hundreds every month but very impressive, all tiled bathrooms and four-poster beds. That was when the cash had not run out and I had managed to arrange the accommodation at a time when there was money in my pocket, which as you may gather was an infrequent occurrence in my life.

On other occasions it would be a rather different situation. We would be lying in a mouldy bed with a ceiling full of flaky white paint already threatening to drip down in long strips on to the off-white sheets the hotel had been kind enough to allow us to use that night. Hotels like these were dotted around Maida Vale. They had the advantage of being cheap and being anonymous. Once the manager had the night's charge in his back pocket he couldn't have cared less if you were splattered with blood and carried a sign announcing you were Jack the Ripper. The advantage to me was that this anonymity meant I could spend the night in totally carefree abandon knowing the police searching for Morry the Head were not likely to trouble me.

The disadvantage was that I would wake and wonder where all the money had gone. I would make a pot of coffee, wake my girlfriend and we would discuss what we wanted to do that day.

So it happened that one night I was in the club when in came a friend with a couple I had never met before. He acknowledged me with a sign that indicated I should keep my distance until he was able to come over and have a chat.

This was quite normal. It might be he was bringing in some people he had only recently met and was on a scam, trying to take them for what he thought they were worth. If that was the case he might have adopted a different identity and the last thing he would want would be for me to come up and say; 'Hi, Malcolm,' when he was telling all and sundry he was 'Baron Hopstein' from a defunct German ancestral tree which had nothing left but a title and a few millions which he needed help with spending.

So I bided my time and waited at the blackjack table for him to come across. Sure enough, after about a quarter of an hour he sat down beside me and introduced himself as if he was a stranger meeting me for the first time.

'Don't look around,' he told me. 'But that couple you saw me come in with is one of the richest in New York.'

Naturally enough he had grabbed my attention. But since the casino was full of exceptionally wealthy people, I felt no particular excitement, except a need to ask him who were these people.

'You will be surprised, Morry,' he told me, looking at me with one of those glances which are intended to tell you they know a great deal more about the situation than you think they do.

I played dumb. I was on a winning streak and just let his comments pass until he was so wound up he actually grabbed my arm.

'OK,' I said to him. 'What is it you just have to tell me?'

'I'm having it off with the woman,' he blurted out.

'So,' I said, 'you have a new girlfriend. Well, she looks attractive enough. Beautiful, even. And obviously married.'

He laughed and suggested we take a break from the blackjack table.

We got up and went across to the corner where you could get a cup of thick, black coffee. We stood there, a little apart from the small group clustered around the coffee table. I was determined not to let him know my interest.

'He's one of the biggest jewellers in New York.'

'What!' I said. 'This husband?'

'That's right. Probably one of the richest men in this casino right at this moment.'

Immediately an idea formed in my mind. If he was rich enough to be over in London and stupid enough to be allowing his wife to have an affair I thought he would not miss a few of his diamonds.

First I had to establish just how rich he was. I suggested my friend find a way of introducing us.

'He knows his wife is having an affair,' my friend said, as a way of warning me to be careful.

'That's all right,' I said. 'He must know it's you.'

'Not exactly,' he replied. He was giving me one of those embarrassing stares which tell you the person looking at you has just done something a little bit naughty, if you know what I mean.

'I don't understand.'

'I am by way of being a "family friend" who is looking after them in London. He knows his wife is seeing someone else and he has asked me to keep a good lookout and find out who it is. He is not best pleased.'

I still didn't get it. My friend was starting to relish this moment. It was a little while before he spoke again.

When he did it came like a bombshell. 'I told him it was a bald-headed man.'

I looked across the smoke-filled room expecting to see the

angry husband striding across the carpet wielding a knife or pointing a gun.

'You what! What on earth did you do that for?'

'I had to deflect attention away from me. Anyway, it's no great worry. Morry, you're not the only bald-headed man in London. Just take a look around you.'

I did and it didn't comfort me. Maybe it was one of those nights but I could count just three other men with the same hair loss. It did not look good. But I had a stroke of luck. One of the croupier's sisters came over right at the moment the New York couple made an appearance and I grabbed on to her for dear life. I could see she was a bit shocked, though pleased in fact, because I was making out that she was the closest thing to a fiancée I had ever had in my life.

Anyway, there was no aggravation and we were to meet up in the Victoria for several nights. However, a plan had formed in my head and I set about putting it into action almost straightaway.

This man could not avoid talking about his business in New York and I soon understood my friend had not exaggerated about how important he was. This was a seriously high-class jeweller. He had one of the finest jewel houses in America.

I was determined to rob him.

So, a few days later, I set off with The Swan to do this jeweller in New York who's about second or third only to Harry Winston, the tops. His wife, who was an extremely attractive girl, was now getting regularly fucked by this friend of mine.

Over the next few weeks, The Swan and I robbed him of thousands and thousands of pounds before coming back to Britain.

However, things have a habit of not quite working out the way you intend. After flying back and selling the jewels it was not many hours later before I was back in the Victoria Casino, where who do you think I should bump into but this jeweller himself.

He was enraged. He was really enraged. He knew his wife was getting fucked and he thought it was me who not only was fucking the wife but had now added insult to injury by robbing him. He had found out I was a jewel thief and he naturally assumed it was me who had robbed him although he had no evidence linking me with the theft. But that was not the point. The silly comment about the bald-headed lover boy had really put him on the wrong track.

This could do me real damage. But no matter what I said he refused to believe I was innocent. Of course, I was not about to admit to him that he was kindly funding my gambling right at that very moment. But he was no fool. He decided that if the police could not catch me he would find a way to get me sent down, knowing my reputation as that of a regular thief.

The action he took was to send out a worldwide text giving every detail he knew about the two men that had robbed him. Of course, top of the list of descriptions was the fact that one of the men was a bald-headed bloke. This 'Wanted Notice' went to every jeweller in the world he could think of sending it to. He badly wanted me caught.

Anyway, when The Swan wasn't working with me, strangely enough, he worked with another bald-headed fellow, Manchester George. And they too were wanted all over the world for jewel thefts.

I was about to get lucky.

Unbeknown to me, my friend and this other bald-headed fellow went to Los Angeles, where they found themselves on one of the smartest roads in the city, if not in all America, Rodeo Drive. There, among the film stars and the Hollywood producers, they were soon inside a jeweller's shop relieving it of several hundred thousand pounds' worth of diamonds.

Suddenly one of the assistants remembered the worldwide

Wanted Notice: 'Two Englishmen, one tall with bushy eye-brows and one bald-headed man.' Bang. Without my friends knowing, the police were called, quickly surrounded the shop and the end result was that they were nicked. So that was The Swan and Manchester George down the nick for a while.

Of course there's one man who's jumping up and down with joy at this particular piece of news.

The New York jeweller thinks I am the bald-headed man. He's rubbing his hands with satisfaction. He thinks the thousands of dollars he's spent trying to catch me is money well spent. I decide not to cross his path for a while. Maybe the fact I am now 'caught' can be of some use to me.

My friends are well and truly busted and are eventually sent to Green Haven Faculty, Upper State, New York. They get three or four years inside.

I have come into a little money and as a result have taken a beautiful flat in St John's Wood. All of a sudden, one night a few months later, the telephone goes in the middle of the night.

It's the international operator.

'Hallo, is that Mr Spurling?'

I was still half asleep. She was asking if I would accept a call from Green Haven Faculty Prison, Upper State, New York.

Instantly I was wide awake. I knew then who it was. It was The Swan now languishing in prison with his other bald-headed jewel thief of a friend.

'Hallo. How are you?' says The Swan.

'All right, how are you?' I reply.

'Can you come and see me?'

'All right. What do you need?'

'Well. Have you got a pen and paper there?'

I should tell you something about The Swan. He's always eating. This fellow eats for Ealing. He can eat all day and all night. He's a chain-eater and he's not fussy about what he's shoving into his system. When he's finished his dinner he starts on something else. In between eating he's chewing cigars like W.C. Fields. You light a cigar and he lights one, he's finished it as you are having your first intake.

So when he said: 'Got a pen and paper there?' I knew it was going to be a long night.

The list of things he wanted seemed never ending. I filled up a pad of Basildon Bond writing down what he wanted.

Of course it is the early morning and I am getting a bit tired, not having been asleep for too long when he calls. He is also wearing me out with his detailed demands for food to be brought to him in prison. Eventually we reach the end of the list and he pauses before raising his voice and telling me he wants Callard and Bowser toffees.

'Whatever you do I want Callard and Bowser. UNDERLINE IT. Underline the name,' he orders me. 'Just remember Callard and Bowser. Eight or ten packets.'

All this is to be bought at a delicatessen on Fifth Avenue. I know the place quite well. I am relieved he does not want anything bringing over from London. It is a long list.

He gets off the telephone and I wonder what to do. I have never liked visiting people in prison. It brings back too many nasty memories. I often think that once inside I might not get back out again. But visiting someone in a British prison is reasonable. Flying across the Atlantic for a few hours to an American prison could be silly. But I thought to myself I wasn't doing anything, so I may as well spend a grand and go over and see him.

Before putting the phone down he had made one last request. I should bring plenty of nickels and dimes. He suggested a hundred pounds' worth.

A few days later I was in New York and walking down Fifth Avenue in the pouring rain on my way to the deli.

I took out the sheets of paper on which I had written my friend's order and handed them over to the assistant behind the counter. She was a kind-looking woman who I could see was dying to ask what sort of party I was giving. She got on with filling out the order. But one item she can't help with is the Callard and Bowser toffees.

'Ooh,' said the assistant, 'we haven't got those, sir.'

'Is there anything like it?'

'Oh yes.' And she gives me eight or ten packets of something else.

The box of food was so big I had to hail a yellow cab in order to get it the short distance back to the hotel I was staying in that night.

The following morning I was in Times Square waiting with my massive box of food to catch the bus which would take me to the prison. The World Cup was on that day in Brazil and people were in a good mood. My friend had told me we would have all day together. I was feeling quite pleased with myself for getting him all this food and I had not forgotten to bring a hundred quid's worth of nickels and dimes. That was certainly the strangest request I have ever made of a bank.

There's no mistaking the prison. It is a massive complex of forbidding buildings and if that isn't enough there are guards everywhere you look. Each one is carrying a machine gun and it seems every one of them is pointing at me.

Once inside I have to declare everything. The visitors are searched more than the convicts. We are all lined up and checked by a big group of mean-looking prison officers. It seems to take for ever.

Nothing prepared me for the visiting room. They say everything in America is bigger. They certainly went out of their way to prove it with this visiting room. It was like walking into an aircraft hangar. The place is packed with people, prisoners, visitors, mothers and fathers and sons and daughters. I feel quite lost and am definitely getting worried about getting out again.

I have to wait a while but eventually out comes my friend. And do you know what? The first thing he said to me, and I mean the very first thing he said to me, was: 'Where's my order?' Not, 'Hallo, how are you? Thank you for coming,' but: 'Where's my order?'

So I showed him it. Whereupon his mood changed and he started to mellow.

'Oh,' he said. 'Good. A big box.'

He seems quite satisfied and genuinely pleased I have made the effort and got him all this food. Next he asks if I remembered the nickels and dimes.

I take out the bag and show them to him. By now I'm dying to know what on earth he plans to do with them. So he takes a handful and marches over to one of the walls telling me to come with him. It was the first time I had paid attention to the edges of the room. The place was so big and so full of people you didn't notice what was going on over there. I'm not joking when I say the walls were lined with one-armed bandits. It was like being in Las Vegas. There were hundreds of slot machines and one-armed bandits. Every one was full of food. Apple pie, roast beef, salami, sandwiches, biscuits, cheese . . . You just had to put nickels or dimes in them to get at the stuff.

He spent most of the visiting day on the machines just eating. In between meals he starts whispering to me.

'Don't talk loud but that fellow over there's got three hundred years, the one beside him's got six hundred years and that other one's doing four hundred years. I've only got five years. I'm a relative short-timer.'

We seemed to be getting on really well. I thought it was because he was so grateful to me. Not only had I flown all the way from London to see him in jail but I had come complete with more food than Father Christmas.

At that moment he looked inside the box. He started to pick through the tins and wrappers to see what I had brought him.

There was everything you could wish for, smoked salmon, Dutch cheese, herrings, rye bread, you name it I seemed to have bought it. Then he looked up. Just like a child whose favourite toy's been broken. I thought he was going to cry. Nothing prepared me for what was about to happen.

'Did you get the Callard and Bowser?' he said, sounding a bit angry.

'No.'

'You didn't! Do you mean to tell me you've come all this way without getting me the Callard and Bowser?'

By now he was drawing the attention of the people sitting near us. I was a little embarrassed. He was in his element.

'You got another make!' he went on, much louder than before. Now he's really shouting and two or three guards are giving us funny looks and stroking their pistols. 'Are you some egg? Are you some nitwit? I told you a hundred times I want Callard and Bowser.'

I pointed to the box. 'Look at all the stuff I got you. The deli didn't have any Callard and Bowser.'

This just seemed to get him going even more.

'No Callard and Bowser's. They make more toffees than anyone in the whole world. They send them everywhere. How can you come halfway across the world and tell me you've got no Callard and Bowser's.'

And he's shouting and shouting. Froth was even coming out of his mouth.

I just felt ridiculous. I'd gone all the way to New York to see him. I'd spent a lot of money. And there we were having a row over toffees.

I didn't know what to say, so I turned away and at that point we were showered with coffee. The table went up in the air spraying us with food and drink. The Swan stormed back to the one-armed bandits and started playing them with a passion not seen outside Vegas.

This fellow who's doing three hundred years leans across to me. 'Excuse me,' he said. 'What's with the Callard and Bowser's?'

After a few hours of roast beef, apple pie and cigars The Swan had calmed down. But even as I left after spending the whole day in that dreadful place he was still sore about my failure to buy the right toffees.

It was a relief to get back to my hotel. I was staying at the Lexington Hotel in Lexington Street, opposite the Waldorf Astoria, but I decided to start the night off with a drink in The Peacock Alley of the Waldorf. It's a place where every famous personality in the world has walked through and there was the most beautiful, beautiful girl sitting there. She had legs as long as Fifth Avenue and she absolutely took my breath away. I mustered up courage and went into action and I said: 'Excuse me.' The old shit that I've always used. 'I must tell you this. You're the most beautiful woman I've seen all day long and I've been out since five o'clock in the morning.' It's now six o'clock in the evening.

And she says: 'Oh, really. What a lovely accent you've got. You're a Limey?'

'Yes. I'm a Limey. I'm here on my own and I'm looking for company.'

'Oh, really.'

I had an erection standing there talking to her and she knew it. 'Oh,' she says, 'look at YOU! Aren't you a big boy?'

'Well. I've been known to be rather big.'

'Well,' she says, 'it's your lucky day. I'm waiting for Frank.'

'Frank?' I ask, wondering who she's talking about.

'Yes, Sinatra. He's flying in from Lake Tahoe.'

'Well,' I tell her, 'what chance have I got? A mere mortal, a mere lonely Englishman, with Frank Sinatra.'

To my utter amazement she said: 'I think you've got every chance.'

We had a drink. Fifteen minutes later we were in the Lexington Hotel, in bed with her lovely, lovely long legs wrapped right round my head.

She was a playmate, a Bunny Girl.

The next day I thought I'd look around the jewellery quarter on spec, like I've done all my life. This was the first time working with this Bunny Girl as the distraction. I found myself looking at an advert for a shop selling diamonds. When I got there the place appeared to be open but it was locked. I knocked on the front door and a man opened it and invited me inside.

I told him I was looking for a couple of presents to take home. It didn't take me long to select what I wanted and I offered him a cheque.

Now one point I should stress. If you want to bounce a cheque you better make it a big one. Mind you, this was long before electronic systems were introduced which made investigating a person's funds so much easier. But this jeweller could still have waited until he was able to ring my bank. If you plan to convince somebody you have money you must adopt a certain attitude along with the obvious tricks such as a well-tailored suit and a smart appearance. Wealthy people have a kind of arrogance which tells people they are so used to getting their own way in the world that no one is going to turn them down. If I had presented the cheque in a nervous manner or even asked if he would accept a cheque I might have been turned down. As it was he automatically assumed an Englishman in New York in the Sixties would not enter a top-class jewellers unless he had the money to pay for his purchase. Instead of umming and ahhing he came right out and told me how he had an associate in London who would be able to cash it for him. Good of him to be so obliging. I told him that was OK by me. So I gave him a cheque for twenty thousand pounds for a beautiful diamond stone.

It was nearly midday, and I've got the stone and I'm on my way to the airport after bidding goodbye to my Bunny Girl. While I'm riding along in the yellow cab I take this diamond out of the box and I wrap it in tissue. I put it in my pocket. All the way from uptown New York I'm feeling this stone, stroking it through the material of my trousers. It's quite safe. A lovely stone worth twenty thousand, all for a cheque not worth two bob.

So all the way through the streets of New York I am touching this beautiful diamond through my trousers and thinking God is good. I've done the right thing by visiting my argumentative friend in jail and God has repaid me by saying: 'Right. You've done well, son.' Bang! I've got the stone and so I'm as happy as a pig in shit.

I've arrived at the airport about three or four hours before the plane is due to leave. So I thought to myself: 'Morry. It's time for a large vodka and bitter lemon and ice.'

I'm sitting at the bar, relaxing and constantly patting my pocket, all the while stroking this lovely stone which is going to be sold in Hatton Garden the next day. So I've got money.

Along comes this guy. Huge. He had to be American. The first part of him I noticed approaching was this massive pair of shoes. He was wearing very heavy thick brown brogues. He had feet like an elephant, they must have been size fourteen shoes. He's bigger than Cassius Clay and is coming towards me. He had on a blue jacket, brown shoes, a yellow shirt, a red waistcoat, green trousers. Nothing matched. The Americans are the most terrible dressers, the worst in the world.

He comes and plonks himself down next to me at the bar where I'm enjoying my large vodka.

I'm beginning to feel the vibe of the alcohol plus a few other excitements and generally I would say I'm on a high. And every time I touch my pocket, which I do frequently, there's that lovely stone wrapped in the tissue.

As I order the second large vodka, this guy says to me: 'Hi. You're a Limey. I'm just off to England.'

Well, it transpired he was going on the same plane as me and he was in some sort of business.

We share stories of romances, travel, anything you can think of. You name it we're talking about it. There's a lot of time to kill before we can board our plane. He lived in Phoenix, Arizona, where I had some friends, so we had something in common.

After about the fifth large vodka my speech is becoming rather slurred and my faculties are not a hundred per cent. Now we are both enjoying the bag of bollocks that we're shooting to each other. All of a sudden I'm touching my pocket and I have the most terrible sneeze. I take out the tissue with my beautiful stone in, wipe my nose and put the tissue back in my pocket. The Tannoy goes for our flight. He says: 'I gotta make a call. See you on the plane, Morry.'

I start to saunter towards the boarding gate. And like the hundred previous times I touch my pocket. I freeze. I can feel the tissue but I can't feel the diamond. The effect of the vodkas had addled my brain. I couldn't imagine where the stone had gone. I dropped my cases and flew back to the bar.

What do you think? He'd been on the phone, gone back to his large Jack Daniels and was standing there finishing his drink before he joined me on the flight.

And I don't know why in Heaven's name but I just looked down at his shoes, shoes fit for an elephant. He was standing with his foot half raised up balancing his massive shoe on its heel.

I yelled at him: 'Don't move your feet.'

Under that shoe there was a little twinkling star. My lovely beautiful diamond.

It must have been lying there ever since it slipped out of the tissue when I sneezed. This American looked at me as though I had gone half mad and asked what was I doing.

I said I had bought a present. 'It fell out my pocket, can you believe it. Let's get on the plane. Let's get drunk.'

One day I was introduced to some Irishmen at Royal Ascot. Unbeknown to me they were top members of the IRA and they wanted to back a horse and have several thousand pounds on it. Someone said I was a big bookmaker. I was dressed immaculately. So I became a bookmaker.

You see, in all my fifty years of racing, we have always obtained money off bookmakers, by some way or means. Not physically but simply by them being gullible and us conniving, us being the likes of myself and The Swan.

These IRA members gave me ten grand. I laid them the bet, I never put on the money and what won? The horse won. Of course now I had the IRA on my back looking for me wherever I went. They had their money to come. They went to White City Dogs looking for me and then they gave up and that was it. I never heard or saw them anymore.

I didn't have a sixpence, I was dressed up like a millionaire, big cigar, lovely silk suit, crocodile shoes, never had a shilling.

Years ago, up north, I met a man who was the biggest bookmaker-entrepreneur-boxing promoter there was in the north of England. His name was Gus Demmy.

I was standing at what we call 'The Rails'. The biggest bookmakers only operate on the rails, Chandler's, Hill's, Ladbrokes and so on. Didn't have a shilling, looking for what we call 'A Move' to get a pound. But everybody thought I had millions, by the way I looked, by the way I presented myself and carried on. I was standing talking to The Swan, who, I think, had three quid. A beautiful girl appeared and she was with a young man who turned out to be the son of Gus Demmy. As they walked by me he said in that nice northern accent: 'Hallo. I'm going to the bar. Would you like a drink?'

Well, I didn't know who he was. So I went in the bar and had a drink, looking at the girl. He knew that I knew his father.

Something else was important to this. Before this happened I had spoken to a feller at the races who worked for a bookmaker and his name was Curly. This was about a quarter of an hour before racing.

Curly came up to me. 'Hallo. How are you?'

'I ain't got a shilling. Where can I get some money?'

'I don't know. I'm the same.'

He left me and later this young man, Selwyn Demmy, approached me.

So we're now in the bar and I'm staring at his girlfriend and he's regaling me with that lovely northern accent.

'I've known you for years,' he says. 'I know yer name, Morris isn't it?'

'Yes.'

'You knew my father.'

'Yes.'

'Do me a favour,' he says, 'tell me something. The man you were speaking to earlier, Curly, is he all right? Is he sound?'

'Why do you ask that?'

'He's got an account with me and he hasn't paid.'

Now, remember I never had a pound. 'Well, I don't know about him. I wish *I* had an account with you.'

'Mr Morris,' he said, 'you can have what you like with me.' Now this is the biggest bookmaker in the north of England. Well my heart missed a beat when he said that.

'You can have what you like. You're a pal of my late dad's. It's no problem. You're a good punter. Why don't you have a bet with me?'

I said: 'I'll think about it.'

He said: 'I've got to go to work now. If you need me you know where I am.'

When I got my breath back I started planning what steps to take. It was like an invitation to rob a bank.

So, I stayed in the bar figuring out how to get my act together, took another big Churchill cigar out of my pocket and said to The Swan: 'I think I've got a chance here.'

Now I'm waiting. Waiting for what we call 'The Day's Good Thing'. With a bookmaker you can call a bet, you either give him the cash, or if you've got an account you don't pay on. So I waited for the good thing of the day. It was what we call an even money chance, one for one, you have a pound on you win a pound, ten thousand you win ten thousand. Exactly level stakes.

So there was this 'Good Thing' and there was an even money chance and I didn't know how much to have on it, a hundred quid, a thousand pound, two grand, so The Swan said to me, 'You better have five grand on it. Get some money. It's gonna win.'

I thought, 'I wonder if he'll take the bet.' I'm acting on that advice given to me years earlier by Roper the Doper. I was at a coursing meeting called The Waterloo Cup which is held near Aintree every year round about February or March. Coursing is where they drive the hares into the field. And he told me one thing as regards racecourse 'Moves', that is scams.

'Morris. Whenever you're going to have a bet with a book-maker always come up on his blind side. Never let him see you approaching him.'

You come round the back of him and then appear so that he doesn't have an opportunity to think of an excuse for refusing the bet.

So now we're at Ascot and I'm going to approach Selwyn Demmy. Anyway, this was a long time ago. I thought of what my tutor Bill Roper told me. So I walk round the back, it's Royal Ascot, a hot day, thousands of people milling about, champagne flowing all over the place, cigars smoking everywhere, money passing hands, and I came right round his back side.

He was shouting, 'Evens on the field,' which means evens, one to one, yours to mine.

'Even five thousand pounds.'

'Aye,' he says, 'Mr Morris. Even five thousand pounds.'

So the reaction was good. I walked away. I didn't give him any money because I didn't have any money. So I proceeded to go into the stands and watch the race. And the horse won. So I've got five thousand pounds to come which was like winning The Lottery. I ran down the stairs whereupon I banged into The Swan.

'Get some money,' I told him, 'we'll have a bottle of champagne.'

I think we borrowed a tenner or something and there we are in the bar quaffing champagne.

'What are you going to do?'

'Get the five grand.'

'You shouldn't really. If you don't get the five grand the image of you will go up.'

I thought to myself for a minute: Five grand. It's a million pounds. I can get out of trouble.

'Look,' I says to The Swan. 'I'm gonna draw it.' So I let time go by, I didn't immediately go up to him. I let another race go by and then I walked up to him.

'Ah. Mr Morris. Give Mr Morris five thousand pounds.' Whereupon I got it in my pocket, thank you very much.

Well, the result of that episode was I finished up owing Mr Selwyn Demmy thousands upon thousands upon thousands. After that five grand, which I'd got in my pocket, I never backed a winner and I didn't pay. And he phoned me every weekend there was, because he had my number. I couldn't avoid it.

'How are things, Morris?'

'Terrible. Could you send me a few quid?'

'I like your style,' he said. 'Don't worry about the five thousand pounds.'

'I got news for you, Selwyn. I'm not worried about it because I haven't got it.'

Anyway the shine wore off after a few months and he phoned me.

'Morris. I must have this money.'

A couple of years later I bumped into him in a place called The Lygon Arms in Broadway where he always stays for the Cheltenham Festival.

'How are you?' he asks.

'Not good. You couldn't lend me a couple of hundred quid, could you?'

And he laughed. 'Get out of it, you're a scallywag.' And he laughed again and walked away.

As usual, back in the Fifties, I was broke but we had access to all the false and the forged white five-pound notes. And we were using them all over the country with bookmakers. We had thousands of them, millions of them. I was at York and a horse called Troy was running. It was five to two on, for every five you put down you win two, it was a certainty and I had five thousand pounds on it in crooked fivers and it won. I had it with a man called Colin Webster who's still in operation today.

So when I gave him the five thousand pounds which wasn't worth five bob he took the bet. But he knew. He realised that he'd been done. And Troy won. Now I got seven thousand pounds which I'm hoping is real money. To his credit he never screamed or anything. He gave me the seven thousand pounds but he gave me back the five grand that I gave him which I thought was a bit of a liberty, and only two grand in real money.

We worked what we used to call 'Sniede Fivers' during the fifties all over the country. Sniede is a slang word which I think comes from German and means false or no good.

38

Ten Years to Serve

In 1978 the Belgians eventually stuck me in one of their jails. After serving about nine or ten months in prison I'd made friends with a fellow from the Middle East. He'd lived in Damascus and he liked me and I was making plans with him to go over there. Anyway, I was walking around during exercise time taking in the fresh air and looking forward to freedom in another couple of months. At that time my main home was in Canada although I was actually in limbo. I didn't know where I was, I didn't know where my clothes were. Right at that moment one of the principal officers called me in to the office.

'There's a letter for you from the British Consulate.'

I opened the letter. 'This is to inform you that in your absence you have been sentenced to ten years' imprisonment and you will be deported to Great Britain at the end of your sentence.'

Well, I was looking at the letter and just could not believe it. I just could not believe what was happening. The next day I had to believe it because they told me to pack my bags.

'You're getting moved to another city en route to being deported home to Great Britain to serve your ten-year sentence.'

Obviously I was distraught. 'What's happening here?' I thought. 'This can't be right.'

But apparently it was because they moved me from there to Ypres, from Ypres to another place and then on to another place to finish up in Bruges.

I realised they were shifting me as near to the coast as possible in order to be picked up by whoever was taking me home.

Early one morning in Bruges they came for me, handcuffed me to two plainclothes Belgian detectives, took me outside the prison whereupon a lovely English voice said: 'Hallo, Morris. How are you?'

The voice belonged to one of two flying squad officers from the Metropolitan Police. One knew me, I believe his name was Sags or Snags, and he said: 'What have you gone and done to get a ten-year sentence?'

He couldn't believe it himself.

'You tell me.'

'The judge has gone off his head. He's gone berserk.'

You'd have thought I was a vicious bank robber because I was surrounded by so many detectives. The Belgian detectives had been told that they weren't to release me until the ferry got to Dover. The British detectives didn't like that because I was really their property, but that's how it worked out. They wanted the handcuffs off me. In my mind I was forming a plan – I wasn't going to go to Dover. I'd either run off or dive in the water. I was thinking like James Bond at this moment.

We got on the ferry with the two British detectives still unhappy with the Belgians and insisting the handcuffs be taken off me. Finally, they persuaded them. They knew me, they knew my modus operandi. I wasn't a rapist or a robber or a murderer, I was a thief.

The boat was rocking up and down, the water was high, it was a freezing cold December day, and I asked: 'Can I get a bit of air?'

The detectives said: 'Yeah, let him go.'

I went upstairs thinking I was going to throw myself in the water and swim back to the shore. But when I saw the sea I thought I'd rather face the ten years.

We got to Dover and the Belgians went back. I came down the gangplank from the ferry and we bumped into a very large fat woman bigger than Frank Bruno who was wheeling a baby in a pram. One of the detectives bumped into her and she turned round and said: 'Special Branch.'

I couldn't believe it. A baby in a pram with a twenty-stone woman. 'I hear you've got a prisoner on board. Is everything all right?'

'Yes, no problem.'

The detectives looked at me in awe.

We caught the train to Victoria and then they took me to Vine Street Police Station off Piccadilly.

I was brought back under the Fugitives' Offenders' Act. They produced me at Bow Street court the next day. The magistrate slung me into Wandsworth Prison. The actual ten years was imposed because of the theft of a watch, but it didn't make sense to anybody.

After a sojourn in Wandsworth Prison I was told I was going to be sent to, of all places, Parkhurst on the Isle of Wight, which is for train robbers, murderers, life sentences. And among this crowd of criminals there was little old me.

So I was sent down to Parkhurst in the spring of 1979 and I finished up with IRA bombers and the like.

After a couple of weeks of walking round scratching my head thinking, 'What am I doing with a ten-year sentence for stealing a watch?' I got a letter from the solicitor who was battling away on my behalf.

He wrote to say that he had called in counsel. The leading exponents in this country as regards extradition are two brothers called Nicholls. They advise the government on anything to do with extradition. Two brothers, two eminent QCs, and I had a solicitor who was into them. He was also into a counsel called Dermot Wright, who sat as a Recorder somewhere. After looking at my case and what I was doing at Parkhurst saddled with ten years, he wrote to me and said: 'Don't hold your breath, but I don't think you should be there.'

Of course, this was like putting petrol in an empty car. I thought: 'Aye aye, what's this?' Whereupon I got another letter to say that Dermot Wright had taken my case to the Nicholls brothers and they said that it seemed I had been brought back from Europe illegally. It's like when the Israelis went into Argentina or whatever and kidnapped Eichmann, they did it illegally. He still got topped. But it was an illegal act to bring me back.

I'd now been in Parkhurst for about ten months with hardened criminals. And everybody was talking about it in Parkhurst. Then I got another letter to say my case was due to go to the High Court in London in front of Lord Justice Webster.

I was quite friendly with the legal aid officer of the prison and the welfare. I seemed to get on with them, as I didn't give them any hassle. They were full of hope for me.

The day of the hearing came. 'When will I know?' I asked them.

'Some time today.'

Round about two o'clock in the afternoon I bumped into the legal aid officer who seemed quite cheery.

'Any news?'

'I can't really tell you.'

That answer gave me a bit of hope.

To cut a long story short, after a while I get called to the governor's office. I thought that the governor was a bastard. He was the nastiest man in the whole world. He's sat there in all his power. A bag full of nothing he was and he thought he was God's gift to whatever. And he starts talking to me.

'I have to tell you you're a free man.'

'What?'

'You have won your case in the High Court and when I get the warrant you can go and the quicker you go the better.'

Well, I was stunned, even though I half expected it.

Now you can't be released from prison unless you get the document from the court saying you're released, no matter who rings up. If the Queen says you're to be released you can't go straightaway, not until you get that bit of paper.

When I found my composure and realised I was no longer really a prisoner and I had nothing to lose, I got saucy.

I looked at the governor and found something to say.

'Do you know, sir, it's a privilege to get away from the likes of you, who would put everybody including God, if you could get hold of Him, in jail. It's a pleasure leaving you.'

His face was black as thunder. 'Spurling. You're not going until I get the paper.'

When the prison heard that I'd actually beaten the system they were banging on their doors. It was like the Cup Final.

The legal aid officer phoned my friend in London. My friend put his wife on the ferry to the Isle of Wight with the document. I was released about eight o'clock at night.

By the time I got to Waterloo about midnight I was pissed out of my head.

On arriving home, I think it was St John's Wood, someone

said to me: 'Morry, you've been locked up for a year, you can claim off the Home Office.'

I made an appointment to see Mr Dermot Wright, this barrister who really got me out of it. I took him a lovely case of red wine and a box of cigars, which he appreciated.

And I said: 'Now look, Mr Wright. Can we get any money off them?'

'I thought you were coming to that,' he said. He reclined in his big leather chair and twiddled his thumbs as most barristers do, before replying to my question.

'Look, you may well get some money off them. But you've annoyed them by winning the case. If I were you I wouldn't take any action . . .'

I'll always remember his next words '. . . because you will stir up a hornets' nest.'

In other words, they would nick me for walking along the street, looking at the sun or taking the dog out.

So I didn't and that was that. That was the tale of the ten-year sentence.

39

Lust for Diamonds

The only piece of advice my father gave to me which I ever paid any attention to was this: 'If you meet a mug you gotta take his money. If you don't, there's a long queue behind you who will.'

I never steal from individuals. That's been a strong point in my life. Always, I take from shops and warehouses and auctions. But to take a private diamond from a beautiful woman, no, that's not my style at all. But where shops and businesses are concerned, it's equal opportunities all the way for Morry the Head. Sometimes pleasure and work really do come together.

After a run of good luck in Britain I decided to leave for a while. The police were not on to me but I had done so many shops and hotel showcases in the past four months I was running out of places to take from. I'd never been to Marbella before and decided to give it a try. It's now very popular but back then not many people had visited it from England. It was a resort for the rich. A wise friend had whispered to me that there was a bit of money to be made.

After bundling my few possessions into my Volkswagen car I drove out of London heading in the direction of Dover. On the ferry I went out on to the deck and puffed a small cigar and waved goodbye to the White Cliffs of Dover. Before making my way to Spain I planned to make a few calls a little closer to home.

From Calais, I set off for Belgium and visited a few places I had been to before. They were not to disappoint me. I was stealing from jewellers and fencing the goods by midday. There were always plenty of people to buy my wares. There aren't as many honest people around as you might think. Offer them a diamond ring at a third of the shop price and you've just found another crook. So I was doing well, even allowing for a little bet before continuing on to another town.

Crossing the border into Germany I had really got no idea where I was planning to visit first. Then I recalled that on an earlier trip I used to stay in the top hotel in Munich, the Bayerischer Hof, which I would say is equivalent to Claridge's in London. My mind was made up, Munich it would be. I was travelling with a considerable amount of money on me. It had been a fortunate trip, not only for diamond stones but gold chains as well. My pocket was full of money and I meant to cash in on my luck and get a bit more. It's a bit like a run of luck at the races – when good fortune smiles you must keep paying attention to her. You'll know soon enough when things start to go wrong!

It was early summer and the sun shone brilliantly as I drove towards Munich. At the Hotel Bayerischer Hof I found there was a room; my luck was in. I knew that was so the minute a sophisticated young lady approached me as I was having a quick vodka and tonic at the bar.

'I see you are English, sir,' she said with the sweetest smile a woman has ever had.

'My accent gives me away, I suppose.'

'No. It was not your voice. It was the way you dress. I love the English clothes, you know.'

I muttered something and then asked her if she cared to join me for a drink.

'I would love to do so.'

After the second vodka I was starting to become rather relaxed.

She touched my knee, resting her hand gently on it for a few seconds. I knew it would turn out to be a good night.

Work always comes first with me. You can spend your whole life chasing after the pleasures of a woman but I am afraid that at some stage work must reappear otherwise you would be so poor nothing would ever happen in your life.

I was not thinking of work when the young lady touched me on the knee. I had money in my pocket and a plan so I responded in like manner.

'Shall we go upstairs?' I asked her.

'I would love that,' she replied. 'I don't come cheap, you know.'

I realised she had targeted me as a wealthy businessman for her services as a hooker. I could afford her. So we went up to bed and discussed everything but the price of jewellery. Much later I returned to the bar after bidding a fond farewell to the lady of the night.

After ordering the next vodka and tonic I left it on the bar and went off to find the concierge.

'Excuse me,' I asked him, 'would you be good enough to tell me where the jewellery auction is? I have been before to the splendid one you hold in this hotel.'

'I'm sorry, sir. The auction is no longer held here.'

My heart fell. It seemed this was going to be a waste of time.

'But if you're interested, sir,' the concierge continued, 'although the auction is finished the woman who used to run it has opened a shop just a hundred metres up the road. Perhaps you might care to pay her a visit?'

I thanked him and set off to have a look. It was as he had described.

The following morning I had a light breakfast and went down to the shop to say hallo.

'What a lovely shop you have here,' I told the woman who came to the door. She wore a yellow silk dress and a smile hotter than the sun. She greeted me with a warmth you don't often find from jewellers.

On entering the shop I looked around and saw it was filled with some marvellous items, some wonderful jewels. Instantly I knew the trip had not been a wasted one. The woman took me by the hand and led me across to one of her display cases.

'Would you care to see this out of the case?' she enquired.

Naturally enough I agreed. 'That would be most kind.'

She took out some of her prize possessions, a diamond ring here, an opal brooch there, a beautiful string of pearls, a couple of ladies' diamond watches. I listed a number of items I was interested in buying. I told her I had a shop back in England and was looking for a substantial amount of high-class stock for my richer customers.

'Are you in a hurry?' the woman asked.

'Not at all. I often come to Munich and enjoy spending some time here. Fortunately I am in the position of being able to combine business with pleasure. I don't think either should be rushed. Do you?'

'I quite agree.' By this time we had exchanged names. I was Sam and I shall call her Heidi.

'Come, Sammy, and sit down beside me while we look at these diamonds over a cup of coffee.'

'Splendid, Heidi. Splendid.'

She brought over a small table which she placed beside two lavish Regency high-backed chairs and proceeded to cover its surface with some beautiful pieces.

We talked for some time, our bodies touching frequently. It was clear she fancied me and I certainly fancied her. Her skirt was one of the shortest I have ever seen; it was summer after all. Her legs were as long as the Edgware Road and the tan was the kind you get after a month in the Caribbean. She would have been about thirty-five, with long, blonde hair and extremely large breasts which were having trouble being restrained by her clothing. My type of woman.

She explained she had left the auction in the hotel and had opened this shop independently in the heart of Munich. The goods she was showing me were worth up to £50,000 each, the cheapest would have been at least £10,000. The area around the Hotel Bayerischer Hof is a rich one and they are used to selling expensive jewellery. I thought to myself, 'I'm going to get the prize here.'

'Would you care for some whisky, or perhaps some schnapps?'

It was approaching midday but I had nothing better to do. I couldn't believe my luck, fancy a jeweller flirting with me. She went over to the safe and bent down to extract a bottle of schnapps and another prize diamond. She made no attempt to stop her skirt riding up over the tops of her thighs. I couldn't have stood up and left even if I'd wanted to.

'Do you like this bracelet?' she asked, showing me a huge monstrosity worth thousands, littered with sparkling diamonds. It was too obvious to look good on even the most beautiful woman in the world. It was also a little too big for me to get away with. Consequently, I did not like it.

'Not really,' I replied.

'Well, how about this?'

This was a ring encrusted with emeralds and diamonds. It would have been worth £20,000 to £30,000. A really pretty little thing which would easily have slipped into my pocket.

'I do,' I assured her.

'You know what you like and what you don't,' she commented, giving me the teeniest little wink.

It's midday, broad daylight, a hot summer's day and we both have a problem. Someone else is in the shop. Tucked away at the back must have been a small workshop where I occasionally heard the sound of someone humming and singing away to himself.

'I won't be a minute,' she said, turning away to go to the rear of the shop. Standing beside the wall she shouted something through to the workshop.

'It's my brother,' she told me. 'I have suggested he might care to take the afternoon off. It is such a beautiful day he may as well go off and enjoy himself with his girlfriend.'

A few moments later a handsome young blond-haired man appeared with something of a grin on his face. He had needed no prompting from his sister to leave the building and give up work for the rest of the day. As he left the shop she carefully and obviously locked it. She was making her intentions crystal clear. She gave me a good long look and then went across to the blinds and drew them down quickly, cutting off the bright rays of sunlight which covered the slatted pine floor. Moments later we were in a dimly lit room which gave us a feeling of being inside a bedroom in a smart hotel in the middle of the night, but with the advantage of all the fresh energy of the morning burning inside our bodies. She spoke perfect English.

'Thank God he's gone. Now, my darling, we are alone. Let's have some fun.'

There, right in the middle of the shop, surrounded by her finest diamonds, rubies and emeralds – half a million pounds' worth at a rough guess – she unzipped her little yellow dress and slowly let it drift down onto the floor. She was wearing nothing more than a pair of white panties the size of a delicate lady's handkerchief. These she removed with one swift movement, all the time indicating that I better start doing a similar operation on my clothes. She came across the room and helped me unbutton my Huntsman suit trousers. After caressing me as gently as I had touched her diamonds she stood back.

'Do you like me? Do you like this?' she said, slowly turning round.

'Well, I think you're lovely. You're as beautiful as the Koh-i-noor diamond, my sweet.' She was standing there with a beautifully bronzed body, her breasts standing to attention like the guards outside Buckingham Palace.

She surprised me then by suggesting we get straight on with the job in hand. She told me in no uncertain terms what she wanted. I told you her English was good. Well, she was also in full command of basic Anglo-Saxon. Although, what we proceeded to do was more than just the basics, it was high-class German sophistication meets experienced English travelling gentleman.

After half an hour the sweat was pouring off our bodies. We rested over another schnapps and cuddled each other on the floor. She had found a rug which she laid out right beside the table.

Someone knocked on the door. I froze. She didn't move a muscle.

'Leave it. They'll soon go away. No one can see inside.'

Our energy returned, we stood up and resumed our love-making. I had turned her away from me so she was facing the table with the half a million pounds' worth of jewels. It was made of oak, thick and quite sturdy. Strong enough to hold her weight as she pressed down on the edges supporting herself by holding both sides with her delicate hands. My hands started massaging her neck. I stroked her shoulders and gently worked my fingertips down the sides of her body until my hands reached her waist. Holding her firmly, I summoned up all my vast reserves of energy to make love to her once more with as much expertise as I could manage. We were rocking and rolling all over that table, although she was careful not to knock off any of the valuable stones. But in the height of her passion her head kept moving from side to side, so much so that sometimes she seemed to be in a dream, gazing at her cabinets of jewels lining the walls of the shop. I saw my chance and manoeuvred my body into position slightly to the left of her. With each thrust into her I was getting closer and closer to the diamond and emerald ring which was perched near the edge of the table. I bit my lip as I took my final chance and as our bodies thrust once more into the table I removed my left hand as if to steady myself and seconds later had the ring firmly cupped in my fist.

As we slumped exhausted to the floor I rolled over and quickly slipped the ring inside my trousers.

We lay there for a while gently touching each other and whispering sweet nothings. Then we decided the afternoon was wearing on and we had better get dressed and go about the rest of our business.

I buttoned my shirt and pulled up my trousers. As I did so it looked as though I was about to be found out. She wanted to do it again. I couldn't believe her energy. She was making it impossible for me to do up my trousers, but what was worse still, she was rubbing one of my thighs with one of her hands. If it had been the other hand on the other thigh she would have felt something even more familiar and the game would have been up. I pretended to have an appointment back at the hotel.

'Did you enjoy that?' she asked, rather unnecessarily in my opinion.

'I'm coming back tomorrow.'

252

'We'll have more, yes?'

'Yes. We'll have more.'

As she let the blinds go back up and unlocked the door she threw her arms around my neck and gave me a final, warm, wet kiss of love. 'Forget the jewels. Let's have some fun tonight. Where will you be?'

'Still at the Hotel Bayerischer Hof.'

'I'm coming to you at about eight o'clock tonight. And perhaps afterwards we can have some dinner.'

I restrained myself from patting the pocket containing her lovely diamond and emerald ring as I walked up the street back towards the hotel. I knew she was watching me every step of the way.

Once in the foyer I stopped moving at a passion-exhausted leisurely pace and rushed up to my room. Throwing my things into my bags, I looked once around the bedroom checking to make sure I had left no evidence of my identity. Then I went down to reception and paid the bill, in cash, as fast as I could. Within ten minutes I was in my trusted Volkswagen car and heading out of Munich for sunny Spain.

The following day I sold her ring in the Casino Nueva Andalucia in Marbella for about £7,000. I sold it to an Arab whom I had befriended. I could have got much more but I wanted the money there and then.

There was something of a sequel to this adventure. I told a few close friends about my success in her shop and they naturally enough made their way over to Munich to try for themselves. I was travelling with them but keeping very much in the shadows. 'This is an easy coup,' I had told them. 'You'll get some money here.' So, after travelling halfway across Europe they went inside the shop only to emerge about half an hour later.

'Was that easy, Morry?'

'What happened?'

'Easy, you said. Easy as hell. Not only wouldn't she show us one single piece but before we got inside the shop we had to show her our passports, identity documents, driving licences and nearly our birth certificates.'

One final question you may be asking. What did I feel like having to miss that passionate lovemaking session, which had been promised to me in the evening? I have only one answer and it is this. I wonder how she felt when she arrived at the hotel and found out I had gone?

King of Diamonds or Knave of Diamonds. What do you think?

In the 1980s I had a wig made in Australia by a theatrical costumier, a woman. It took three months to make and cost several hundred dollars. She took the hair out of my neck, blended it in and made me the most perfect wig which I've still got today.

Some years later it still fitted like a glove and I was enjoying a beautiful hot summer's evening in Paris where I frequented a restaurant which also housed the best gambling club in Paris, the Aviation Club de France. Top French gamblers and well-to-do people used to eat and gamble there. I became a member and I was staying at the Hôtel Maurice, my name in French, which was on the rue de Rivoli. A lovely hotel. I was very active at that time. I was all around Europe doing bundles and bundles of money. You name the town and I'll tell you the jeweller's shop in it. You name the country and I'll tell you all the towns with the jeweller's shops. I was living in Toronto at the time and I had flown over for a few weeks to meet some people there.

I had several thousand pounds in my pocket and I had gone to the Aviation Club de France for dinner about ten o'clock at night. I had spent the day at a jewellery fair where I got some money.

That night I wore the wig. You wouldn't know me in this wig, no one would know me. It was good for my work because it was such a first-class disguise. At two or three o'clock in the morning I am completely penniless, I have done every shilling, I've done Swiss dollars, Canadian dollars, American dollars, French dollars, my dollars, everybody's dollars. I thought, 'Argh. Here we go again.'

I come out, look in my pockets whereupon I discover I've got no money for a taxi even from the Avenue des Champs-Elysees, up near the Arc de Triomphe where the club was, down to the rue de Rivoli where the hotel was. So, I have to walk. It's about three o'clock in the morning, the Parisians are all sitting out drinking, listening to nice music and I'm thinking, 'What have I done to myself, what's going on here?', and I start to walk. I've done thousands and thousands of pounds and as I'm walking along my hand brushed my side pocket and there's some francs which total about a hundred quid. I think, 'I could have got a taxi,' but I'm halfway there, so I carry on walking.

As I'm walking and crossing over, I think it was the Place de la Concorde, I'm muttering to myself, and along comes a tiny little Fiat car. It sidles up alongside me, the window comes down, there's a beautiful girl in it and she says to me 'Hallo, cherie. Would you like to come home?' She's a hooker.

I looked at her and I thought, 'I've done every dollar. I might as well do the rest.'

'Where do you go?'

'I'm a few miles from home . . .'

'I'll tell you what I'll do,' I said. 'I'm staying in Room three one nine at the Hôtel Maurice, the rue de Rivoli, you come to me.'

'OK.'

Lovely. I carry on walking. I get to the hotel. I go upstairs. I think, 'If she comes she comes, if she doesn't she doesn't.'

As I closed the door, before I could get into the shower, there are three knocks on the door. I could hear, 'Hallo, cherie,' in a sexy quiet whisper.

In she comes and she was gorgeous. She says: 'We have fun, cherie,' in a really sexy voice.

She didn't mess about because she was experienced. She stripped off and she said: 'I must have the money.'

'There you are. Take those francs.' I'm going to be broke in the morning, might as well be broke at night and enjoy it.

'Come, cherie. We have a nice time.'

We get on the bed, she starts messing around with me and not before too long I'm very aroused and we wanna fuck.

'You lie back, darling,' she says, 'I take care of you.'

And I'm lying back on the bed but I forgot I've still got the wig on. 'Oh darling, you're lovely,' she's now saying, 'you're a handsome man, I like you,' and she's fondling me and caressing me and kissing me and obviously I'm getting a bit hot and excited. As I get excited I can feel the wig slightly slipping back off my head and she's kissing me and she's got my cock in her mouth and she's doing it to me and the more she's getting me at it the more I can feel the wig slipping. She's got her eyes closed, she's very experienced and she's giving me all the treatment.

Eureka! I've given her all that she wants in her mouth. As I've done that the wig slips off and falls onto the floor. The moment she's drained me of every bit of whatever I had in me she's opened her eyes and looked up at my face, both of us smiling in satisfaction. But as she's opened her eyes and – remember this is well gone three o'clock in the morning – she lets out one almighty scream of a type I've never heard before in my life.

She's gone to bed with a man with a lovely full head of hair and opened her eyes only to find a bald-headed guy who she's just given the most perfect blow job to. She doesn't know what's happened. She thinks somebody else has got in the bed or something, or there's two of us like a Jekyll and Hyde.

She not only screams but she runs off the bed, grabs the money, opens the door, in the nude, runs down the corridor in the nude, the most established hotel in Paris, screaming her head off.

I was laughing and laughing and laughing.

The next morning I walked down to the rue du Faubourg St-Honoré, the Bond Street of Paris. I went into a jeweller's shop with the wig firmly back in place, had no money and like a thousand times before, a woman came up to me.

'I'm looking for . . .'

'Oh yes. Sit down.'

She brought over a box of the most beautiful diamond bracelets of which I extracted two, shook hands with her, left and bid goodbye to France for a few months.

40

The Frying Pan

Later in life I went to this loony bin in Buckinghamshire, this psychiatric place in Grendon Underwood, and there was an author there – I believe his name was Tony Parker. He got permission from the Home Office to live in the prison. He wrote a book called *The Frying Pan* and I was in it as The Gambler. There was The Violent Man, who's now died, Jim Gilbert, there was The Junkie, and a whole host of characters. We got quite friendly. He asked me a question. 'Morris. If I was a judge and you came in front of me with your convictions what would you like me to do with you, other than send you to prison?'

I couldn't really answer him sensibly. I look upon it like this. If he had given me a chance, and I underline the word if, that magistrate, and not sent me to prison for my first offence, my life might have turned out better. But the magistrate was just an idiot and he sent me to prison. Tossing me in the jail, if he'd have only known, was the worst thing that could have ever happened. If he hadn't have thrown me in the jail I wouldn't have got up to all the pranks and tricks that I got up to after coming out of the jail. Any man could learn.

A friend of mine had a phrase: 'Do you know the worst punishment you could have in the world?'

'No.'

'A judge to sentence you to back horses for the rest of your life.'

Anyway, there I was in this psychiatric hospital with the doctors doing test after test on me to see if they could cure me of gambling.

This goes on for weeks until one day I am in the chief psychiatrist's office. It's a bleak room with a large desk and he's sitting in his chair thumbing through his papers. He asks a question, I give an answer, question answer. This goes on for hours and all the time I am watching his face. He keeps scratching his nose and furrowing his brow. All the time I am trying to stay one step ahead of him.

This is one of the country's top psychiatrists. This man, Bernard Marcus, has to give his opinion before any major criminal, murderer, lifer, you name it, is released from prison and he's dealing with Morry the Head. He looks just like Phil Silvers from the Sergeant Bilko shows and he's the cleverest man I ever came across. You would think he was the easiest man to con from the way he looks but you have this feeling that he's sitting there just reading your thoughts as though you were a book.

So, just when I thought the session was never going to end, he exhales a large sigh and scribbles something on his private notes, notes which the patients are never allowed to read. A minute later he pushes back his chair and stands up.

'Won't be a minute, Morry,' he says placing his hand firmly over the page he has just been writing on. 'I've got to have a quick word outside.' And with that he ups and leaves the room. Quick as a flash I lean forward and swing round his notes and read what I know he wants me to read.

Right at the end he has left a gap and then put down what seems to be a final statement.

'Morris Spurling is a lifelong gambler. After long and careful consideration I have reached the following conclusion about the prospects of him being able to live without gambling. Prognosis: Hopeless.'

I could have told him that weeks before when I entered the hospital.

41

The Sting

You do make some good contacts in prison. Out of one of them came The Sting.

The Sting originated in Wormwood Scrubs where I was spending a little time on remand for theft of an antique diamond brooch valued at about £20,000 which fell into my pocket out of a jewellers in Burlington Arcade in London. This was in the late eighties.

Whilst luxuriating in Wormwood Scrubs I was introduced to a gentleman who came from Brazil and was detained on some passport charges. He didn't speak English and I was asked to be the interpreter as I speak quite fluent French.

We got quite friendly and to my delight he was interested in buying diamonds. He'd heard of me and of my escapades from other inmates. At the end of the day I could see what I call 'A Move'. I saw some photos he had of his ranch in São Paulo and I gathered that he was a very wealthy individual. We agreed to meet one day in the future. The arrangements were to meet in the Portman Hotel in

Portman Square which I used to use quite a lot for break-fast.

He was a very distinguished character who disliked the English. He was extremely short-sighted and had several pairs of glasses. He told me he wanted to buy as many diamonds as I could get hold of to take back to Brazil, whereupon I thought of a sting.

I had a friend who had a jeweller's shop in the East End. The shop itself was not much – dirty, grey, nothing nice. It was in a very poor quarter of London but this Brazilian multi-millionaire who's got a ranch in Rio didn't know anything about the area, was nearly blind. I approached my friend who had the jeweller's shop and I said: 'Look. If you have a couple of hours off, leave the shop, give me the keys and let me put my own staff in the shop.'

He did trust me. One doesn't rob their own – it's honour amongst thieves.

'You leave for a couple of hours and take your two assistants for coffee somewhere. I'll give you quite a bit of money.' I explained what I was going to do. My friend agreed to this sting. I had to tell him the whole plan.

Now the man I was going to conduct the sting on was called Armand Atlan. I met him in the Portman Hotel and told him that I had approximately £100,000 of diamonds for sale at a very cheap price. He was overjoyed and we took a taxi from the hotel to the jewellery shop in the East End.

The taxi dropped us off at the shop and we made our entrance. In the front of the shop were two girls who I had been living with, stealing with and whatever with. As I walked in they said: 'Good morning, Mr Morris.'

In the back room was my best friend sitting with a big Havana cigar, a Savile Row suit and diamonds all over the desk. Well, Mr Atlan was very impressed. Behind my friend were bottles of champagne, whisky and scotch.

'Good morning, Morris,' says my friend.

I introduced him to Atlan and of course I spoke French.

Mr Atlan sat down at the desk and we deliberated on the sale of the diamonds. I put in front of him twenty or thirty packets of what were supposed to be diamonds but were in fact pieces of glass which I had bought in Woolworths. To my great surprise Atlan knew absolutely nothing about diamonds. He professed to be knowledgeable but I knew that he didn't know, which made it quite easy for me. After an hour's discussion we came to a price of round about £65,000. Of course, I'm wondering how the sale's going to be done.

He turned round to me and he said: 'If I can ring up my bank and give you a cheque they'll pay you.'

So I let him use the phone and he phoned up a bank which was in Cannon Street or Moorgate in the City, whereupon he wrote out a cheque, told me how to get there and I went to this bank while he waited in the shop.

I introduced myself in the bank. The manager called me into a strongroom.

'Mr Atlan's been in touch with me. How would you like the money?'

'All at once, please.'

He laughed. It was the denomination he meant.

And then came the money over the counter.

Well, I was broke and it was a million pounds to me. I got back to the shop within the hour, parcelled up the 'diamonds' for him and we left together for the Portman Hotel where we had a bottle of wine.

Upon leaving him I took another taxi back to the shop. There were my friends and the owner of the shop. They all looked at me and I said: 'Eureka!' I laid the notes on the table.

We cut up the money.

The story ended there for the time being.

*   *   *

Then I was approached in a betting office one day by what I call the local gangsters, in fact one was a stuntman on TV. This stuntman said: 'Oh, I don't like to see you. You have conned thousands of pounds off this fellow.'

'Yeah? And what business is it of yours?'

'We want . . .'

'I'm sorry. There is no money. And that's that.'

The reason I was so defiant was I knew that if he came across in a heavy manner I had my own heavies to deal with him. I heard nothing more until strangely enough about eight months later I walked into The Portman. Coming towards me was Armand Atlan. Of course, I froze, but Atlan was so short-sighted he walked straight past me without seeing me. And there endeth the lesson of the sting. But I found out that the £65,000 was like a cup of coffee to him, it didn't mean anything. Obviously, I reproached myself for not taking more. It was a hell of a lot of money at the time but it could have been much more because I didn't know how wealthy this man was. However, I did get a bit more money off him before bidding him goodbye.

He was a gambler and when we had got back to the hotel after the diamond sting he asked me if I could back a horse at Clare Fontaine in France for him. He had his own horses running over there. In this country you can't back horses in France but when he said he wanted five grand on it I told him I'd my own bookmaker who would accept it.

He gave me the five grand to put on the horse and I phoned up this bookmaker in another form of sting. I let Atlan hear the conversation on the phone and I put on the five grand. The horse won and I disappeared. I disappeared with his winnings. I had invented the bookmaker. In other words I phoned up myself to place the bet.

42

Going, Going, Gone!

For ninety pence every Tuesday midday you can get all the information about all the auction houses in this country and in Europe from *Antiques Trade Gazette*. And I've done every auction house in this country and a lot in Europe from the information coming from this paper. The auction houses were the easiest to do, because two days before the auction you have the public viewing. All the diamonds and jewels are on display and you can examine them. All the buyers can inspect them. They may be in cases but you ask for the number and they bring the case out and show the diamonds to you. By distraction, or by switching or by hoisting or by whatever plan you want to use, you can get what you're after.

For example, in the early 1990s I went up to Scotland when Christie's were having an auction and on view there was a three-carat stone for about twelve grand. I asked for it and the boy behind the counter gave it to me. It was in a box. I opened the box, took the ring out, gave him the box back. He put it away and then I went on to another number. He didn't even open it up to see if it was still there. Some of these people working there are so bored they're not concentrating properly. That's happened on numerous occasions.

One day in Bonham's in Montpelier Street opposite Harrods they had a Sunday view of expensive jewels. I walked in there and an American lady had a box out with all the lovely jewels, whereupon I stood next to her and I remarked: 'That's a lovely diamond you've got on.'

'Yeah, it is rather nice,' as she smiled at me. 'I bought it in Texas.'

As she said that I had my hand on another diamond which was next to it and just proceeded to walk out. It was worth fifteen to twenty grand. It was like taking candy from a baby.

One day I was reading through the jewellery magazines and I came upon an advert of a man called Dr Crott. He had the finest new and secondhand watches in the whole of Europe in his shop at Aachen in Germany. On one of my trips, I visited this shop and I could see he certainly did have the best watches you could ever come across. He knew me as Mr Jacobs. I tried to perform my acts in this shop but I just couldn't and then he told me he had a huge exhibition of watches and jewellery at the airport in Frankfurt. He thought I was a big buyer. I told him I would be coming to the exhibition.

On that day I got there very early. I drove over there with very little money, as per usual, and I arrived well before he did. The women there knew me from my earlier visit to the shop. They had the most gorgeous watches I've ever seen in my life. All the best makes were there: Vacheron Constantin, Patek Philippe, Rolex. I had arrived at the right time because the best time to get to any place is when they're just preparing and they're at loose ends and they've got all their stuff all over the place.

I had my eye on two diamond Vacheron Constantin watches.

'Can I have a look at those?'

'Well, Dr Crott's not here yet, but knowing you, Mr Jacobs, yes you can.' And they placed the two diamond watches in my hand whereupon I proceeded to get near the exit and I was just going to go. But something stopped me and I don't know what it was. It was just a sixth sense. As usual I was desperate, with no money.

The miracle of all miracles, I didn't go. As I was making towards the exit in came Dr Crott. He looked at me and at his two watches in my hand.

'I was thinking of buying these,' I said.

'Oh yes, they're lovely. Come on, have a drink.'

So it's a good job I didn't go out because I'd have bumped into him. It's fate. Fate rules everything.

'I'll be with you shortly,' said Dr Crott. 'Sit down.'

'Yes,' I replied and walked into the next room where there was a little bit of a gathering, a crowd round a man who was displaying diamond rings and watches and lots of nice stuff. So I got involved in it. I held up these two diamond rings which were worth ten or twenty thousand pounds.

'I'd like to see them in daylight,' I said. Now the man was from Berlin and he looked at me as if to say 'Who are you?' and Dr Crott said: 'That's all right. That's Mr Jacobs.'

Dr Crott didn't know anything about me except for the impression I caused with my big cigar and my Savile Row suit and crocodile shoes.

I walked to the exit to have a look at them in daylight and I walked on, got in my car and drove away – the proud possessor of a couple of diamond rings.

Funnily enough, there is a postscript to this. I drove from

Frankfurt as fast as I could to Calais. I still had the two diamond rings with me.

Somewhere down the motorway I was overtaken by half a dozen German police cars which all swooped on me. 'This is the end,' I thought, 'they know about it.'

But they didn't know about it. They stopped me purely for speeding. One big German took me to the nearest police station. Apparently it was an operation in which they had caught about half a dozen cars. Over there, for speeding, it's an instant on-the-spot fine. I had about forty quid and the fine was about eighty.

After arguing with them for some time during which I said I'd send it on to them, they let me go. Thank God they didn't search me!

I get back, I sell the rings, I do the money and it's the same old story. Like a washing machine, it goes turning round and round over the years, for sixty-eight years.

Anyway, about eighteen months later I go to a fair in Frankfurt and as I'm walking round the fair I see a young fellow looking at me. I can't place him, so I carry on walking round looking at the merchandise.

I placed the mystery stranger ten minutes later all right because two armed police officers stopped me with guns.

'Komm' mit.'

They took me to a little room and then I remembered. He was Dr Crott's son and he remembered what happened with the two diamond rings and I was arrested, put into prison and given a year's probation for it.

I believe in fate. Everything in life appertaining to me is fate, especially my game, searching for diamonds. Manchester George and I flew from Malaga to Bangkok. In the heat of Bangkok we were searching for jewellers. I couldn't find one.

I bumped into a rabbi in Bangkok. There can only be two rabbis in the whole of Thailand and I bumped into one whose brother owned a diamond factory. It's incredible. Now this is an absolute miracle. How do I bump into a rabbi in Bangkok? After speaking the few words of Hebrew that I knew he said: 'What are you doing here in Bangkok?'

'I'm looking for diamonds.'

'My brother has a diamond factory. Tell him I sent you.'

I go to the diamond factory and I steal a fifty-thousand-pound Caversham sapphire diamond ring. It's fate.

I'd booked into the hotel in Bangkok for a week and I left in a day because I'd got the prize there.

Another quick turnaround happened on a trip to Israel. The Swan and I arrived at three o'clock in the morning and left the same night. A most unusual occurrence in that country. What happened was that The Swan and I had an introduction to a diamond manufacturer, but he was in the Bourse in Ramat Gan and it was impossible to get in to without leaving your passport. So, as we were travelling on our own papers, we decided to leave on the next plane back to England.

We had some time to spare before leaving for the airport so we wandered into the Tel Aviv Hilton for afternoon tea. After a pot of tea, a pastry each and a couple of very small sandwiches up came the bill. It was equivalent to about twenty-five pounds in English money.

I looked at the bill and I was furious. The Swan says my face changed from peaceful to mad and all my pent-up frustration at coming all that way for nothing burst out.

'Bloody Ladbrokes,' I said in the loudest voice I could muster. 'They get all my money in London. Now I come here for a cup of tea and they rip me off here as well.' I was shouting at the waiter who, although he spoke good English, had absolutely no idea what I was going on about.

Ladbrokes the bookmakers firm had recently acquired all of the Hilton hotels outside America. So I was incensed that the bookies got my money and on that occasion without even having the pleasure of having a bet.

The Swan started laughing and eventually I too saw the funny side.

It was harder getting out of Israel than getting in. And *we're* two Jews. We underwent a stringent interrogation at the airport. Even though we had done nothing wrong I thought we weren't going to be allowed to go. The security is so strict there. That was one of the very few times we came home empty-handed.

The second time I had a gun stuck up my nose happened in Belgium. I relieved a shop in Antwerp of a diamond ring then went straight to Brussels, and decided to go into a high-rise apartment block which had a well-stocked jewellers. I was in the lift when all of a sudden a feller pulled out a gun and pointed it at me with the words: 'You were the man who stole a ring in Antwerp.'

The two shops, the one I was going to and the one I'd relieved of the ring, were combined and I didn't know it.

Baden-Baden is one the smartest towns in Germany. It has a wonderful casino and several marvellous restaurants among other attractions.

I was on my travels all over Europe with Tina from Canada. One day, while walking in the Square looking at the jewellers' shops in Baden-Baden, to my amazement I saw two loose diamonds sitting on a black velvet pad and a card on the pad which said: 'This is the property of Baroness Von Thyssen.'

Immediately I was attracted. It was a simple exercise to get hold of those diamonds. I had twenty or thirty false ones,

Cubic Zirconias, which fortunately included the exact sizes. So I did what I normally do and had 'The Dummy Run'. I walked in to see what it's all about but without any intention of doing anything. Tina came in with me. To everyone I looked like I was the sugar daddy and she was the glamorous model.

The next day we went back and a young man asked what I wanted. After telling him I was interested in Baroness Von Thyssen's jewels he put those diamonds in front of us. Tina was giving him the glad eye and the come-on treatment. He told me they were worth 50,000 Deutschmarks. Stuck in my top pocket were the two fakes. After five or ten minutes of talking my two false stones were now on the lovely black pad which had earlier been brought out of the window. Tina was smooching with the young assistant. I left saying I would need to go and get some money.

We left the shop with me trying not to laugh, it had all been so easy. I couldn't stop myself from glancing round and on doing so I burst into fits of laughter at the sight facing me. Clearly visible in the window of the shop was the assistant complete with bright yellow duster. What do you imagine he was doing but carefully dusting the glass. He was wiping the duster over the tops of my little fake stones, worth all of twenty quid. In my pocket were his stones worth twenty thousand pounds. For all I know the fake ones might still be there. At least there'd be no dust on them.

One operation was in Wiesbaden using 'The Switch'. I used to go abroad with hundreds of replica diamonds, the cubics: one carat, one half carat, two carat, round-shaped, pear-shaped, square-shaped, you name it. I had them all in case I ran into the right thing.

About five o'clock one afternoon I came out of the Wiesbaden Casino and I was desperate and when I'm desperate logic goes out the window. I don't care whether it's the Mafia after me, I just don't know what I'm doing, it's like a boy wanting food, if he's hungry he'll steal anything. I didn't have a penny on me.

I was friendly with a feller called Alfie Haines who helped in the next operation.

I had looked in a shop window where I spied a lovely two-carat stone and fortunately I already had the replica. I thought to myself, 'This'll be all right,' and so I went inside and the woman owner sat me down. She was very nice.

On the next table, within reach, was the telephone. It was just a little bit awkward for me to switch the stone. So I formed an idea.

'I'll be back tomorrow morning at nine o'clock.' I went back to the hotel and I packed my bags. I had the replica and I was ready to go. I phoned Alf, God rest his soul. He was the master of what they call 'The Jar Game'. The 'Jar' is a false diamond and he has done publicans and bookmakers all over the country. Alf would go into a pub and get friendly with the landlord. At the time he would be flashing an expensive diamond ring, usually a three-stone gypsy ring. After a while he'd say: 'Do you like this? I can get you one if you like.' He'd come in the following night with a real ring and say to the landlord: 'Here, take that away. I don't want no money now. You take it to a jeweller and have it valued.' The next night he would come back and the landlord would be all over him. He would hand over the money and stand him a drink. Now, after a while Alf would say: 'Show me yours against mine.' Both men would take the rings off their fingers and compare them. Alf would now switch the rings giving back his which was nothing more valuable than a two-bob piece of glass.

One thing about Alf, he was very punctual. If I said five past nine it was five past nine.

'Alf, if you phone this shop at five past nine tomorrow

morning and hold the lady on the phone I will get a very valuable stone.'

'OK.'

I got in the shop at nine o'clock, I sat down, she showed me the stone, I looked at the stone. The telephone rang as I have the stone in my hand. I knew it was Alf in London and I could hear him.

'Oh. Good morning.'

And as the lady turned her head and was talking I put down my worthless piece of diamond which cost about two quid and I finished up with a twenty grand piece, which had been the plan. Then I made my excuses to her, left, caught the train to Frankfurt and I was then in possession of a beautiful stone.

I flew in and out of Tokyo within the day returning home to Heathrow with another beautiful stone.

I went from Heathrow on Aeroflot via Moscow. When we changed at Moscow and went through the terminal all you could see were rifles and nobody smiled and nobody said hallo. It was the most horrible flight I've ever had. I picked Aeroflot because it was the cheapest. Serves me right. The Swan reckons there was nothing wrong with Aeroflot but I hated it. Different people, different memories.

I got into the high-class district of Japan which is called The Ginsha. And there I relieved a jeweller of a diamond worth approximately £20,000 and flew out the same day.

I thought there'd be a lot more but I was wrong. I was lucky to get this stone. But I was frightened about going back to the airport because all the police had swords down their legs. I was frightened that I might get stopped.

Once back in this country I sold the diamond and I was broke within a few days.

I was looking for money in this country and on the A1 I had

a near-fatal car crash. I know nothing about the car crash except if I was a cat I would be down one life for sure. They sewed my broken hip while I was in the ambulance.

Ironically, I broke my knee looking up a mini-skirt in London, on the same date a year later. Her skirt was up to her neck and she had a gorgeous pair of legs as long as the A5 so no one can blame me for that. The date was August 10 so I avoid August 10 these days.

Anyway, getting back to the car crash. I woke up in the Lister Hospital in Stevenage on a life-support machine. At the same time I was a man wanted by every jeweller in the country. I was hallucinating thinking I was in Tokyo because I had been there recently. The police had phoned my lady friend and said: 'We can't cut him out the car, he's dead.'

They did manage to get me out of the car and I'm still alive!

I've got pipes up my bum, up my nose, my ears and everything to keep me alive. So when my friend, Sue Donnelly, visits me the first question I ask her is: 'What plane did you catch to get here?' She thought I'd gone off my head. She'd only travelled from Northampton to Stevenage. And to cap all of that, resting next to me a couple of feet away in the adjoining bed is a man swathed in bandages, you just see his eyes and his nose, and who does he happen to be but none other than a Thames Valley policeman who has also just had a near-fatal accident. After a while he turns as much as he can in my direction and croaks a greeting: 'Are you all right, mate?' I chatter away, glad he doesn't know I'm more wanted than Lord Lucan.

To this day I don't know what happened. The two people in the other car weren't hurt. I was surrounded the next day by police all round my bed taking statements; being very nice and kind and sympathetic not knowing I was Morry the Head, thinking I was someone called Dennis William Hillyard. Morris

Spurling was temporarily living under another identity. I had met someone who sold me the identity for a thousand pounds. Well, of course this also started to cause problems.

The family of Dennis William Hillyard picked up the local papers and read that he had been in a car crash horror. It didn't worry the real Dennis. He was sitting at home watching the television, probably feet up on the sofa with a can of beer gawping at *Coronation Street*. But with newspaper headlines stating 'Dennis William Hillyard Critically Injured in Crash' the relatives reading the papers down in Bletchley rushed to the hospital and to my bedside.

'That's not him,' they said. 'That's not Dennis Hillyard.'

There they all are pointing at me. I'm supposed to be the uncle of all the kids and everything. They've rushed out the house and seen me instead.

So the police came back to see me after getting these worried calls from the relatives, some of whom were becoming seriously confused. But I am at death's door so on their arrival the nurse said: 'You can't disturb him, he's on a life-support machine.' The matter resolved itself when everyone discovered Mr Hillyard was at home and still alive and I was going to take some time to recover.

The name change came about when I first moved to Buckinghamshire. For three years out of four I was living as this man. Some people still know me as Dennis because they had always known me as Dennis Hillyard.

In one casino in Britain I use when I've got a quid or two they know me as Harold Kay, because I was living as Harold Kay before I became Dennis Hillyard. I had the Harold Kay driving licence. I bought that as well. Then I bought all the documents for Hillyard. I've got a friend who does passports and other documents, he's a master, the best in the world. He does it all to perfection.

The real Dennis Hillyard is a football coach in Bletchley.

But he'd never gone out of the country before in his life. So I bought all his ID. He is about ten years younger than me.

I've often been to bed with a woman who's been trying to arouse me as I've been reading the *Sporting Life*.

'Am I pleasing you?' she says.

'Yeah, lovely,' but I'm looking at the card for Leicester tomorrow. That's pleasing me more, trying to work out what's going to win. I do try to avoid mixing business with pleasure but sometimes it becomes a difficult task.

I'm on the phone in a London hotel with a problem. I had some jewellery on me and the man I regularly used to sell the stuff to was abroad, so here I am looking to sell abroad through another party. I natter away on the phone for a while and get a good suggestion.

Half an hour later I am in Church Street, going to Alfie's antique centre where I enquire very subtly who's the buyer. So somebody who I knew said: 'She's the buyer, over there.'

I looked to where he was pointing and this vision appears. She's either Iranian or Palestinian or something similar and a very good-looking girl she is with a lovely figure, big tits, which I always love. I go over to her. 'Would you like to buy a couple of things?'

'Let me have a look.'

We sat down together and our bodies brushed against each other, arousing me. She bought a couple of things from me. She was very nice to me and all the time she is giving me this lovely smile.

'Anytime you have anything, I'm a buyer.'

Bang. I have a car crash. Now I'm on crutches, not that it stopped me from working. I employed a driver to take me around the shops. He would put me into the car, drive me to the scene of the robbery, lift me out of the car, I would hobble up to the shop, go inside, do the business, hobble back and he would carefully place me back in the passenger's seat before making our getaway. Ironically, the crutches were a help to me. When you go into a jeweller's shop on crutches it arouses a little bit of sympathy.

This all went on for quite a while. One day we're back in London, as usual I was broke, still on crutches, but I had a couple of diamond rings and went back in to see her and she bought again.

One thing led to another and I started to chat her up.

'You're a nice person,' I told her.

'I am married,' she says.

'Would you care for a drink one night?'

'Perhaps, when I finish work.'

I knew she wanted to.

Crutches or no crutches, I was broke and I was in trouble and I was scheming and plotting and thinking and I thought to myself: 'I'll use a scam with her.'

I walked in one day without any diamonds but with an idea of how to get some money off her. I had concocted a plan involving two fictitious American buyers supposed to be holed up in the Hilton Hotel, who wanted to buy top quality antique jewellery, just the kind of stuff which she had. I told her all about it.

'Can't they come here?'

'No, they're too busy. They're in the film business. They've got a couple of bimbos with them and they want to impress them.'

'Shall we go there?'

'That'll be a good idea,' I reply, as she swallows the bait. So we made an appointment.

I knew exactly what I was going to do. Now, I'm on crutches, remember. At some stage during the conversation her hand went over mine and mine went over hers and I thought 'Aye, aye, this is it.'

The next stage of the plan was to get hold of a friend of mine who's known as The Rat.

So I'm describing the plan to The Rat. 'I want you to get a car and at a certain time of the day I want you to draw up your car at the back entrance of the Hilton and wait for me to come out. I'll be on crutches. I want you to help me into the car and just drive and you'll get some money.'

'Lovely,' he says.

We arranged the time and I then arranged the time with this lovely lady to get in her car to drive to the Hilton. My plan was as we arrive at the Hilton I'll say, 'Darling, you drop me off.' I'll go through the front entrance, tell her I'll meet her in the St George's Bar but I was going to go right through the back with the beautiful jewellery, into the car and away.

The day of reckoning came. My two fictitious characters are there, it's round about midday, it's a nice hot day and she's wearing a lovely blouse which I can see through. I hobble up to her on crutches.

'What have you got?' I ask.

'Will this do?' she replies, opening a box full of beautiful rings, five grand, eight grand, two grand, ten grand. I thought, 'Wow. This is it.'

So we get in the car in Church Street, outside the supermarket. She helps me in the car with my legs and she's wearing a lovely short skirt and she gets in the car and we start it up. As she puts it in gear she puts her hand on my leg.

'Darling,' she says, 'shall we really go to the Hilton?'

I was astounded. So I said: 'I think we'd better, don't you?'

I looked at her and she looked at me and we were so close together in the car that I couldn't stop myself from putting a hand on her breast.

'Oh,' she says, 'that's lovely.'

I said: 'I think you're lovely.' But I'm more interested in her little box of diamonds.

As we're going down Park Lane she's stroking me all over the legs.

'You're making me excited, a man on crutches,' I complain.

She laughs. 'Don't you think we should go somewhere before we go to the Hilton?' she suggests. 'Then we can have fucky-fucky.'

I'm interested in the diamonds although by now she's getting me right at it. She's got her skirt right up and I've got my hand in between her legs.

I don't know what to do now. I don't know whether to have a fuck or get the money. But I thought I ought to get the money. I can always have a fuck somewhere. She's taken off the Rolex watch on her hand and put it in the box as well. She wants to sell that too. Oh, and I really could've have given her a fuck, even going down Park Lane. She was truly nice. She kissed me and said: 'I really think we ought to go somewhere and do something.'

'Yes. But later, we'll have a drink.'

So now she's pulled into the forecourt of the Hilton and there's nowhere to park, thank God. I don't want her parking.

So what happened was, I said: 'Well, darling, give me the box. I'll go into the hotel and I'll see you in the St George's Bar.'

'All right, darling.' She's given me the box of rings and I haven't got a shilling. It's exactly the time that The Rat is supposed to be at the other exit. All I have to do is hobble through the Hilton, go past the lifts to reach The Rat and safety. Anyway, her skirt's now round her neck, she's panting for a fuck. 'Shall we book a room?' she asks me.

'No. We'll do it afterwards, darling.'

'All right. Be careful.' She's playing with me and I'm all excited.

'I'll park round the corner,' she tells me.

'OK.' And I've hobbled into the Hilton. Well, fuck the crutches. I was going through the Hilton like Linford Christie. I'm hobbling as though I'm in the paraplegic sports. I'm flying down the corridor. I don't want her to park the car and catch up with me.

I get to the end and now I'm looking for The Rat and there's no car. The sweat's beginning to pour down on me. I've got this lovely box and I'm on my crutches. Now what do I do? Where is that fucking Rat? He's nowhere. I don't know what to do.

Where can I go? I'm hobbling down Hertford Street, into Park Lane, into Piccadilly, out of breath, I can't walk, I can't get a taxi, busy, busy, busy. I fly into the Meridian Hotel opposite Simpson's. I sit down. I'm exhausted. I look at the box and there they are, the lovely beautiful diamond rings and a Rolex watch.

Time passes and I find a buyer who comes over and takes the stuff off me. I get a nice bit of money for those goods.

The next day The Rat phones me.

'Where were you?'

'Oh, dear. I went in the betting shop. Have I got some money to come then?'

'No you haven't. No show, no dough.' That was the end of it. But the aftermath were the screams all over London.

She screamed. She went to the police and I found out afterwards she is one of the biggest crooked buyers in London plus the fact this happened to her before for about a quarter of a million pounds – by somebody I know well who's now in France and can't come back to this country.

She complained to the police. But they took no action.

She was crooked, desperate for a fuck. I was crooked, desperate for her rings. She wanted a fuck in Park Lane in the midst of all the traffic. Can you believe it?

43

A Ferryful of Gold

The easiest thing to sell in the world, even easier than diamonds, is gold. And strangely enough for ten years I switched from diamonds to gold because I had done all the best places for the diamonds.

Gold is a better currency, which makes it easier to sell. Gold is also a much easier commodity to steal in the first place than diamonds. There's no trace with gold, as there is with diamonds. You just sell it as scrap or you sell it to private individuals. You don't even have to melt it down first. And for ten years I dealt mainly with gold because gold is the most requested commodity in the world. If I'd had any sense I'd have bought a country mansion, a penthouse flat in Mayfair, two Rolls-Royces, a Ferrari to impress the girls and a couple of holiday homes and a Mediterranean yacht. My sons would go to Eton and I'd mix with lords and top politicians. And to make it all seem above board I would also have bought a few legitimate businesses. Many have done so and now they're among the most respected businessmen in Britain, with seats on all the top committees and their wives lecturing young men about the need for responsibility.

The most successful criminal type is the so-called 'Mr Big' who sets up crimes and gets other people to do the work for him. Some could have taken a risk in smuggling drugs or arms, of which I don't approve and have never got involved myself, and be living peacefully every after. A nice little country cottage would do me just fine. In this country, people respect money and they don't ask questions about where it came from. Nowadays I could tell them I won the National Lottery. But I'm a gambler and what goes into my pocket on a Monday morning comes out by Monday afternoon.

Well, this gold thieving didn't half prove promising. I got gold from all over Europe. On one trip I had so much gold sitting in Calais that I had to telephone Britain for three people to come over and bring it back for me. Three people I trusted met me in Calais. They put the gold around their legs, their arms, their necks and just came over on the ferry with it because I couldn't carry it all. Out of that one Calais trip I reckon I would have got twenty grand. Now twenty grand's worth of gold is a lot of gold. I sold it to a dealer. If you walk into a dealer with any amount of gold they'll give you the fixed price for that day, no questions asked. You see notices outside the shop: 'We buy gold.' I picked out the lovely pieces I wanted and sold the rest as scrap for convenience so I got paid all in one go. Now the real shop value of that gold was much higher. At a guess about a hundred grand, maybe more.

If you walk into a shop and ask a man for a gold chain or a bracelet the difference between that and walking into a shop and asking a man for a diamond is enormous, because everybody wants gold chains or bracelets, whereas diamonds sometimes make the hairs on his neck stick out; they make him much more security conscious.

So after going all round this country taking gold chains and bracelets from every shop, I decided to go to Europe.

I used to put the car on the ferry, arrive in Calais, work out a route, then spend a week away at a time. At the end of the week I had thousands of pounds' worth of gold, £20,000 to £25,000 a week of gold. I couldn't move, you couldn't walk for the weight of the stuff. This was mostly by standard 'Palming'. I even went as far as East Germany – Leipzig, Dresden, Mainz. I was in the former East Germany without knowing I was there funnily enough, because there's no border now.

I'd sell part for scrap and part privately. I've got buyers. Everyone wants gold. Buyers all over the country. On my last trip I arrived in Calais with about fifty quid in the world. My first stop was Lille, because I know the road very well, in between Calais and Aachen. It was nine o'clock in the morning and there was a big jeweller's shop being refurbished with a sign up saying: 'No Business Today. Not until another two or three days' time. We're refurbishing.'

The manager was at the door and saw me looking.

'Can I help you?' he asked.

'You're not open, are you?'

'Yes, sir. If you want something we can help you.'

I said I would like a couple of gold chains and bracelets to take to my customers in some other town I concocted on the spot. He brought out some trays of eighteen-carat gold with some diamond rings in them. And at five past nine that morning I must have had three of the best diamond rings that were in the shop. There I was stealing gold but just couldn't escape from being offered diamonds.

It's all a fluke, being in the right place at the right time. He wasn't even open and I secured the prize.

Did I feel guilty about that? No, is the answer. To me it's like a profession. It was just a day's work.

But it was fate. If I hadn't been outside that shop at that particular time I wouldn't have been invited in.

I used to go over to mainland Europe twice a month. The total amount which I have stolen in gold comes to an absolute fortune. It could be as much as five million pounds. That's what it was worth in the shops, not what I got for it.

I wish I had that money now. Forget the money I earned out of diamonds, which was tens of millions, I could do with what I earned from the gold. Now I haven't even got the price of a fare to London.

So fancy that. After working with a string of girls I ended up using a string of boys to help me out. Not the same attraction and useless as distraction but they were very helpful in the job. After working the Continent I used to get back to Calais where I would book into a certain hotel from where I would phone the boys and get them over on the ferry, pay their expenses, give them perhaps a hundred quid each, buy them a beautiful meal and they came back wearing all the gold under their clothes.

These were boys that I'd met and trusted and knew. It was like a Sunday trip. I mean, everybody goes to France on a Sunday now on the ferries to do their shopping.

I didn't entirely give up on the diamond side of the business, however.

I went on Eurostar to Paris for the day. I was being financed for this trip, meaning someone was putting up the expenses in return for a profit, so I had to return with some good money. Businessmen don't like laying out good money for no return and with me, if I fail to do my job, they automatically think I've done the money in a casino, betting shop or at the races. So I caught the 08.23 from Waterloo, with three hundred pounds' expenses for the day. A hundred and fifty-five pounds for the train gets me to the Gare du Nord. I got on the Metro with three calls in mind. I arrived at the most fashionable district in Paris which is the Place Vendôme, rue de la Paix, and promptly go into Cartier's. I tried to do something there but I wasn't worried because all the time I knew I had an ace up my sleeve. No luck in Cartier's, I went to Chaumet, no luck there either. I'd done these two firms before for thousands and thousands of pounds all over the world. Ring up 'No Sale' at Chaumet but still I have this ace to play. The train was coming back at five o'clock. So I went to the ace, a gold shop. Over the years I've had a lot of money out of this gold shop but they don't recognise me. Every time I go in they think I'm a different person, with the wig, without the wig, with the trilby, without the trilby. I went in and before you could say 'Jack Robinson' I have got a lump of gold on me and all of it eighteen-carat beautiful chains. I got money, not a lot of money, but it was Christmas money, helped me out a bit, two or three grand in gold chains.

I caught the train home and that was it. And that's how life goes on.

44

Morry, You're Nicked!

In 1993 I was in the money. I was working away quite happily both here and abroad, when the time came for a spell in Exeter Prison. I'd done hundreds of jewellery shops in the previous year. All of that came to an end when I was picked up for stealing gold from a jewellers in Devon. I ended up being given twelve months.

I had taken £1,200 worth of goods from a jeweller's shop in Okehampton and been caught on the video. A picture was put out and an alert which didn't really bother me. I was no longer in Devon, but to my great misfortune an off-duty police officer was on holiday in Torquay. He picked up the newspaper one day and instantly realised it was me, The Head, by the modus operandi of the job – the stick, the hat, the limp, the educated London voice. But I was still free and completely unaware of what had gone wrong back in Devon.

So I am waltzing down Oxford Street on a bright sunny day without a care in the world with the money from the Devon job long gone. I decide on the spur of the moment that it is about time I bought myself some new clothes. I was not as well off as in the old days when I would have been heading down towards Savile Row. Marks and Spencer would have to suffice for now. Into the store I go and wander around for a few minutes until I find myself in the suit section trying to make up my mind what to buy. All of a sudden I hear a voice behind me.

'Morry. You're nicked!'

I turned round and it was another off-duty policeman. This time a City of London police officer who knew that I'd been on the run for three and a half years from Birmingham where I was wanted. I was in the wrong place at the wrong time.

He was buying a lightweight suit to go to Uganda where he was going to do a month's work. Cruel fate for me was that day but in a way it turned out it was the best thing that could have happened to me.

During my time on the run, posing as Dennis Hillyard, I did nearly every shop in this country and abroad. If that hadn't happened in April, in May the local Devon police had submitted me to go out on the BBC's Crimewatch. They were looking for Morry the Head and couldn't find him. If I had gone out on the May edition of Crimewatch, jewellers would have come from all over the country. I would have had hundreds and hundreds of charges as opposed to the four that I did have.

Whilst in the nick in Devon with a few thousand pounds that I had left, I gave every shilling to the bookmakers in Buckinghamshire, by means of the telephone. I was sending the money out of the prison to the bookmakers for what they call a deposit account. Once the bookmakers received the money I was then backing horses on the telephone and I went broke. Eleven thousand pounds down the drain and I never got out of the nick. I got down to my last five grand in the whole of the world and even that went in the end. So despite being in the prison I'm gambling and I'm going broke.

Nearly a year after gaining my freedom once again I was in trouble and had occasion to write this letter to my new solicitor:

'I was released from Exeter jail last October, that's 1994, after serving a twelve-month sentence. I was on probation for two months after my release, which I successfully served, and I was placed into a housing association hostel where I've been living ever since, for over a year. This association normally has a strict rule whereby three to six months is the maximum period of stay. During this three to six months' time I tried to get housed both by the Milton Keynes Housing Association and South Northants' Housing Association but because I had no ties with the area they would not accept me or house me. My only chance to leave the hostel where I am and get my own home was in the private sector.

'I tried very hard for this but it was of no consequence. In the meantime around August of this year I received notice to quit from the hostel because I had overstayed the normal stay. I was desperately worried as to what I was going to do because I may have been put into the street at sixty-seven years of age. I'm on income support getting £67.10 per week and I supplement this by going to early morning markets all round the country as in the past I have been a market worker. All the time I have been at this hostel life has been very hard and I steered away from crime. But when I got the notice to quit I was extremely worried as I had to find the initial money to get a home in the private sector after which the DSS would have contributed to the rent.

'On a Saturday morning in September I decided to go up to Darlington to see some friends and perhaps they might have helped me since I've known them for years. I arrived at Thirsk on the A1 to stop, have a coffee and use the toilet. About a mile outside of the town a police car had started following me and I was a little bit anxious until I realised I never had my seatbelt on. And the reason I didn't have my seatbelt on was that I get trouble with my upper arm and shoulder due to an horrific crash I had in 1992. I was on a life-support machine for days at Milton Keynes General Hospital.

'Anyway, I pulled into the market square in order to use the toilet and have a cup of coffee and the policeman who had followed me stopped the car and he came up to me and he said: "Sir. You've been driving without your seatbelt on. Please don't do it again."

'I told him the reason why it's very difficult to wear it owing to my shoulder injury. He warned me it was an offence and I said: "Thank you very much I won't do it again. I'll put it on."

'And he left me.

'I went to the toilet and as I came back I noticed a jeweller's shop. Again, I stress this was not a premeditated act on my part. I went into the jeweller's shop and I looked at some chains, some gold chains. In the back of my mind was the terrifying thought that if I didn't get any money within a couple of weeks I would be kicked out of the hostel and I would be homeless.

'On a mad impulse I put five chains in my pocket and I walked out. I knew I had done wrong and I was terribly, terribly worried. For one instant I was going to go back into the shop and say: "Look, I'm sorry." But I thought to myself, I'll be in trouble if I do and I'll be in trouble if I don't. And all I did it for was to get the money to put down a deposit on a flat. I suppose my logic went out the window.

'I didn't proceed further north to Darlington. I turned the car around and I went down to Ripon and sold one chain for £80 and then I went to Harrogate where I sold four chains for £190. So for the paltry amount of £270 I have finished up in this mess.

'I drove south and on the way and in order to try, now that I have done it, to get the thousand pounds or whatever was needed to move into a flat for a month and a month's rent I lost the money en route. By the time I got back to the hostel I never had a penny.

'This has been the story of my life every since I can remember. Three or four days later I was detained by the Milton Keynes police on behalf of North Yorkshire police.

'I was arrested and held for approximately two days in custody until I was brought back to Northallerton Police Station where I made a full confession.

'I understand now that I'm going to be charged with two additional charges of deception, i.e. in selling the chains I have by law deceived the buyers that they were mine. I also understand that the police believe everything I have said about the story but unfortunately the chains were sold on by the actual buyers. So all in all for £270 I've got myself in a jam again after a year out of prison just living a very sad, morose life. I have no home and am living in one room all the time which has been like a prison.

'I would now like to give you some background which I hope is relevant to my present situation.

'I have served many long sentences both here and abroad for similar offences to Thirsk, purely in order to have money to gamble with. I have had treatment for gambling. I have seen specialist doctors, I was one of the early members of Gamblers' Anonymous. Where gambling is concerned logic goes out of the window. I just lose control. I've gambled every shilling away, I've lost family, friends, homes, businesses because of my compulsion.

'I am sixty-seven years of age. I've had two major operations in the past four years. As I've already mentioned, there was the car crash from which I was cut out of the car by the emergency services, and then I broke my knee so I suffer very badly and am registered disabled. During the last four years of living in Milton Keynes I have befriended a family, Sue and Steve, who are very close to me.

'I'm treated like a member of the family and they are very near and dear to me. They're very upset at my position. They've given me lots of help in the past and are quite willing to speak for me at court whenever the date shall be.

'I've come to a time of life when I am penniless, no great hopes, except that I'm in the middle of writing a book with a journalist friend of mine, Mr Paul Drewitt, who thinks my story should be exposed both for myself and other people who've lost their way through gambling. I am the epitome of a sad gambler. This is a compulsion that only a gambler would admit to and knows about. People who don't gamble can't understand the mental make-up of a gambler. I've sold the overcoat off my back, the lights on the walls. I hope that if I ever get to finish this book it will benefit other, mainly younger people, advising them not to follow in my footsteps. Prison has ruined me, it's destroyed my whole life. I've been described in court as a sad figure. I suppose I am sad, I'm completely alone and apart from the Donnellys and Mr Drewitt himself I have no friends due to the fact that I have abused them all for want of gambling.

'Days I can go without food in order to gamble. It's just a sickness. But I would like to say, without craving sympathy, if I hadn't had notice to quit from the hostel I would never have committed this offence as I've gone a year from coming out of prison being a normal citizen, however hard it may be.

'It's quite obvious that if I'm sent back to prison for this offence my life will not be worth a candle. If I lose the love and friendship of Sue and Steve because of being incarcerated then life's got no meaning at all. I realise that what I did was wrong and the only thing I can say is that it was on the spur of the moment and I don't know what came over me. But the notice to quit had really upset me.

'I've never had a chance. I've always been sent to jail. I find the most difficult period in life is the aftermath of a jail sentence because I've had nowhere to live. I've had to go into hostel after hostel and at the age of sixty-seven it's not very appealing.

'It's quite obvious that at my age, or at anybody's age, I don't want to go to prison. Social workers and welfare workers in the past have canvassed on my behalf for me not to go to prison and if solicitor and counsel can argue that I would respond to any other sentence, i.e. probation, or a suspended sentence, which I've never had, I would abide by the rules or conditions. The lengthy spells I've spent in prison have in fact made my life worse, made me morose, depressed and very lonely and I ask for the chance to be dealt with in a way other than custodial.

'At my age I'm terrified of going back to jail for a stupid act such as I have committed and beg the court to give me a chance.'

The outcome of that was that I was given that chance. It was a wise decision to put me on probation because it stopped me from stealing diamonds and gold and other jewels. I wish I had had the same treatment at the other end of my life, it might have saved me from a life of crime.

45

One Room in a Hostel

A lot of people ask about how much I have enjoyed this life of gambling. It doesn't annoy me but it irritates me in a way. Of course it's not been enjoyable. Enjoyment is kids running about at home, dogs by your feet, a nice fire. I've got no place to live, I'm ashamed of myself. The only enjoyment, actually, is on that spur of the moment when I'm gambling. When I'm betting on the wheel, or the horse, or the dice, I'm oblivious to anything else in life except that moment.

These days people don't dress to go out but I used to dress to go to the Ritz, or Crockfords or wherever. When I used to walk through the entrance of wherever it was, casinos mainly, always it was 'Good evening, Mr Spurling.' The adrenaline starts running and I'm on cloud nine, I'm hyped up. Ah, that's wonderful, going into a casino. I love it, I still do. I love the aroma, the environment, I just like being there. If I've got to gamble I'd rather gamble in a casino than at the racetrack or the dogs or anywhere else, there's no atmosphere there. But in a smart casino there's the excitement, the buzz, the aroma, it's like a woman to me. All my troubles, all my debts, nothing matters bar red or black, high or low, odd or even, at that moment in time nothing counts. My head'll hurt after but it doesn't hurt then.

I only want to gamble. I don't want to hold a conversation. That drives me insane. I don't talk to anybody when I'm in the casino, I just gamble.

I've won lots of money gambling, won in casinos, won at racetracks. At casinos I've won fortunes, particularly at Baden-Baden.

I won tens of thousands one time at Baden-Baden. Normally, when I'm in a casino, I'm like a horse with blinkers on. I'm not thinking of anything else. I go to a casino to win. As I walk into a casino I get an erection, I get a sexual stimulant. I'm buzzing, I'm alive. I can't wait to get in to cash my money to play. Only if I've gone broke do I become a socialite in a casino. Then I start looking at girls and I want to fuck or I want to talk or I want to borrow money. But while I've got units on me I'm in that casino to win. I'm the same in a betting shop. If I was surrounded by naked women I wouldn't notice. I can be the rudest man in the world. People have said 'Hallo' to me and I've ignored them because I'm only interested in what's going to win the two o'clock at Lingfield. In fact it's been said that you cannot talk to me in racing hours. I'm concentrating on what I'm doing. What you want to say to me, tell it to me before the first race or after the last race, then I'm sociable, then I'm a normal person.

In casinos I play the first available table I get to, blackjack, baccarat, dice, roulette, it's whatever table fate destines me to play at, whatever I come to. Say it's roulette, then I get a notion in my head, I don't know where it comes from, red, black, high, low, odd, even, you name it and the first instinct I get in my brain I play. There's no such thing as a system, I don't play a system. It's like doing the National Lottery. Just pick a few numbers, that's what happens. I don't win as much as I lose but I've won. I've won lumps of money. I haven't won as much at gambling as I've earned at thieving diamonds and jewels.

The biggest wins I've had in casinos came when I was forced to play against high-rollers. You've got to have a lot of money in the pot to get into one of these games and the losses can be truly horrendous.

It's all fate. One morning in New York I found myself in East 47th Street where I walked into a shop. What did I see but a huge box of diamonds waiting to be shipped to Saudi Arabia. When I asked the man if he had any others he turned to look into the safe and I helped myself to the box that he had on the table. It's sheer fate and being in the right place at the right time.

Also, you must have the nerve to do it. My hand goes out automatically. I've been into wholesale manufacturers in New York, I've given cheques, I've stolen millions. This is not a bragging enterprise, because I'm a fool. Right now, nearly seventy years old, I don't have a penny after possessing millions and millions of pounds' worth of diamonds. Each big robbery might be equivalent to what a salaried person, a professional person, might expect to earn in a year. It's not been a Great Train Robbery nor a Brink's-Mat affair. Rather it's been a consistent, fifty years of steady jewellery theft. Every day I've earned what professional people might expect to get in a month.

Take this country, for example, before I retired. I'd just jump in the car with twenty quid, go to Scotland, to Wales, go all over and just steal diamonds and sell them, gamble in the betting shops on the way. I could be away for weeks earning fortunes. That's what it's like. There is no town in this country, in the whole of Great Britain, that I haven't been to and haven't stolen jewellery from. For me, jeweller's shops are like cashpoint machines. I've gone to shops where I've stolen fifty quid. I've been to shops where I've stolen fifty grand, it's all fate. It's being in the right place at the right time.

I owe fortunes. I tear my little bit of hair out some days when I've got money. Before the last court case I found myself with about £1,700 quid in my pocket, after doing whatever it was. I hadn't had that for ages. A miracle happened. It was the end of the month. So I paid the phone £280, the car £440 which gave me another four weeks' breathing space. I'm left with £1,000. I don't know who to pay first, I was just in a terrible state. I'm not inventing this as an example, it's the truth. I owe so much I don't know what to do. So I thought to myself, 'Oh dear, who do I pay?' Some sixth sense got hold of me. I thought: 'Oh fuck it, I'll pay George.' I drove to London and I gave a man £850 that I owed him. And the reason I gave it to him in preference to the other people was that during the time I owed it to him, for about five weeks, he never once asked me for it. He never drove me mad for it.

He said: 'Thanks very much.'

I left myself with £140, which I lost. So now I'm broke. But at least I got rid of one debt, paid that, right. In the meantime, I owe someone else chunks of money, which I can't pay at the moment, I owe another man £1400 who phones me every day for it.

I pipedream. I'm like Walter Mitty. I keep thinking I'll wake up with three or four hundred quid and I'll back five or six winners but I don't, I go broke every time. The other day I had £400. It went in an hour.

It just goes and I wake up broke again with a sore head. I just don't know what to do. And I'm terrified at the thought that at 68 years of age I'll fall by the wayside and get pinched again.

One afternoon recently I was due to ring someone at seven

o'clock. We had made an arrangement. Well it was five o'clock, I'd just come out the betting shop. I don't know why I went in there, because I had no money. I had nothing to do until seven. What are the alternatives until then? I had a cup of coffee somewhere and took stock of myself and tried to think, 'What is there to do?'

I had to ring him at seven. That means I had to go round there at half past seven. What do I do between five o'clock and half past seven in Milton Keynes? No flat, nowhere to sit down on a couch. If I go back to the room where I live I've got to sit on the bed. I'm talking to myself over a cup of coffee.

This life has led to a man who has nowhere to go, no chair to sit on, no friends, nothing to do, at five o'clock in the evening.

These days my only buzz is when I get the *Racing Post* and the *Sporting Life*. In the morning, I go to John Lewis's for my coffee and two slices of toast, if I've got the two pounds to buy it. First of all I steal the papers. I go to a shop and I take the *Racing Post*, the *Sporting Life* and the *Daily Telegraph*. I love the *Telegraph*. Now I've got those three papers, I go and have my coffee and toast. I don't want anybody in the world to speak to me. I'm out of this world reading the *Racing Post* and the *Sporting Life*. I am the happiest man in the world looking at those papers. Then I'll look at the *Telegraph* to see what happened in life and I'll look at the crossword, kid myself I'll do two or three clues. Then throw that away and go back to the *Sporting Life* and the *Racing Post*. Nobody in the world could speak to me. I don't want to know if there's been an earthquake in Fuengirola, if there's been a goldrush in Siam, if John Major's had twins with Margaret Thatcher or if World War Three's started. I don't want to know about anything except the *Sporting Life* and the *Racing Post*. I'm working out all the form, seeing what's what, the bets and everything, whether I've got money in my pocket or whether I haven't. I just must have the *Sporting Life* and the *Racing Post*. It's like a cocaine addict must have his fix. I must have them.

I've found a new place, BHS. You can have two slices of toast and marmalade and coffee for £1.80p and the girl gives me a lovely smile in the morning. She now knows I'm the regular.

One morning she said: 'You'll have to send a doctor's certificate if you can't make it one morning. You're always here.' I've got my little table in the corner and no one touches me, no one interferes with me. That's a half hour every morning.

Why I'm reading it without money in my pocket I don't know. I don't pay for the papers. I cheat for the food. If I go into a Motorway Service Station I get chicken and chips, a coffee and a sweet and cheese and biscuit and I don't go to the till, I go out the back way, so I eat for nothing. Instead of paying seven quid I eat for nothing. Big time Charlie Potatoes, me. Thousands and thousands on the horses and dogs, can't pay seven quid for a meal.

So. I'm trapped.

These are things people need to know about. The other day I never had a pound. I went into Marks and Spencer's and didn't know what I was doing. I had a bag. I put cheese, wine, fruit into it and I walked out, never paid for it. Man's had thousands, gambled all over the world, finest hotels, finest casinos, walked into Marks and Spencer's and got fifteen quid's worth of food and walked out.

My friend Brian has had lottery money. He's had more than me and I've had fortunes. He's had double fortunes. He was busted and nicked. What do you think he was nicked for? A tin of fish in a supermarket. Stealing a tin of fish. Wasn't even the best fish, it was salmon in brine. It's pitiful, isn't it?

*   *   *

Can get in my car tomorrow morning because thank God it's Wednesday and I've got sixty-five pounds to come. At nine o'clock I go to the Post Office and I get sixty-five pounds. I'm a millionaire. I'm talking a lot of shit but I feel like a millionaire. I put fifteen quid's worth of petrol in the car, leaves me with fifty quid. Now where do I go and what do I do? The lunatic in me would have a thirty-quid bet but I mustn't because I'll have no food. Now what do I do? How do I live? How do I get my money for the car and the phone? I don't know. Crime? I don't know what to do. Sometimes I think I might just as well get some tablets and end my life. But I haven't got the courage and I don't know where to get the tablets.

I never had a shilling last week. I was starving, to be honest. A pal gave me a couple of hundred quid. I said: 'Arthur. How am I going to pay you back?'

'Don't worry about it.'

He phoned me today and asked, 'Are you all right?'

'Arthur. I could burst into tears at any minute. I just don't know what to do. Unless I get a home to settle down in I'll be seventy shortly and homeless or stuck in one room.'

He didn't know what to say to me and I don't know what to do.

I keep thinking about my childhood now. I could have everything I wanted. I could have a new suit every day, a new coat every day. I could have new shoes every day. I had a motor car when I was four, a toy motor car to sit in. My life was too good, I could have everything. At the click of my fingers I could have anything. I think that was my undoing. There was no such word as 'Can't'.

I believe that, bless them, my parents contributed, unfortunately, to my downfall by giving me everything I wanted. That's what I believe. Had they taken a sterner line with me life may've been different. Had the magistrate not sent me to prison, life may've been different.

There are a lot of people doing what I do in the gambling game, especially today. In today's day and age when every day a new possibility to gamble is coming out, day after day after day after day. Women are gambling, children are gambling, no matter what it is. It's becoming part of the national psyche. You see, it's hard to moderate gambling. It's expanding so much, gambling. In a matter of years, four, five or six, maybe shorter, this country will be like Las Vegas. That's what I think. I believe this country is coming to it by being able to watch so many sports on satellite television and gamble on the results. Not to mention the Lottery. Ten years ago what was the evidence of gambling on the high street? A shop front with no windows. You weren't allowed to look in and watch this dreadful activity taking place, this ruination of man happening in the high street but beyond your vision.

Now you can't get away from it. They're inviting you in. There's an attraction, prime time TV, eight o'clock, BBC1, Saturday night.

Coral's shop in Milton Keynes is a just one example. How many hours do I spend in there? You wouldn't walk into a butcher's or a baker's if you didn't need to go in there. You don't need to go into Coral's but it looks so attractive you go in. And once you're in, you're hooked. Make no mistake, you are hooked. A lot of that is due to technology. Of course, in my day we never had the technology there is now. You had to wait half an hour to get a result, now you get it in seconds.

To be honest, a day in my life in the past few years has been the equivalent of waking up in a prison cell. I would wake up at seven thirty, sometimes earlier if I was going out to get some jewellery, rob some wholesaler or shopkeeper when he opens at nine o'clock in the morning and he's still got sleep in his eyes, which I've said is the best time to work.

If I was not doing villainy I would wake up at half past seven, go to the communal bath, scrub it out, have a hot bath, feeling very, very depressed. Nothing to do, living out of half a dozen suitcases, clothes all packed tightly in the cupboard. If you've got two people in the room at the same time it appears very crowded. I'm very depressed all the time until I'm in someone's company, then I don't let them see I'm depressed.

After a bath, I clean my teeth, drink a fruit juice if I could afford one from the night before and a bowl of cereal if I've got the milk to go with it. I've got a fridge in the room. Turn on Radio 4 and listen to the news. Then I clean my shoes, which I do regularly, I've only got one decent pair left. I used to have about thirty pairs. I don't ever dress smartly any more, I don't even wear a jacket. The day ahead is a battle from the moment of getting up.

I might have twenty or thirty quid. If I've got fifty quid it's a lot of money. There is no future in the rest of the day because I can't and won't do anything wrong in this country. Sometimes I go to a Little Chef where a pot of tea and a couple of slices of toast is under two quid, or perhaps go to the café at Woolworths.

I then go into Coral's to read the racing papers and have a bet with what I've got in my pocket and make sure the bet lasts the whole afternoon so I can watch it. There are bets which take up all the day before the final result. It's sort of meeting against meeting and it takes six races to decide the winner. It's better than having one bet. If that goes beat then I've got nothing to do for the rest of the day.

And if at the end of the afternoon at five o'clock or whatever it is I've got any money, I'll head straight for the casino, whichever, Luton, Northampton, and stay there until the money runs out. Even a year ago I'd have been down the

Victoria Sporting Club, now I can hardly afford the petrol to get to London.

What time I go back to my 'prison cell' depends on what money I've got in my pocket. Normally I'm broke and have left myself just enough for the coffee and toast in the morning and petrol. If I'm broke I won't even put the television on, I'll go straight into bed and sleep away my troubles and then tomorrow's another day.

And that's what happened really for the past fifteen months since I came out of jail in Exeter, except for the fact that I've borrowed and I owe. Being on probation now for two years I can't go stealing jewellery and I suppose for the first time in my life I'm frightened to do it. If I get caught, then as the barrister said, they'll throw away the key and I'll die in jail.

All in all it's a very dismal future that I face.

On a Wednesday morning I am very affluent because with the £65 I draw in the morning I can now concentrate on the day's horse racing. I don't buy food. The £65 is my gambling money. So I go to Coral's and invest units of the £65 on quite a few bets. Nine times out of ten by five o'clock in the evening I kick myself for not buying the food because now I haven't got the money. And if I have got some money then I go into Marks or Waitrose, buy the bits and pieces which I can take home with me, and a bar of chocolate perhaps and then go to the casino and gamble until I either get money or go broke.

In between I go to friends in Northamptonshire, Sue and Steve, where I'm welcome to put my feet up, watch the television, which I do very often.

I've got no time for reading, I've got no time for women, I've got no time for anything except hoping that I turn the £65 pounds into £650 and then turn the £650 into £6,500 and then I won't be satisfied until I've either turned it into a lump or into nothing.

I'm always optimistic. During the day I always think things are going to get better, every gambler does that. No gambler thinks he's going to go broke. When a gambler goes to the betting shop or casino he never ever believes he'll lose all his money.

I never think of tomorrow. No gambler thinks of tomorrow. Whenever I've got money in my pocket I never ever think I'm going to go broke.

Looking back on my life I think I would rather have done anything else than stealing. I would have liked to have been a lawyer, I think I would have been very successful. I would have liked to have been a brilliant pianist and to have been multi-lingual. I speak fluent French and bits of other languages. They were my three ambitions in life.

I've been described by a very eminent lawyer as irritating, frustrating, amusing and intelligent. I don't know in what order you would want to put them. But from being the flamboyant, egotistical, amusing 'Man about London' I've now become a cabbage in Milton Keynes. I used to love to go home about five or six o'clock in the evening, get in the bath, lay my clothes out, get dressed. I'd be going to a casino, a racetrack, a dogtrack, womanising, nightclubbing. There were no days off. Same thing, same style. I've been known to be the first one in a casino at one o'clock when it opened and the last one out at four o'clock in the morning.

Since I had my near-fatal accident people say, 'Oh well, you're lucky to be alive.' But I sometimes wonder if it wouldn't have been better if I'd died in that car crash. I was unconscious, didn't know anything about it, I could have just died and that would have been it. Over. But I'm not bitter. You see, what I think about myself is this: I don't think I'm a bad feller. I think that I've blotted a lot of copybooks because I've done a lot of wrong things. I've done a lot of desperate things in my life which I regret and that's why I'm alone now. People are sick and tired of me, driving them mad for money to gamble. I'm really sad about that, pissing people off.

My life's been a battle, everything's been like a war but I was winning the war for a long time. Morry the Head! International jewel thief – diamonds in my pocket. And now? A sixty-eight year old on social security. Only a couple of months ago I was reduced to asking for a crisis loan.

They gave me twenty-six pounds and what did I do? I walked straight back to Coral's and had a twenty quid bet with it. I did keep six pounds which was a miracle for me. I suppose it's an addiction that will never leave me.

Do you know I often wonder why God never gave us the right to see years ahead of ourselves. I mean, I am sixty-eight and I wonder when the penny's gonna drop.

Let's take it in its context. It's nine o'clock on the evening of Tuesday February 20, 1996. Now really, in spite of writing this book, getting up in the morning is certainly nothing for me to look forward to, except for my £65. I suppose really the only thing I look forward to is getting into bed, getting under the covers and going to sleep. If that is not depression, what is? I mean, if you take me back six months I would have been in bed already, getting up at five o'clock in the morning, going to Wales, Lancashire, Hampshire, wherever, to steal jewellery. But there's nowhere left for me to go to steal and besides, I'm frightened to do it. For the first time in my life, after the last court appearance, Teesside, I'm frightened.

I feel very sad. It's reality which has made me sad. You see, every gambler is a pipedreamer. He just thinks of how much he's going to win. But the reality when it strikes is something different.

In a strange way, if I'd been sent to jail this last time for a number of months, I might have been better off. Why? I'll tell you. Instead of that prison – the hostel – that I've been in for fifteen months I'd have been in a proper prison. My clothes would've been stored with Sue. I would have come out, gone to the hostel, had a few months' notice given to me. I would have gone out and I would have stolen jewellery without the fear of probation hanging over my head.

Perhaps they were cleverer than I thought by giving me probation because it's like a noose round my neck ready to be pulled the moment I do any wrong. Then they'd throw the keys away for years.

So where do I go from here? The child of wealthy parents with a network of family and friends all set on giving me the best possible start in life and I end up in a back room of a hostel on social security. So much for the glamorous lifestyle of an international jewel thief! Where are the good times now?

Would I live my life in a different manner if I had my time over again? Who can answer such a question? I don't think I'll ever give up gambling but I hope never to return to thieving because I don't want to spend the last years of my life in prison. I don't look back with regret because there have been so many good times.

But the memories are fading and I wish life had turned out differently.